Learning to Question, Questioning to Learn

Related Titles of Interest

The Teacher's Guide to Flexible Interviewing in the Classroom: Learning What Children Know About Math
Herbert P. Ginsburg, Susan F. Jacobs, Luz Stella Lopez
ISBN 0-205-26567-7

Up and Out: Using Creative and Critical Thinking Skills to Enhance Learning
Andrew P. Johnson
ISBN 0-205-29731-5

The Pocket Mentor: A Handbook for Teachers
Chris A. Niebrand, Elizabeth L. Horn, Robina F. Holmes
ISBN 0-205-29693-9

For more information or to purchase a book, please call 1-800-278-3525.

Learning to Question, Questioning to Learn

Developing Effective Teacher Questioning Practices

Marylou Dantonio
Southwest State University

Paul C. Beisenherz
Southwest State University

Allyn and Bacon
Boston • London • Toronto • Sydney • Tokyo • Singapore

Series Editor: Traci Mueller
Series Editorial Assistant: Bridget Keane
Marketing Manager: Stephen Smith

A Pearson Education Company
Needham Heights, MA 02494

Internet: www.abacon.com

Library of Congress Cataloging-in-Publication Data

Dantonio, Marylou.
Learning to question, questioning to learn : developing effective teacher questioning practices / Marylou Dantonio, Paul C. Beisenherz.
p. cm
Includes bibliographical references and index.
ISBN 0-205-28036-6
1. Questioning. 2. Teaching. I. Beisenherz, Paul C. II. Title.
LB1027.44 .D38 2001
373.13′7—dc21 00-055866

Printed in the United States of America

10 9 8 7 6 5 4 3 2 04

This book is dedicated to our family:
Walter and Alice Beisenherz, parents,
Eugene and Louise Dantonio, parents,
our children Andrea, Michael, and Christopher,
and Lovey, our dog, who faithfully kept us company
while we wrote.

Contents

Preface xiii

The Book's Approach to Learning to Question and Questioning to Learn xiv

Self-Study Learning Techniques Used in This Book xv

Acknowledgments xvii

PART I Our Journeys into Questioning 1

1 Marylou's Journey 3

Journey to the Student Response 3

The Power of Questions as Student Learning Tools 6

Evolving as a Teacher Educator 8

References 10

2 Paul's Journey 11

Are the Concepts Relevant? 11

No—It's the Process That's Important 12

Duane Returns 13

References 15

PART II Inquiries into Questioning 17

If Good Teaching Is a Dialogue, Why Does the Little-Red-School-House Method Survive? 19

References 22

3 **A Story Full of Sound and Fury** **23**
Facilitative Set 23
Process-Centered Instruction and Questioning 23
Classroom Observation Research 24
Higher-Level versus Lower-Level Questioning Research 26
Cognitive Correspondence Research 27
Summary 28
References 29

4 **A Story of Light through Yonder Window Breaks** **32**
Facilitative Set 32
Teaching and Learning for Understanding 33
Conceptual Thinking 34
Instructional Conversations 35
Effective Questioning 36
Questioning Sequence 37
Questioning Patterns 40
Metacognition 43
Productive Questioning Practices 45
Summary 45
References 46

PART III Learning to Question **49**

References 50

5 **Questioning for Understanding: Empowering Student Thinking**
Facilitative Set 51
Conceptual Understanding 51
Qu:Est Instructional Strategies 54
Inquiry Suggestions and Questions 59

6 **The Nature and Function of Productive Questions** **60**
Facilitative Set 60
Vignette: This Thinking Stuff Is Serious Business 61
Self-Study Discussion 66
Inquiry Suggestions and Questions 70
References 70

7 **Collecting Strategies** **71**
Facilitative Set 71
Observing and Recalling Strategies 71

Observing Questioning Strategy Chart 72
Sample Observing Lesson Design 73
Self-Study Discussion of the Observing Strategy 74
Curriculum Applications 76
Analyzing Lessons: Observing (Ob) 76
Recalling Questioning Strategy Chart 79
Sample Recalling Lesson Design 79
Self-Study Discussion of the Recalling Strategy 80
Curriculum Applications 82
Analyzing Lessons: Recalling (Rl) 82

8 Bridging Strategies 86
Facilitative Set 86
Comparing and Contrasting Strategies 86
Comparing and Contrasting Questioning Strategy Chart 87
Sample Contrasting Lesson Design 88
Sample Comparing Lesson Design 89
Self-Study Discussion of the Comparing/Contrasting Strategies 90
Curriculum Applications 92
Analyzing Lessons: Comparing (Cm) and Contrasting (Ct) 92
Grouping Strategy Facilitative Set 96
Grouping Questioning Strategy Chart 97
Sample Grouping Lesson Design 98
Curriculum Applications 100
Self-Study Discussion of the Grouping Strategy 100
Analyzing Lessons: Grouping (Gr) 101

9 Anchoring Strategies 105
Facilitative Set 105
Labeling and Classifying Strategies 105
Labeling Questioning Strategy Chart 107
Sample Labeling Lesson Design 107
Self-Study Discussion of the Labeling Strategy 109
Curriculum Applications 111
Analyzing Lessons: Labeling (Lb) 111
Classifying Questioning Strategy Chart 114
Sample Classifying Lesson Design 114
Self-Study Discussion of the Classifying Strategy 116
Curriculum Applications 118
Analyzing Lessons: Classifying (Cf) 118

PART IV Questioning to Learn 121

10 Everything I Really Needed to Know about Life I Learned by Asking Questions 123
First Try 123
Second Try 125
Third Try 126
Fourth Try 129
Fifth Try 132

11 Closed Questions: Do You Understand? 134
Facilitative Set 134
Vignette: Opening Closed Questions 135
Self-Study Discussion 137
Inquiry Suggestions and Questions 139

12 "Who Asks a More Beautiful Question" 141
Facilitative Set 141
Vignette: Cueing Thinking 142
Self-Study Discussion 149
Inquiry Suggestions and Questions 152
References 153

13 "Always the Beautiful Answer . . ." 154
Facilitative Set 154
Vignette: Back and Forth We Go 156
Vignette: Making Conversation 159
Self-Study Discussion 166
Inquiry Suggestions and Questions 173
References 173

14 Dealing with Correct and Incorrect Responses 174
Facilitative Set 174
Vignette: Student Misunderstandings: Students Have Some Wild Ideas 175
Self-Study Discussion 177
Inquiry Suggestions and Questions 178
Vignette: Tracy Discovers How Christy Thinks 178
Self-Study Discussion 180
Inquiry Suggestions and Questions 181

Vignette: Clearing Up Student Misconceptions Is Not So Simple 181
Self-Study Discussion 185
Inquiry Suggestions and Questions 187

PART V Journeys into the Study of Productive Questioning 189

References 191

15 Steve's Journey into Learning to Question and Questioning to Learn 193
Status of Questioning as a Learning Process 193
Lessons, Transcripts, Coding, and Reflections 195
Vignette: Reflections on Erosion—Moving the Thinking of Students 210
Closing Remarks 212

16 The Talent Development Model 214
Facilitative Set 214
Reflective Practice 215
The Talent Development Model 216
Types of Rehearsals 217
First Rehearsal: Line Tryouts 218
Framework for Lesson Design 219
Second Rehearsal: Blocking 221
Framework for Coding 223
Third Rehearsal: Dress Rehearsal 225
Collegial Coaching 227
Closing Remarks 228
References 229

Index 231

Preface

For more than 24 years, Paul and I have been studying teachers' questioning practices. Our interest in the study of questioning is twofold: First, as teacher educators, we are curious about how teachers acquire productive questioning practices; and second, as teachers, we are absorbed in experimenting with productive questioning practices to determine their effects on student thinking and understanding. Like all teachers, we are continually engaged in the frustrating experience of how to construct meaningful learning experiences, learning experiences that enable students to deeply understand concepts. Likewise, we want our students to think well and to have the ability to monitor their learning processes.

The research on teachers' questioning practices has provided many insightful understandings about what to do during classroom interactions and has granted a wealth of information regarding effective questioning. Numerous books, articles, and staff development initiatives have attended to the development of effective teacher questioning practices; yet, the research on classroom observation reveals that teachers are not using effective, productive questioning practices aimed at the development and refinement of student thinking during instruction. For the most part, teachers ask low-level, rapid-fire recall questions that require at most one- or two-sentence answers. The question we pose is "Why?"

In this book, we examine productive questioning from two directions: how teachers learn to use productive questioning practices, and second, how productive questioning practices contribute to the dialogue between teachers and students to effect meaningful and purposeful instruction. This is a book aimed at the development of productive questioning practices for teachers. It is not a book about teaching students how to ask questions, although the use of productive questioning practices has a powerful impact on students' use of them in their own learning. The instructional strategies, Qu:Est (Questioning for Understanding: Empowering Student Thinking), described in this book, have been inspired by the instructional strategies of Hilda Taba (1964, 1966), have been embellished by Lyle and Sydelle Ehrenberg (1978), and have been refined by Dantonio (1990) to emphasize the importance of using student responses in guiding the development and refinement of student conceptual thinking.

Concomitantly, we draw on the literature of classroom questioning practices, teaching for understanding, brain-based research, constructivism, and how children learn as a foundation for the design of the Qu:Est Instructional Strategies. As we continue to study questioning and to gain insights from our experiences and the experiences of other teachers using the Qu:Est Instructional Strategies, four questions continue to guide our inquiry:

- What are the experiences of teachers as they learn to use Qu:Est in classroom interactions?
- In what ways does learning about Qu:Est impact teachers' thinking about curriculum, students, and learning?
- How is instruction affected as teachers implement and reflect on Qu:Est? and
- What effects does Qu:Est have on student learning?

It is our hope that readers will find this book informative as well as interesting to read. As teachers and teacher advocates, we are sharing our experiences and the experiences of our students (teachers struggling with how to make learning more meaningful and relevant to students) in an attempt to connect with readers who, too, are sincere in their efforts to create more productive, worthwhile learning opportunities for students. We believe that Qu:Est Instructional Strategies are important instructional practices that can be used in bridging the gaps between academic concepts and students' life experiences.

THE BOOK'S APPROACH TO LEARNING TO QUESTION AND QUESTIONING TO LEARN

We are writing this book to be a useful resource for teachers desiring to enhance their instructional interactions and conversations with learners. Our purposes in writing this book are to:

- introduce Qu:Est Instructional Strategies as an approach for developing and refining student conceptual understandings through instructional conversations;
- illustrate, through teacher stories or vignettes, the complexities encountered by teachers in learning to question productively; and

- portray the challenges faced by teachers as they engage learners in instructional conversations.

After much contemplation, we decided to divide the book into five parts. Each part invites readers to awaken their conscious deliberation on productive questioning from different perspectives. In order to facilitate the reading of the book, we have tried to keep the literature and research references confined to Part II and the introductions to each part of the book.

In **Part I: Our Journeys into Questioning**, we present several personal vignettes about and reflections on our teaching experiences that led to our interest in teacher questioning. **Part II: Inquiries into Questioning** delves into the literature impacting teaching for thinking and teaching for understanding. We also present the literature on questioning that was instrumental in designing the Qu:Est Instructional Strategies. The individual Qu:Est Strategies are described in **Part III: Learning to Question**, followed by **Part IV: Questioning to Learn**. Here we explore the subtle issues related to productive questioning that make for successful instructional conversations using the Qu:Est Strategies. In the last part of the book, **Part V: Journeys into the Study of Productive Questioning**, we share one of our student's experiences learning to question and invite our readers to join us in the study of productive questioning. Additionally, we offer a talent development model we have used in our professional development work with teachers.

SELF-STUDY LEARNING TECHNIQUES USED IN THIS BOOK

You may have discovered this book yourself and are reading it on your own. If it says something important to you, you will encourage others whom you value to read it. However, from our experience, we have found that the most enjoyable way to learn about questioning and to use it productively in your classroom is to learn with others who have a similar desire. We encourage our readers to seek out other teachers who share an interest in questioning and to organize a collegial self-study team that meets regularly for the purpose of discussing and practicing productive questioning. To mediate our readers' personal and collegial journeys into learning to question and questioning to learn, we have set up the following learning tools in Parts III, IV, and V of the book.

> ***Facilitative Set:*** At the beginning of each chapter, a brief description of the thinking operation or critical issue of productive questioning is introduced. The facilitative set describes the thinking operation or critical issue, why it is important to conceptual understanding, and how the chapter will be organized.

Self-Study Discussion: This is where the thinking operations or critical issues of productive questioning are examined carefully, using a vignette, lesson plan, or transcript as a reference. Each thinking operation or critical issue is assessed carefully by providing examples of productive questions, what to do with on-focus and off-focus student responses, and procedures for analyzing instructional interaction patterns.

Inquiry Suggestions and Questions: The questions at the end of each chapter invite the reader to investigate a Qu:Est Strategy by examining a transcript of a dialogue or by observing a critical issue of productive questioning within a classroom context in order to personalize learning. The inquiry questions are designed to probe into the instructional practice so that readers can develop persistent insights about conducting instructional conversations.

In Part III, the Qu:Est Instructional Strategies are described using the following learning devices:

Sample Lesson Designs: Sample lesson plans are provided as a guide for planning and conducting each Qu:Est Instructional Strategy. They also can be used for practicing the Qu:Est Strategy with learners or other teachers.

Parts IV and V of the book contain the same structure as Part III, except the lesson designs have been changed to vignettes and reflections on practice.

Vignettes: Vignettes are clips of teaching episodes that illustrate in narrative form the central issues of the chapter. We are using teacher vignettes because we believe that they are an effective way to evoke recollections, organize critical points, and make meaning of learning and teaching experiences (Jalongo & Isenberg, 1997). We find that teacher vignettes are springboards for reflecting on development of one's talents as a teacher.

We have included vignettes from our experiences as well as from other teachers. Some of the vignettes are long, approaching a short-story length. This is a deliberate decision on our part in order to convey adequately the techniques within the Qu:Est Instructional Strategies. Although the practices of productive questioning are simplistic, in reality they take time to conduct, and only through the telling of an extended event can we communicate to you the subtleties of the practices.

Reflection on Teacher Learning: After each vignette, a teacher reflection or teacher educator reflection is provided that comments on the vignette. The reflection assists the reader in understanding how the teacher or teacher educator perceives the learning taking place during the vignette.

Finally, to learn anything well, we must experience it. Quality in questioning requires enlisting our minds to participate in reflective practice and committing our hearts to the delivery of exemplary instruction as we teach for conceptual understanding. Our delivery of quality instruction can only be as effective as it speaks to the hearts and the minds of our students–fellow educators.

We believe that understanding occurs for our students, and for us, as we immerse ourselves in *practice combined with reflective action*. When we practice teaching, we can continue to do what feels comfortable to us, without thought and continued improvement. Or we can inquire into how we teach, critically looking at our practices to determine if they truly contribute to sound educational theory and are consistent with what we believe about how students learn.

Through our active efforts to inquire into our own questioning practices and participate in the shaping of sound instructional practices of other educators, we become a valuable member of the universal education community. By blending our practitioners' insights with scholarly theory, we can evolve and share a more sophisticated understanding about how to accomplish productive ways of teaching for thinking and conceptual understanding. We also know that through sharing our personal teaching experiences with each other, we weave the fabric of "quality practices." As you investigate Qu:Est Instructional Strategies, gather your own teaching and learning experiences that speak to your hearts, entwine them with ours to create an informed tapestry of how teachers learn to question and how we use productive questioning to affect student learning. Then, share your insights with us. We can be reached through email. Email address: challou@maxminn.com

ACKNOWLEDGMENTS

This book is the result of many people who have influenced our thinking and nurtured our investigations into productive questioning. We have shared our thinking with many educators over the years. Always, we have been rewarded by their enthusiasm, keen insights, and commitment to providing quality educational experiences for children. We are especially grateful to our students, and to public and private school educators, who have contributed significantly to our growth and development.

The vignettes in this book have been submitted by many talented, sincere educators throughout the United States. We thank all the gifted teachers who think seriously and critically about teaching students to think, especially the teachers of Jefferson, Orleans, and St. Tammany Parishes in Louisiana for their contributions to refine our work. The stories they have shared with us about their experiences using Qu:Est and other methods of teaching for understanding have served to refine our thinking about the ways students learn best.

We extend our appreciation to our mentors and colleagues who have supported our efforts to develop as educators. Their never-ending support and guidance have enriched our lives and challenged our thinking.

We are grateful to Jeff Jones of National Education Services for returning copyright to us for Marylou's first book on questioning. The chapters on the Qu:Est Instructional Strategies could not have been as complete without his assistance.

Our appreciation goes to the following reviewers for their comments on the manuscript: Loren Baron, Richard Montgomery High School; Linda Hall; Sandra P. Baker, School Town of Munster; Joan Isenberg, George Mason University; Lorraine Gerstl, Santa Catalina School; Susan Lyman Ross, Michelangelo Middle School.

Finally, and most importantly, thank you, Christopher, for putting up with us, enduring our long discussions over cappuccinos when you really wanted us to simply be with you.

REFERENCES

Dantonio, M. (1990). *How can we create thinkers? Questioning strategies that work for teachers*. Bloomington, IN: National Education Service.

Dantonio, M., & Paradise, L. V. (1988). Teacher question-answer strategy and the cognitive correspondence between teacher questions and learner responses. *Journal of Research and Development in Education, 21*, 71–76.

Ehrenberg, S. D., & Ehrenberg, L. M. (1978). *Building and applying strategies for intellectual competencies in students*. Miami, FL: Institute for Curriculum and Instruction.

Jalongo M. R., & Isenberg, J. P. (1997). *Teachers' stories*. San Francisco: Jossey-Bass.

Taba, H. (1966). *Teaching strategies and cognitive function in elementary school children*. (U.S. Office of Education Cooperative Research Project No. 2402). San Francisco: U.S. Office of Education.

Taba, H., Levine, S., & Elzey, F. F. (1964). *Thinking in elementary school children*. (U.S. Office of Education Cooperative Research Project No. 1574). San Francisco: U.S. Office of Education.

Learning to Question, Questioning to Learn

Part I

Our Journeys into Questioning

Somehow, we must all find our teaching selves. Many times it is a path of gaining experience with each year that we teach, savoring our experiences to enrich the next year's instruction. From our challenges and successes we are able to bring together a repertoire of instructional practices that influence who we eventually become as teachers. It is an evolutionary, self-actualization process that is never ending. In Part I, we share some pivotal moments of our experiences in learning to question and questioning to learn.

Marylou's journey was stormy. She was thrust into her role of teacher, feeling quite unsure of herself as a teacher, yet committed to doing it her way. Throughout her first years, she encountered a hostile administration, nonsupportive of her experimentation with instructional methods. She, nonetheless, challenged the norms of the school and succeeded in discovering her teaching self. Through her relationships with her students, she serendipitously formed insights about teaching and learning that were to influence her thinking about instructional practice and the role productive questioning plays in teaching learners to use their innate thinking abilities.

Paul, on the other hand, had a smooth transition from his preparation program to his first position as a teacher. As a high school science teacher, he believed in the laboratory approach to teaching science. His approach to instruction was fairly traditional: He introduced science concepts through the text or in lectures. He was most proud of his labs, where students were able to apply and verify the concepts. However, in pursuit of a doctoral degree, his interactions with other doctoral students dramatically changed his view of instruction. Inquiry education and the science process skills influenced his understanding of the role of teacher. As a teacher educator, he continues to struggle with how to sharpen teachers' inquiry approach to teaching and learning.

▶ 1

Marylou's Journey

JOURNEY TO THE STUDENT RESPONSE

I began my journey into questioning in 1974. The heat of a Midwest summer and my furious search for a teaching position had not had time to cool when I secured my first job as a teacher of high school English. Like other novice teachers recently graduated from a teacher preparation program, I had been well schooled in the classics, as well as in writing processes. What I was not prepared to do was teach tenth-grade grammar and literature. I was lost and needed time to study the textbooks that were given to me. I was not sure that I could teach.

To cover up my lack of preparation to teach, I decided to have my tenth-grade students write short stories for the first two weeks of the semester so that I could be free to study the grammar text and read the stories in their American Literature text. What I did not know was that my ignorance of effective instructional methods, serendipitously, would lead to establishing my pedagogical practices.

My students and I embarked on a journey of self-expression and learning that was to shape my beliefs about student learning and my teaching. We became colearners in the instructional process. Because I knew nothing about the interests of my students, I decided to have them select topics for stories and to question the ideas they came up with for characters, plot, themes, conflict, and settings. As they shared their ideas with me, I asked them questions to help them create details and descriptions. When they read their finished stories to each other in class, we all were delighted with our effort. Their stories were not only good, but they had learned that writing could be stimulating and that they were capable of using grammar correctly. It was at this point that I began thinking about the power that questioning has on student learning.

In 1975, in my second year of teaching, I was introduced to the *Taba Teaching Strategies* by Lyle and Sydelle Ehrenberg, the Institute of Staff Development. This was the first time I had encountered a systematic way of asking questions. One of my earliest memories of using Taba's instructional strategies was in a course called The American Dream Machine. In that course, a student named Shelly taught me a lesson about questioning that jarred my thinking and inspired my growth as a teacher and teacher educator.

Shelly was a tenth-grade student in my American Dream Machine course. During the first week of the course, she sat sulking in the back of the room. I had been struggling with how to create a classroom environment that would help students understand American society as depicted in art and literature. I decided to try Taba's Concept Development Strategy as a way to integrate art, literature, and historical events so that students could see the emerging concepts and relationships among the disciplines.

About the second week in the course, I decided to scrap what we had done previously and start over. I began by asking the students to rearrange their desks. Slowly and skeptically they slid their desks from the confines of straight, vertical rows into a liberating, but threatening U-shape. This was very unsettling to the class. Shelly, in particular, was most uncomfortable. I noticed that she became more withdrawn, sitting with her eyes cast down most of the time and slumping lower and lower in her seat as though she were trying to become invisible. After completing the data gathering process, which required two days of students observing the artistic elements and content of American paintings, she approached me after class.

Shelly stood before me, awkwardly. The sullen expression that she usually wore on her face as she sat in the farthest corner of the classroom had been replaced by a whimsical smile as she asked, "So, what are you doing?"

"What do you mean?" I replied.

"Just that," she said. "You're doing it again. You are expecting me to do the thinking."

"I think you got it." I smiled.

Shelly looked confused. "This is so different. I've never been in a class where the teacher asked so many questions. And you never tell anyone that they are right or wrong. You just keep questioning their answers."

"Does that bother you?" I inquired.

"No, it just makes me think, like which one of the answers is the one you're looking for?"

"Give me an example," I said.

"Like today when we were looking at a picture of Wyeth's *Distant Thunder*, all you asked is what we noticed about the picture. You recorded everything on the board and then asked us to point to what we were talking about. When we did, you said, "What do you mean by 'She's relaxing'?" When Jim said that she was lying in the field, you said, "What do you notice about her body that makes you say she's relaxing?" It was like you wanted us to know why we believed that she was relaxing."

"Yes," I nodded affirmatively.

"Well, what do you think?" she protested.

"Does it matter?" I queried.

"No, everyone has an opinion." she replied.

Since Shelly had not made an observation during class, I asked, "What did *you* notice about the painting?"

She responded, "Well, I noticed that she had a cup of something she had drunk and a pint of blueberries by her head. I guess she was enjoying the summer."

"What makes you say that it was summer?"

"Blueberries are in season then and she had a hat covering her face." She added, "Also, the dog's eyes looked lazy."

"In what way did they look lazy?" I queried.

"You know how a dog looks when something wakes him out of a deep sleep. The eyes are half closed. My dog does that all the time."

"What makes you think that the dog's eyes being half closed has something to do with summer?" I pursued.

"Well, summer is hot and he was lying on the grass, looking up dazed. The sun in the summer makes me tired and lazy, so he must have been."

"Ok," I said, "what makes you think that he was awakening from a deep sleep?"

"His head is just hanging there—up, not down like his body. Like he heard something," Shelly said and then her eyes flashed. "You know, I just thought of it—the picture's name is *Distant Thunder*. The thunder woke the dog!"

"Hmm," I responded.

"You know," she said with a twinkle in her eyes, "I like this. I can feel my mind thinking." She smiled brightly and floated lightheartedly out of the room.

"Yes," I thought, "Shelly, you do have it."

The next day she returned, sat in the front of the class, and said assuredly, "I'm ready!" This was the beginning of Shelly's empowerment as a student.

Reflection

I am determined that if I can reach Shelly with these questions, I can definitely reach other students. I am determined no matter how frustrating and difficult it is to pull out ideas from students that this approach can be an effective way to teach. Students have to think for themselves. For me, covering the content of American literature is not enough. I want my students to know how and why this material is important. I also want them to *own* their learning. I know that I have the talent to assist them in their journeys to become actively engaged in their own thinking and learning processes. In talking with Shelly, it dawned on me that it was *her answers to my questions, and not my questions,* that sparked her understanding. Wow! I need to find out more about questioning student responses. This is powerful stuff!

THE POWER OF QUESTIONS AS STUDENT LEARNING TOOLS

About midyear, my principal surprisingly appeared in my classroom to observe me. He stood tall, flooding the doorway with his body. No one dared enter or leave the room. After the bell rang, he nodded and took a seat in the back of the room. I wasn't sure why he decided to visit my classroom, as he had observed me for evaluation only a week ago. Nevertheless, I was glad he was there because I was going to conduct a lesson on the attributes of the characters in the short story "The Outcasts of Poker Flat." I knew that I was well prepared, and I was excited about using an inquiry approach that would assist students in making inferences about characterization. I thought that this would be a great opportunity for him to see how expert I was at drawing out student ideas and using their own life experiences to bring meaning to a piece of literature that was difficult reading. We began our discussion.

"Who remembers some of the characters in the short story?" I asked. I listed the characters on the board as students recalled them.

Beginning with the first character, I asked "What do you recall about this character?" Several students responded with facts from the story. I asked students giving a response to clarify and verify their information. I also asked for other students to add further details from the story or their own life experiences in order to exemplify the qualities of each character. We continued this activity until all the characters listed on the board had been addressed.

The board was arranged in three columns. The first column had the character names; the second column had facts from the story (things the characters said or did and what other characters in the story had to say about the character under discussion). The third column was labeled "Inferred Qualities." Under that column the students placed the qualities they believed were true based on the information we had in the second column. In order to support his or her inferences, I asked each student making an inference, "What is your reason for believing that (the character) was or is (the quality)?" As students responded to the question, other students would agree or disagree with the inference. For each agreement or disagreement, I would ask, "On what basis do you agree or disagree?" This question resulted in students talking freely with each other and asking each other for evidence from the story concerning the quality. The class noise level was high, and often students talked on top of each other in their zest to state and support their ideas.

When we finished with the lesson, the board was covered with information generated by the students. I felt ecstatic! The lesson worked, and the students were excited about how much they knew about the story. We were all proud of ourselves.

The principal left without a comment, bumping into desks as he strutted to the door. Later that day, I received a note to meet with him after school. I was sure that he was going to tell me what a great lesson I had conducted. Still high from my day of teaching, I bounced into his office. As I sat down, a dark feeling came over me.

He began, "You ask a lot of questions."

"Yes, I really think it's the best way to get students thinking and involved with literature. Using their own experiences and being able to associate those experiences with the characters make the literature come alive for them. And you know, I've discovered that if I continue to question each student response, they provide deeper information and connect it to their lives. I believe they truly do understand how literature reflects life." The words bubbled out of my mouth.

Character Names	*Story Facts*	*Inferred Qualities*
John Oakhurst	gambler imprisoned philosophical	sees though things courageous likable
Mother Shipton	used bad language	mean wicked
The Duchess	acted hysterically	insincere mean-spirited
Uncle Billy	leaves town	dumb hostile

"Uh-huh," he said, adding, "Do you tell them to ask these questions in other classes?"

"Yes," I said, unaware of the implication. "I tell them that these questions are a way of helping them understand information. I've told them that by asking for clarification and evidence that they can get the information that will help them understand whatever is not making sense to them."

"Do you realize that when students question their other teachers with these questions that it threatens the teachers?" he asked sternly.

"What!" I jumped and began to tremble fearfully. "I can't believe that. We're supposed to be teaching kids to use their minds. These questions help them process information. I can't help it if other teachers don't want to be asked these questions. If the students are using these questions in other classes then I think that they are beginning to think for themselves. I admire that! What I am doing in my classroom is working if they are using these questions to learn in other classes," I protested.

"What goes on in other classrooms is none of your business," he retorted.

I was struck dumb. He continued, "I am suggesting strongly that you caution the students in your class about using these questions in other classes. You still have a lot to learn about teaching and how to influence young people."

Reflection

I felt like I had been slapped. I didn't know whether to be angry with myself, the students, the other teachers, or him. I left his office deflated. I could not believe that anyone could object to students' need for knowledge and figuring out how they arrived at their knowledge. Again, I realized that this questioning stuff was powerful in my classroom. Now I found out that students were using it in other subjects. *What was an emerging method of teaching for me was becoming a tool of learning for my students.* And yet, my enthusiasm was damped by finding out that other teachers could not see its value. Why?

After years of pondering this experience and other similar events, what I didn't know was that, in the early years of my teaching career, I was exploring the principles of pedagogy based in the teaching for understanding. It defied the usual traditional methods of fact-based learning. I couldn't stop, even at the risk of becoming viewed as a rebel by my colleagues.

EVOLVING AS A TEACHER EDUCATOR

As the winter snow melted in the early spring of my second year of teaching, what I *did know* was not only that I was determined to use this method for my own instruction, but that I also wanted to help other teachers understand the importance of using student responses to guide their questioning practices. I also knew that if I wanted to influence the teaching of other teachers that I would have to prepare myself to work with teachers.

My encounters with students who were turned on by productive questioning and teachers who began talking with me about it inspired my formal study of questioning. I got my doctorate in Curriculum and Instruction with a focus in Teacher Development. It was during my doctoral program that the seeds for Qu:Est, Questioning understanding: Empowering student thinking, questions were planted.

I've come a long way from my accidental use of questioning as a teaching technique. Over the years, I have evolved in my understanding of questioning and using student responses to guide questions. As I continue to learn from my students who are in undergraduate and graduate teacher preparation programs, I believe wholeheartedly that to influence how teachers teach, one must be a model for them. To change teachers' instructional behaviors, one first must change the way teachers *think* about teaching, students, and learning. Misconceptions about teaching and learning occur as a result of not examining carefully our instructional assumptions and practices. Concomitantly, as we explore our pedagogical assumptions, we become more accomplished in our instructional practices.

Likewise, I have found, in my twenty-five years of studying and using productive questioning practices, that sustained behavioral change comes about only as a result of teachers' perceiving themselves being effective with students' learning. This can occur only through practice and reflection on the use of productive questioning in instructional conversations with students. Looking at our instructional practices with a critical eye and possessing an attitude of inquiry about what we do in the classroom, how we learn to do it, and what results with students when we instruct can empower our learning as well as the students'.

Reflection

To question productively and effectively, teachers must be willing to experiment with instruction and reflect on their actions as they are related to student learning and achievement. It means becoming actively involved in collecting classroom data about both our students and ourselves, analyzing it, and reflecting upon it in order to make informed instructional decisions. When we inquire, thoughtfully, into our own learning about questioning, by practicing and reflecting on our experiences, we grow as learners into caring, proficient educators. As we mature as educators, we substantially influence the lives of our students forever.

In observing my students—teachers—as they struggle to understand the nature and function of effective, productive questioning practices for themselves and in instructional conversations with their students, I am always amazed at how much more there is to learn about understanding how students think. My students' productive questioning practices to assist students in thinking profoundly and deeply, and finding ways to connect curriculum concepts, meaningfully, to student experiences, encourage me to continue my work. It is through my students that Qu:Est is nurtured, growing deeper in our understandings of it. As I listen to the stories teachers tell about their progress, or lack of it, I'm always delighted to find that their experiences in learning about and in using Qu:Est are as exciting, frustrating, and rewarding as mine.

REFERENCES

Institute for Staff Development. 1991. *Hilda Taba Teaching Strategies Program.* Miami, Fl.: Institute for Staff Development.

▶ 2

Paul's Journey

ARE THE CONCEPTS RELEVANT?

Every day I venture into my classroom thinking, Science is important! It's relevant to these kids' lives. I've got to get the concepts across to them. And every day, Duane asks, "Why do we have to memorize this meaningless stuff?" My answers never satisfy him. *Luckily, there is only one of him,* I think, as I begin my lecture on cell structure that will prepare them for the next day's lab.

I began my first year of teaching following completion of my master's degree. Like many science teachers prepared in the '60s, the Sputnik Era, I was convinced that the *Biological Sciences Curriculum Study* (BSCS, 1959) approach to teaching science made sense, so I used it. It organized basic concepts into a number of major themes that provided an efficient and sequential structure for my teaching. Presenting the material was enjoyable; the labs were challenging. Getting students to apply the concepts in the lab required that I become a master of organizing time, space, kids, and materials. To this day, I still am a scavenger, searching for items that can be used as lab resources for my students.

Throughout my first years of teaching, I learned well all the BSCS science concepts. I knew that my presentations were well prepared and I felt that students were learning. After all, they did well on the tests. The labs were another story! At the time, it never dawned on me that the students saw very little connection between the concepts of my lectures and their lab experiences.

Looking back, years later, I realize that the labs were considered playtime for the students, possessing very little instructional value for them. We made messes. They oohed and aahed at my demonstrations. However, they made a mess when they did the experiments. I spent hours after school cleaning up the room and planning for the next two days.

Questioning played a role in my instruction, but it was not inquiry-oriented. I asked questions, mostly questions that asked students to validate what I said and to recall information from their texts. Typical questions from my lectures were: "What are the parts of the cell?" "How would you explain cell division?" "Where is the nucleus of this cell?" The students would spit back information using the right language. I was pleased. I believed that they knew the concepts because they could define them and give me appropriate examples that they had memorized from the text.

During labs in a physical science course, I'd say things like: "Make sure you've completed the circuit." "Where are the wires touching in the circuit?" "Who's circuit lights the bulb?" "Who's doesn't?" "Why do you think the bulb doesn't light?" To which the students would reply in unison, "Because the circuit has breaks in it." "Fix it," I would say. And the students would obey my command. Never did I think to ask, "What did you have to do to complete the circuit?" or more importantly, "In what ways does your understanding of the circuit contribute to your knowledge of how things work around your home?"

Four years passed by quickly; yet each year, I was confronted by Duane's question about relevance. Each year there was a Duane in my classes, spoiling my enthusiasm for my carefully planned lessons, challenging the concepts, and creating periods of discomfort in the learning environment. I kept thinking: "There's something missing from my instruction. What is it?"

Reflection

How could students not see the importance and relevance of these science concepts? The labs were hands-on. Science is hands-on. Sure, there's a lot of memory work involved, but the content *can* be applied. If they don't know the concepts, how could they understand the labs? This erroneous assumption by me stood in the way of my students learning for understanding. My strong desire to "cover the content," without giving any attention to how students thought about it or how they organized it so that it would have meaning for them, set me up to misinstruct the fundamental concept in science teaching—*inquiry!*

NO—IT'S THE PROCESS THAT'S IMPORTANT

Learning to teach science by incorporating inquiry and "sciencing" into my personal model did not occur to me until I entered my doctoral program. As a teaching assistant, my doctoral program offered me an opportunity to coteach a preservice, undergraduate science methods course for elementary/middle school teachers.

My coteaching partner over the next four years was Jerry Tucker, an outstanding biology teacher who was both creative and truly able to organize and teach science as inquiry. Teaching the methods course, we utilized selected activities from one of the post-Sputnik elementary curricula, *Science: A Process Approach* (American Association for the Advancement for Science, 1961), to illustrate the use of science process skills (thinking operations used by scientists) to solve problems and to develop science concepts.

We spent many long hours talking about the importance of teaching science through inquiry and the role of the process skills in inquiry and in the development of science concepts. I remember the excitement I felt in working together to develop and modify many of the existing hands-on laboratory activities. During this time, I would often reflect on my first years of teaching and wonder why teaching thinking wasn't obvious to me.

My experiences working with preservice teachers was my initiation into questioning and understanding how questions affect thinking and the understanding of science concepts. Although my lecture habit was hard to break, I had no choice. If I wanted my preservice teachers to use the process skills, I knew that I had to use the process skills in my teaching. Modeling the process skills and having my students experience thinking like a scientist were important to the development of their instructional behaviors and using process skills in their teaching of science. The process skills demanded good, solid questions to focus the thinking needed to observe and collect data to draw warranted conclusions about various situations exemplifying particular science concepts. Using the process skills, I felt liberated.

Reflection

While I felt liberated, there was something missing. The preservice teachers were able to carry out the process skills in their planning; however, they sometimes miss the concept. If they missed the concept, how could they be effective science teachers? I was perplexed by questions: "How does one integrate conceptual understanding with teaching science through the process skills? What can I do to help these teachers understand both content and process skill methods? Which is more important—knowledge of the concepts or teaching for thinking?

DUANE RETURNS

It has been years since I first taught and prepared teachers. I have spent more than 25 years teaching at a university as a science educator. In my role as teacher educator, I have evolved in my understanding of how to teach science from an inquiring, constructivistic perspective. My students are quite skillful using productive questioning to teach science concepts.

They all have opportunities to demonstrate their newly learned skills in field settings. Their work with children in schools is gratifying to them and me. They are becoming teachers who are knowledgeable about science concepts and pedagogical practices need to teach for thinking, and who are sensitive to the needs of children.

Four years ago, I decided to study my former preservice teachers in their first years of teaching. To my horror, I discovered that although they talked a good game about developing the thinking operations of children, their instruction centered mostly on memorization. Was what we learned in my methods class all for naught? Observing them, my first years of teaching came back to haunt me. I stood like Duane, asking them: "Why are you having your students memorize these concepts? They are meaningless to the students."

My students all addressed the same issues: "There is too much material to cover, and I can't cover it by spending time on the process skills." "The class is too noisy when we do labs, and other teachers were complaining, so I don't do them anymore." "I need to make sure the students understand the concepts so that they score well on the standardized tests." They equated exposure with understanding.

Even though I hated to hear these responses, I knew these beliefs were significantly affecting their classroom instruction. My students, like me in my first years of teaching, could not understand how using a process-centered approach for teaching science concepts contributes to students' conceptual understandings. This realization led me to think about how we prepare teachers to teach and the need for ongoing mentorship and professional development during the first years of teaching.

Reflection

Learning how to teach cannot stop at the end of the preparation program. Schools and universities need to work together to sponsor opportunities for teachers to continue the study and development of pedagogical practices. One course in science methods is not enough to influence years of prior experience in learning science through rote memory. Additionally, the demands placed on teachers in their first years of teaching force them to converge on memory learning at the expense of teaching thinking.

Not only do we have to change instructional methods, we must address our beliefs about teaching. We've long held the erroneous belief that if we have students memorize material and they do well on our test, then they know the material. We know too much about learning, how the brain works, and effective instruction to continue to think that memorizing terms is the same as internalizing the concept.

In order for teachers to use inquiry methods of instruction, they must encounter multiple experiences with it as learners themselves. They must be successful in learning through inquiry approaches to see the benefits before they will desire to use such methods in their instruction. Teachers must also be engaged in an on-going, collaborative study of pedagogical practices in safe experimental environments, prior to integrating them into their teaching repertoire. Teachers need time to practice and to reflect on different methods while they are teaching to become competent at their use. Working together to learn new methods of instruction is most reinforcing. Not only does classroom teaching improve, but we engender a warm collegial feeling about each other that often lasts throughout our careers.

To learn to teach well, teachers must be involved in supporting each other in examining the methods of instruction they use to effect student learning. As communities of learners, we must form self-study groups to investigate if our teaching efforts, curriculum, and assessment measures produce students who truly understand and see the relevance of what we teach. Likewise, schools must become learning environments for both students and teachers. Learning experiences for teachers must include opportunities for teachers to practice and reflect on new instructional methods in ongoing, safe contexts where they can sharpen their skills without the added pressure of students having to learn something every time a teacher performs.

In my view, the voices of informed, talented teachers have been long absent from education. Teachers possess the proficiencies to be strong, instructional leaders in the school community. My reason for coauthoring this book on questioning, student understanding, and conceptual learning is to encourage teachers to demand their rightful place in schools as instructional leaders. As educational leaders we hold the responsibility for effecting quality instruction and students who possess meaningful understandings of concepts and the ability to use their minds to inquire into and solve life's challenges.

REFERENCES

American Association for the Advancement of Science. (1961). *Science: A Process Approach (SAPPA)*. Washington, DC: American Association for the Advancement of Science.

Biological Science Curriculum Study. (1959). Boulder, CO: BSCS.

▶ Part II

Inquiries into Questioning

Understanding classroom questioning from both a personal and a scholarship point of view is most important if we are to make sense of our practice. In this part of the book, we provide background literature, both theoretical and research-oriented, that has influenced our thinking about classroom instruction, productive questioning, and our concern for assuring that instruction encompasses teaching and learning for thinking and conceptual understanding. Four questions are addressed by this literature:

1. How does one accomplish teaching and learning for understanding?
2. What is conceptual learning?
3. What are the cognitive operations that students must perform to achieve conceptual understanding? and
4. How do educators use productive questioning strategies to conduct learning experiences aimed at teaching for conceptual understanding?

These questions not only guide our exploration of the literature but also are the basis for the design of the Qu: Est Instructional Strategies (Questioning for understanding: Empowering student thinking) explored in Part III of this book.

In keeping with our belief in storytelling as a profound way to get ideas across, we open this part of the book with a story written by a teacher, Victor J. Moeller. He succinctly captures the dilemma teachers face when using instructional conversation as an inquiry approach to teaching and learning. His story is followed by two reviews of the literature. Chapter 3, A Story Full of Sound and Fury, explores the research on classroom questioning from 1912 to the present. It also draws on the literature of school and teacher education reform. Chapter 4, A Story of Light through Yonder Window Breaks, provides more specific information centering on effective, productive questioning practices. Most importantly, Chapter 4 considers the importance of the student response in guiding, developing, and enriching students' thinking experiences.

Both chapters are written to provide pertinent literature that impacts teaching and learning for conceptual understanding. Fundamental to understanding is students' ability to comprehend and to use, appropriately, cognitive operations as tools for learning and monitoring their investigations of concepts. As educators undertaking this important process, we must be mindful of our learning needs and expert in our abilities to engage students in their inquiry.

IF GOOD TEACHING IS A DIALOGUE, WHY DOES THE LITTLE-RED-SCHOOL-HOUSE METHOD SURVIVE?

By VICTOR J. MOELLER*
Jacobs High School—Algonquin, Illinois

Robert Benchley once remarked that "There are two kinds of people, those who classify things and those who don't." Since I belong to the first group, I tend to classify teachers according to those who still employ the little-red-school-house model of learning (lecture) and those who daily engage their students in active learning. I do so not only because most of my former teachers assumed that they were the most important part of the learning process but also because the lecture method still survives among too many teachers even today. In contrast, the so-called Socratic teacher knows that the student is the most important part of the learning process.

Take my high school American Literature teacher, Mr. Prosser. He began most lessons by stating the objective ("By the end of this class you will be able to identify the characteristics of the 'code hero' in Hemingway"); and then he anticipated the so-what look on our faces by explaining what he believed to be the relevance or importance of this knowledge in our lives ("Hemingway's concept of the 'code hero' will give you standards by which to judge your own ideas about heroism").

The class then proceeded as a lecture. Mr. Prosser knew what a code hero was and he was going to tell us, tell us that he told us, and then ask us to tell him what he had told us. He called this last step evaluation, or "To find out if we had learned anything." Our job as students was to "pay attention," that is, to be receptive and passive and to take careful, detailed notes. We were not to interrupt his lecture with questions or comments; however, we were allowed to ask questions for elementary clarification. For example, "What do you mean by 'pragmatic'?" or "Who is James L. Roberts?" or "Why do you call this stuff 'literary criticism'?" and the like.

We would learn what a "code hero" was because Mr. Prosser knew what it was. His authority and testimony were sufficient; after all, he had a Master's degree. In the end, we were to trust that Mr. Prosser knew best even when we did not know what he was talking about. "Someday you will understand and all will be clear," he would reassure us. Since he had "to check for understanding," his lesson concluded with an objective test ("I am the tester and you are the testees"). However, before the test at the end of his lecture ("To be fair," he would say), he "entertained" questions if we had any. Those students who did ask questions soon became pariahs among their peers for being obsequious, and Mr. Prosser seemed to gauge the success of his lesson by the lack of questions.

In contrast, take my college Contemporary Literature teacher, Kenelm Basil. He began each lesson not by telling us what we were going to learn (he was not certain that we would learn anything although that was, of course, his fond hope) but by posing a major problem about the meaning of the day's assigned reading. He began always with a basic question of interpretation, wrote it on the board, and then asked each of us to write down our own initial answers on scrap paper. For example, "According to Vonnegut's story, "Harrison Bergeron," is the desire to excel as strong as the tendency to be mediocre?" The lesson focused on this problem of discussion since the question had the vital element of doubt about the answer. Because he never gave his own opinion during discussion (he was not a participant but the leader) and asked only follow-up questions to our answers, Mr. Basil convinced us, over time, that he did not have a single "correct" answer in mind. Indeed, the group soon realized that more than one correct answer was possible because elements from the story supported both sides of the issue. In short, our teacher began the discussion with a real question, the answer to which he himself was uncertain.

As students, we had to be active: clarifying our answers, testing others' answers for supporting evidence, resolving conflicting answers with evidence, and listening for more opinions. Learning in Mr. Basil's classroom was not a reception but a conflict of three ideas. The test of truth was reason and evidence, not teacher authority. The lesson concluded with a resolution activity since, after all, questions are quests for answers. We were asked to review our original responses and then to write a one-page essay stating our comprehensive answer to the basic question. Mr. Basil strove not for group consensus or truth by vote, but rather for individual understandings: "Given the answers that you have just heard in discussion, what is your present conclusion or resolution to the problem?"

At last, Liberation! No longer did I have to sit dutifully silent while someone was telling me something that I could just as easily have read for myself, found in a library, or researched on the Internet. No longer did I feel as though I was parroting the thoughts of the teacher. No longer was someone telling me what I was supposed to have learned. More importantly, Mr. Basil gave me the opportunity, indeed the challenge, to think for myself independently and to become responsible for my own ideas. The responsibility for learning had been placed in my own hands and, along with it, the joy and personal satisfaction of arriving at my own insights. I had learned to live with doubt and to uncover questions that answers hide. In short, I had learned how to learn.

Do not misunderstand. Some so-called Socratic teachers, who have not mastered the method of developing the habit of reflective and independent thinking in themselves and their students, do not conduct discussion in the manner of Kenelm Basil. For these, classroom discussion is too often no more than a bull session where every opinion is given equal respect and when one idea begins to sound as good as another. Such teachers confuse the right to express an opinion with the notion that any opinion can be right. Toleration of any and all ideas has become the goal and brain storming (that pathetic analogy) has been enthroned as the process. "After all, don't we all know that everything is relative and that there are no absolutes?"

At the other extreme, pseudo-Socratic teachers engage in the sophistry of the disguised lecture. These teachers pretend to conduct shared inquiry but eventually it becomes evident to a perceptive student or observer that the leader-teacher does have a single, correct answer in mind. These teachers tip their hand in several ways: by asking leading questions ("How can you honestly think Vonnegut would agree with you?"); by allowing opinions that the teacher agrees with to go unchallenged or unsubstantiated, by developing a single line of argument or side of an issue; by injecting their own opinion into the discussion ("I believe that you have all overlooked important information on page six"); by commenting on student answers ("That's very good, James. I'm so proud of you" or, "Maria, I think you had better reconsider your answer. You are missing something"); and finally, by attempting to arrive at group consensus ("How many think the desire to excel is [or is not] as strong as the tendency to be mediocre?").

If what I have said about these Socratic charlatans is not true, how else can anyone explain some of these common student and teacher behaviors?

Teacher: "Whenever I try to have discussion, my students clam up. Only one or two contribute. They just don't get the point. I have to tell them."

Student: "My answer is correct, isn't it, Mrs. Jones?"

Teacher: "Discussion is a waste of time. I have to cover the curriculum."

Student: "But Mrs. Jones, what is the right answer?"

Teacher: "My students' test scores have to improve. I don't have time for the luxury of endless discussions. I have 120 students. Get real."

Student: "Why do you keep asking questions when you know the answers?"

Teacher: "Students don't know how to ask good questions and anyway, discussions are just too chaotic."

Student: "Just let me alone and give me my C. I don't mess up your class."

Teacher: "My students cannot be trusted to think for themselves. They keep coming up with silly answers."

But isn't that just the point? The master-disciple teacher fails to understand that wrong answers are a necessary part of the learning process when real thinking takes place. The genuine Socratic teacher recognizes and accepts false turns and "silly" answers as inevitable when students have the freedom to be wrong. And right. After all, thinking IS difficult and students resist it like a plague: " I don't know." "Why did you call on me? I wasn't doing anything." "Who cares?" "What difference does it make?" "Ask somebody else." In the end, if thinking were easy, there would be more of it.

Reflection

Does not the fundamental difference between Mr. Prosser and Mr. Basil come down to a question about who is finally responsible for learning? Mr. Prosser's conduct in the classroom implies that the teacher is while Mr. Basil's behavior suggests the opposite. Can anyone convince students that they are responsible for their own learning other than the students themselves? And is it not usually through discussion and dialogue and problem solving, not by way of lecture, that students are challenged to recognize what they have and have not learned?

James Howard of the Council for Basic Education recently remarked in an interview on National Public Radio: "Education is what you have left after you have forgotten everything you learned in school." I wonder what Mr. Prosser would make of that sentence. I know what Mr. Basil would do with it.

REFERENCE

*Victor Moeller's Web page: http://user.mc.net/~moeller/index.htm
e-mail: moeller @mc.net

▶ 3

A Story Full of Sound and Fury

FACILITATIVE SET

The year was 1912. Rommiett Stevens had just completed her observations of teacher classroom questioning. She unearthed that teachers asked an astounding number of questions—395 questions a day. The preponderance—two-thirds—of the questions asked were rote memory questions, requiring students to do nothing more than to recite information from text materials. Nearly ninety years later, and after decades of research aimed at understanding teacher questioning practices and promoting the use of effective questioning to teach for understanding, classroom observation literature on teacher questioning practices promulgates that not much has changed in the classroom to dispute Stevens's 1912 observations: *Classroom teachers persist in asking lower-level, recall-oriented questions, requiring students to do little reflective, creative, or critical thinking.*

Why?

PROCESS-CENTERED INSTRUCTION AND QUESTIONING

During the Sputnik Era, researchers promoted the development of systematic instructional strategies as a focus for American curriculum. Scholars and content specialists, especially in science and social studies, developed and studied instructional practices and curricula aimed at inquiry methods based on the nature of the disciplines and the progressive theories of John Dewey. Emphasis on teaching and learning converged around curricular scope and sequence for developing and refining student cognitive processes (Ausubel, 1960; Bruner, 1960; Burner, Goodnow, & Austin, 1967; Smith and Meux, 1962; Suchman, 1958; Taba, 1966; Taba, Levine, & Elzey, 1964). Inquiry- or process-centered instructional strategies such as concept development, interpretation of data, the scientific method, and problem solving were promoted and financed by the U.S. Department of Education, the National Science Foundation, and other funding institutions.

These process-centered strategies relied on teachers' knowledge of how learning occurs. Learning theories expounded by Piaget and Bruner were taken most seriously by the developers of the funded curricular initiatives. Most important to the process-centered strategies was teachers' effective use of questioning to guide and direct student thinking efforts or thinking experiences.

Taba and her colleagues in 1964, like other educators of the 1960s, created three instructional strategies—concept development, interpretation of data, and application of a generalization—each of which cued particular kinds of cognitive operations by sequencing questions to stimulate and to guide the thinking experiences of learners. Of questioning, Taba et al. (1964) wrote: "Questions are the carriers of whatever new cognitive system is emerging" (p. 177). While efforts for the inclusion of inquiry methods in curriculum flourished, enthusiasm was tempered by the classroom observations of Smith and Meux (1962), who reported that discourse in classrooms was about as logical as barroom conversations.

CLASSROOM OBSERVATION RESEARCH

Subsequent to the inquiry-directed curriculum and instructional emphasis of the 1960s, Meredith Gall (1970) reviewed the literature on teacher classroom questions. He depicted teachers' questions as barren—60 percent were low-level recall questions, 20 percent were procedural, and only 20 percent required students to think. A plethora of research initiatives aimed at understanding the relationship between teachers' questioning practices and student achievement roared like thunder in the educational literature throughout the next two decades (Gall & Rhody, 1987; Gall et al., 1978; Hare and Pulliam, 1980; Mills, Rice, Berliner, & Rousseau, 1980; Redfield & Rousseau, 1981; Rosenshine, 1971; Ryan, 1973, 1974; Winne, 1979).

The research on observations of classroom teachers' questioning practices continued to support the rumblings that teachers, in general, continued to ask fact-oriented questions (Gall, 1970; Shake, 1988; Wood & Muth, 1991). Investigations in the content areas echoed that teachers' questioning practices in subject areas were pervasively recall-oriented. For example, Daines (1982) reported that elementary and secondary social studies teachers asked literal questions at the rate of 1.5 per minute. Science educator P. E. Blosser (1980), in a review of the literature on science teacher questioning behavior, concluded that science teachers ask questions requiring mostly recall or recitation. Eight years later, Swift, Gooding, and Swift (1988) found that 85.9 percent of teachers' questions in middle school science were at the memory level. Again, the question resonates: Why?

The year was 1983. *A Nation at Risk* (National Commission on Excellence in Education, 1983) was the first in a series of national reports that launched agendas for school and teacher reforms that has extended into the 1990s (see References for listing of commissions). These reform agendas had two thrusts for learning: *to teach for understanding* and *to teach for diversity***.** Policymakers and educational scholars were resolute in demanding that America must establish "world-class standards" for American education. Calls for reform in American schooling processes were, once again, focused on the engendering of rigorous content standards and the cultivation of student cognitive abilities.

One year later, Goodlad (1984) published a study of the American classroom, *A Place Called School*. Once again, teachers' questioning behaviors were depicted as bleak. Goodlad found that nearly 75 percent of the time that teachers asked questions, the questions were at the recall or recitation level with little or no follow-up on student responses. Concomitantly, Theodore Sizer (1984) stated that in his observations of dozens of suburban schools,

> *There is little opportunity for sustained conversations between student and teacher. The mode [of instruction] is a one-sentence or two-sentence exchange. . . . Dialogue is strikingly absent, and as a result the opportunity of teachers to challenge students' ideas in a systematic and logical way is limited. . . . One must infer that careful probing of students' thinking is not a high priority. (p. 82)*

Howard Gardner (1991) echoes Sizer's perception in his criticism of American schooling, *The Unschooled Mind*. Gardner characterizes educators as seeking and accepting "rote," "ritualistic," and "conventional performances" from children with little attention given to methods of instruction that emulate how children learn. He further asserts, "The relative absence in schools of concern with deep understanding reflects the fact that, for the most part, the goal of engendering that kind of understanding has not been a high priority for educational bureaucracies" (p. 8).

Six years later, Linda Darling-Hammond (1997), in her book *The Right to Learn*, reports that national and international studies consistently disclose that the large majority of U.S. teaching practices emphasize rote learning. The battle cry of school reform, *"teaching for understanding,"* so pervasive in the scholarly literature, has yet to be realized in classroom teaching practice.

In the year 2000, American teachers, as well as the school curriculum, are preoccupied with transmission of knowledge.

Why?

HIGHER-LEVEL VERSUS LOWER-LEVEL QUESTIONING RESEARCH

While observations of classroom questioning practices have continued to publicize that teachers persevere in asking memory-based questions, educational researchers, bent on influencing critical thinking, have ventured into investigating the impact of teachers' asking higher-level questions on student achievement. Many educators and researchers, even today, cling to the presumption that in order to improve student achievement and enhance learning, teachers must ask higher-level questions.

To research the effectiveness of higher-order questioning, Bloom's *Taxonomy of Educational Objectives* (1956) was assumed to be a hierarchy of cognitive operations and was favored as a means of classifying classroom questions. In most research studies, teacher questions intended for the knowledge and comprehension levels were defined as lower-level questions. Teacher questions intended for application, analysis, synthesis, and evaluation were coded as higher-level questions (Hunkins, 1989). It was the contention of scholars that higher-level questions directly related to student achievement. Years of studies on higher-level versus lower-level teacher questions and the effect of these questions on student achievement were at best confusing, and at worst disillusioning.

Higher-level versus lower-level questioning research exposed a paradox. Rosenshine (1971) concluded that students learn best when teachers use lower-level questions. A decade later, Redfield and Rousseau's (1981) meta-analysis on the research on teacher questioning practices promoted that "the predominate use of higher level questions during instruction has a positive effect on student achievement" (p. 241). Winne (1979), after reviewing eighteen research studies, proclaimed, "There is no sturdy conclusion which can be offered about the relative effectiveness of higher cognitive questions for enhancing student achievement" (p. 46). Samson, Strykowski, Weinstein, and Walberg (1987), in a review of fourteen studies, corroborated Winne's earlier finding. They maintained that there is little support for contending that higher-level questioning strengthens student achievement.

Researchers, however, were able to infer some sound information about the effects of higher-level and lower-level questions. Research indicated that question level should be related directly to learner objectives. The use of lower-level questions is an effective way to check for understanding and to teach basic skills that are required for higher-level thinking (Berliner, 1987;

Rosenshine, 1971). Gall (1984) reported a positive relationship between recall questioning and basic skill acquisition for low SES in the elementary grades and that higher cognitive questions appear more productive with older students with average or above-average abilities. And finally, it was discovered that the use of higher-level questions affects the complexity and length of student responses (Cole & Williams, 1973; Lange, 1982), which may aid in comprehension. Even with these seemingly important findings, Brophy (1986) cautioned that higher-level questions are not categorically superior to lower-level questions.

Although the research on higher-level versus lower-level questioning has been pervasive in educational literature, it has not greatly influenced classroom practice. Teachers still favor recall or recitation questions. Gall (1984) proffered that because teachers are insistent in using recitation, efforts should be initiated to assist teachers in doing it well. Even so, the debate between higher-level versus lower-level questioning to influence student achievement continues to the present day, with no clear answers.

COGNITIVE CORRESPONDENCE RESEARCH

The relationship between teacher cognitive questions and student responses is closely tied to the studies on higher-level versus lower-level questioning. This research provides more productive ways of examining higher-level versus lower-level questioning and offers classroom practitioners some sound advice on question asking. Exploring the cognitive congruence between teacher questions and student responses, Mills, Rice, Berliner, and Rousseau (1980) contended that "the results of their study provided a firm basis for dispelling the belief that there is a high correlation between teacher questions and types of student answers" (p. 200). Dillon (1982) posited that there was a 50 percent chance of students answering a higher-level question with a lower-level response. Dantonio and Paradise (1988) found that the correspondence between teacher questions and student response at the recall level was more congruent than questions prompting inferential thinking.

The research on cognitive correspondence between teacher questions and student responses unveiled that the inferred level of thought in a teacher's question is not necessarily the level of thought emulated in a student's response. Questions coded as higher level using Bloom's taxonomy may not require such thinking on the part of students answering the questions. It all depends on the background information students possess and the information available to answer the question. If information is available to students through some form, then they may simply recall the information in answering the teacher's intended higher-level question. "The odds are only about 50-50 that an analysis, synthesis, or application question will be responded to with an answer reflecting analysis, synthesis, or application" (Berliner, 1984, p. 64). In short, cognitive correspondence between teacher questions and student responses is best described as a crapshoot.

Even so, this research does provide classroom practitioners prudent information about the qualities of effective classroom questioning practices. While Mills, et al. (1980) found that there was little relationship between levels of teacher questions and student responses, they concluded that "The clarity and specificity with which teachers phrase their questions influenced the clarity, specificity, and correspondence of the students' answer" (p. 202). As teachers, we can be circumspect of the purpose and clear phrasing of our questions. We can determine if students are answering our questions with the information and cognitive operation intended by our questions. And we can use methods of instruction that assist our students in understanding and monitoring their cognitive operation.

SUMMARY

Decades of initiatives, filled with feverish school reforms, declarations, and curricular innovations, are seemingly silent in American classroom practice. *The sovereignty of memorizing, restricting learning by asking questions requiring students to recall information, reigns soundly and supreme in classroom practice.* Yet, "to teach for understanding" continues to resound in the contemporary literature of education, becoming ever more tumultuous. We can no longer ignore the cacophony of educational reform calls urging us to teach for understanding. The true indication of student understanding, whether our questions are higher-level or lower-level, can be revealed only in our analysis of what students know and how they know it. We must engage methods of instruction that assure that quality of learning means that students have and use their abilities to conceptualize, to problem solve, and to make rational decisions.

The dissonant criticism of American teacher questioning practices cannot lie solely at the feet of classroom practitioners. There are pioneer classroom practitioners who agonize over American society's pervasive preoccupation with equating higher standardized test scores with memorizing content. These teachers know that quality learning means that students must not only score well on tests, they must know how to learn. The efficiency of memory instruction is not sufficient.

Yet, the lay public's ignorance of, and sometimes fear of, educational methods that promote teaching for understanding and conceptual learning prevent well-informed, caring practitioners from using sound, process-centered instructional practices. As Linda Darling-Hammond (1997) so aptly states:

> *[P]olicy makers and educators need to develop also a new policy for pedagogy. This new policy must support the conditions under which teaching of understanding can occur, not as a subversive activity but as a regular part of all children's schooling. (p. 95)*

As researchers and policy makers continue to clamor for persuasive evidence that teaching for understanding is happening in American classrooms, we, as classroom practitioners, must also provide the leadership to educate the lay public's understanding of what it means to learn. Only by joining with, and not standing against, the call for quality in teaching and learning can we orchestrate instruction to assure that teaching for understanding is not full of sound and fury, signifying nothing.

REFERENCES

Ausubel, D. P. (1960). The use of advance organizers in the learning and retention of meaningful verbal material. *Journal of Educational Psychology, 51*, 267–272.

Berliner, D. C. (1984). The half-full glass: A review of research on teaching. In P. L. Hosford (Ed.), *Using what we know about teaching* (pp. 51–77). Alexandria, VA: Association for Supervision and Curriculum Development.

Berliner, D. C. (1987). But do they understand? In V. Richardson-Koehler (Ed.), *Educators' handbook:* A *research perspective* (pp. 259–291). New York: Longman.

Bloom, B. S. (Ed.). (1956). *Taxonomy of educational objectives, Handbook I: Cognitive domain.* New York: David McKay.

Blosser, P. E. (1980). *Review of research: Teacher questioning behaviors in science classrooms.* Columbus, OH: Educational Resources Information Center.

Brophy, J. E. (1986). Teacher influences on student achievement. *American Psychologist, 41*, 1069–1077.

Bruner, J. S. (1960). *The process of education.* Cambridge, MA: Harvard University Press.

Burner, J., Goodnow, J. J., & Austin, G. A. (1956). *A study of thinking.* New York: Science Editions, Inc.

Carnegie Forum on Education and the Economy. (1986). *A nation prepared: Teachers for the 21st century.* Washington, DC: Author.

Cole, R., & Williams, D. (1973). Pupil responses to teacher questions: Cognitive level, length, and syntax. *Educational Leadership Research (Suppl.)*, 142–145.

Commission on the Education of Teachers into the 21st Century (1991). *Restructuring the education of teachers.* Reston, VA: Association of Teacher Educators.

Curriculum Committee of the Holmes Group. (1991). *Toward a community of learning: The preparation and continuing education of teachers.* East Lansing, MI: Author.

Daines, D. (1982). *Teachers' oral questions and subsequent verbal behavior of teachers and students.* Provo, UT: Brigham Young University (ERIC, ED 255 979).

Dantonio, M., & Paradise, L. V. (1988). Teacher question-answer strategy and the cognitive correspondence between teacher questions and learner responses. *Journal of Research and Development in Education,* 21, 71–76.

Darling-Hammond, L. (1997). *The right to learn*. San Francisco: Jossey-Bass.

Dillon, J. T. (1982). Cognitive correspondence between question/statement and response. *American Educational Research Journal, 19*, 540–551.

Gall, M. D. (1970). The use of questions in teaching. *Review of Educational Research,* 40, 707–721.

Gall, M. D. (1984). Synthesis of research on teachers' questioning. *Educational Leadership, 42*, 40–47.

Gall, M. D., & Rhody, T. (1987). Review of research on questioning techniques. In W. W. Wilen (Ed.), *Questions, questioning techniques, and effective teaching* (23–43). Washington, DC: National Education Association.

Gall, M. D., et al. (1978). Effects of questioning techniques and recitation on students' learning. *American Educational Research Journal, 40*, 175–199.

Gardner, H. (1991).*The unschooled mind*. New York: Basic Books.

Goodlad, J. I. (1984). *A place called school*. New York: McGraw-Hill.

Goodlad, J. I. (1990). *Teachers for our nation's schools*. San Francisco: Jossey-Bass.

Hare, V. C., & Pulliam, C. A. (1980). Teachers' questioning: A verification and an extension. *Journal of Reading Behavio*r, *12*, 69–72.

Holmes Group. (1986). *Tomorrow's teachers: A report of the Holmes Group*. East Lansing, MI: Author.

Hunkins, F. P. (1989). *Teaching thinking through effective questioning*. Boston: Christopher-Gordon Publishers, Inc.

Lange, B. (1982). ERIC/RCS report: Questioning techniques. *Language Arts, 59*, 180–185.

Mills, S. R., Rice, C. T., Berliner, D. C., & Rousseau, E. W. (1980). The correspondence between teachers' questions and student answers in classroom discourse. *Journal of Experimental Education*, 48, 194–204.

National Commission on Excellence in Education. (1983). *A nation at risk.* Washington, DC: U.S. Department of Education.

National Commission on Teaching and America's Future (NCTAF). (1996). *What matters most: Teaching and America's future*. New York: Author.

National Council of Teachers of Mathematics. (1989). *Curriculum and evaluation standards for school mathematics*. Reston, VA: Author.

National Council on Education Standards and Testing (NCEST). (1992). *Raising standards for American education*. Washington, DC: U.S. Government Printing Office.

National Foundation for the Improvement of Education (NFIE). (1995). *Touching the future*. Washington, DC: Author.

National Foundation for the Improvement of Education (NFIE). (1996). *Teachers take charge of their learning: Transforming professional development for student success*. Washington, DC.: Author.

National Governor's Association. (1986). *Time for results: The governor's 1991 report on education*. Washington, DC: Author.

Redfield, D. L., & Rousseau, E. W. (1981). Meta-analysis of experimental research on teacher questioning behavior. *Review of Educational Research, 51*, 237–245.

Renaissance Group. (1991). *Teachers for the new world.* Cedar Falls, IA: University of Northern Iowa.

Rosenshine, B. (1971). *Teaching behaviors and student achievement.* London: National Foundation for Educational Research in England and Wales.

Rosenshine, B. (1973). Teaching functions in instructional programs. *Elementary School Journal, 83,* 335–351.

Ryan, F. L. (1973). Differentiated effects of levels of questioning on student achievement. *Journal of Experimental Education, 41,* 63–67.

Ryan, F. L. (1974). The effects on social studies achievement of multiple students responding to different levels of questioning. *Journal of Experimental Education, 42,* 71–75.

Samson, G. E., Strykowski, B., Weinstein, T., & Walberg H. J. (1987). The effects of teacher questioning on students' achievement. *Journal of Educational Research, 80,* 290–295.

Shake, M. C. (1988). Teaching questioning: Is there an answer? *Reading Research and Instruction, 27,* 29–39.

Sizer, T. R. (1984). *Horace's compromise: The dilemma of the American high school.* Boston: Houghton Mifflin.

Smith, B. O., & Meux, M. (1962). *A study of the logic of teaching.* (U.S. Office of Education Cooperative Research Project No. 258). Urbana, IL: University of Illinois.

Stevens, R. (1912). *The question as means of efficiency in classroom instruction: A critical study of classroom practice.* New York: Teachers College Press, Columbia.

Suchman, J. R. (1958). *The elementary school training program scientific inquiry.* (U.S. Office of Education Cooperative Research Project No. 216). Urbana, IL: University of Illinois.

Swift, J. N., Gooding, C. T., & Swift, P. R. (1988). Questions and wait time. In J. T. Dillon (Ed.), *Questioning and discussion: A multidisciplinary study* (pp. 192–211). Norwood, NJ: Ablex.

Taba, H. (1966). *Teaching strategies and cognitive function in elementary school children.* (U.S. Office of Education Cooperative Research Project No. 2402). San Francisco: U.S. Office of Education.

Taba, H., Levine, S., & Elzey, F. F. (1964). *Thinking in elementary school children.* (U.S. Office of Education Cooperative Research Project No. 1574). San Francisco: U.S. Office of Education.

Winne, P. H. (1979). Experiments relating teachers' use of higher cognitive questions to student achievement. *Review of Educational Research, 49,* 13–50.

Wood, K. D., & Muth, D. K. (1991). The case for improved instruction in the middle grades. *Journal of Reading, 35* (2), 84–90.

▶ 4

A Story of Light through Yonder Window Breaks

Question: What role does productive questioning play in teaching for understanding and developing students' abilities to think conceptually?

Response: We cannot look at teachers' questions in isolation. Understanding the relationship between productive questioning and quality student responses must be our first consideration in the development of students' conceptual understandings. How students think about concepts, how they are encouraged to communicate their thinking, and how they monitor their thinking are as central to learning as the concepts themselves.

FACILITATIVE SET

Instructional questions can provide the focus and structure for specific cognitive operations when students engage in the study of subject matter concepts. Our questions can guide the development and refinement of students' cognitive abilities and conceptual understandings if we listen carefully to what students are saying and use their responses as prompts to our questioning. Studies that have explored the teaching operations within the context of teaching subject matter reveal that students improve the quality of their knowledge as well as their cognitive abilities (Ennis, 1989; Swartz, 1991; Prawat, 1991; Nickerson, 1988–89). Beyer (1997) asserts that "teaching or covering only information overpowers students; helping them to improve their thinking *empowers* students" (p. 308).

To empower students' thinking, we must shift our attention from *what students must learn* to *how students learn and how they think*. We must engage in productive instructional conversations as a means to assist students in learning how to learn. By using systematic, productive questioning practices that promote thoughtful instructional conversations, encouraging students to think critically and creatively about concepts, we can more effectively connect school subject matter learning to relevant life experiences. Duckworth (1996) articulates this idea in the following way:

> *To the extent that one carries on a conversation with a child, as a way of trying to understand a child's understanding, the child's understanding increases 'in the very process.' The questions the interlocutor asks, in an attempt to clarify for herself what the child is thinking, oblige the child to think a little further also. (p. 96)*

Student responses reveal their understandings: what students know, how well or deeply they know something, and how they have thought about something. The more we ascertain how students arrive at their understandings, the more we can involve them in rich learning processes that promote deeper and more meaningful understandings of subject matter concepts. In this chapter, we will explore the literature on teaching and learning for understanding, the role instructional dialogue plays in student thinking, and questioning, as it relates to the development and refinement of student conceptual thinking.

TEACHING AND LEARNING FOR UNDERSTANDING

What does it mean to understand? For us, it requires that students make meaningful connections between what they are studying; how they come to know something through their knowledge of, skill in, and monitoring of their thinking; and the relevance both their thinking and their knowledge has in comprehending life issues and solving problems. Perkins (1998), recognized as an authority in this area, defines understanding as

> *the ability to think and act flexibly with what one knows (p. 40). . . . Understanding shows its face when people can think and act flexibly around what they know. In contrast, when a learner cannot go beyond rote and routine thought and action, this signals a lack of understanding. (p. 42)*

Understanding means that what students learn and how they learn it make sense to them. It has meaning and relevance. New learning has links to past knowledge, and the learner is actively engaged in recognizing the connections. Smith (1998), in *The Book of Learning and Forgetting,* underscores the necessity of meaning in the following manner:

> *The official theory of learning says that we have to learn something in order to understand it. Once again, this is totally contrary to fact. We have to understand something in order to learn it. We have to make sense of it. (p. 34)*

Such thinking about understanding is the basis of constructivistic theory that has its roots in the work of John Dewey. Dewey (1938) believed that learning was the result of meaningful connections people make through their interactions with an event, object, person, idea, or activity. In other words, we learn through our experience and our thinking about or reflect on our experiences (Bruner, 1960, 1966, 1990). Meaning is constructed by the learner, not poured into the learner's head. Dewey charged educators to serve as agents to assist learners to achieve connectedness in their development (understanding).

Contemporary thinking about what understanding means embraces constructivism. Constructivist teaching practices help learners to internalize and reshape, or transform, new information. "Deep understanding occurs when the presence of new information prompts the emergence or enhancement of cognitive structures that enable us to rethink our prior ideas" (Brooks & Brooks, 1993, p. 15). Constructivism calls for students to generate, demonstrate, and exhibit their understanding.

CONCEPTUAL THINKING

Conceptual thinking requires learners to gather information, create patterns or relationships among the information, and create names for the relationships that communicate the essence of the concept. Cognitive theorist David Ausubel (1960, 1968) proposed that the most effective and meaningful learning involves the establishment of patterns of relationships among concepts with the larger, more general patterns coming to subsume the more specific concepts. In other words, all concepts can be organized hierarchically.

Bruner, another well-respected cognitive theorist, expounded the idea that learning is an active process through which learners construct new concepts based on their current and past knowledge. There are four principles that frame his theory of learning: (1) students must discover the concepts for themselves; (2) students and teachers must engage in active dialogue to form concepts; (3) the context for learning should accommodate the students' current state of understanding; and (4) the curriculum should be organized in a spiral manner so that students continually build on what they have learned (Bruner, 1960). More recently, in 1996, Bruner brought forth the idea that the classroom should be reconceived as a community of mutual learners with the teacher "orchestrating the proceedings" (p. 21).

If, then, we want to assist students in the development of their conceptual abilities, we must engage them in thinking experiences that promote both attention to the constructing of concepts and the social interactions necessary to exchange ideas and learn from them. Beyer (1997) suggests that by establishing thoughtful environments for thinking to occur, students will become more refined in their abilities to use cognitive processes and more comfortable in doing so. He reminds us that to become proficient in any kind of thinking requires conscious, deliberate practice and understanding of procedures for carrying out a cognitive operation.

> *Improving the quality of student thinking is thus not a matter of employing the skill-teaching techniques described here as "one-shot" crutches or remedial devices. Rather, it is a matter of providing the continuous, systematic instructing, direction, guidance and support that assists students in becoming increasingly self-directed and expert in how they execute their thinking. (pp. 232–234)*

Such practice can be guided only when the thinking students are doing is explicit and available for analysis and development.

INSTRUCTIONAL CONVERSATIONS

Classroom dialogue or talk can be instrumental in developing and refining students' conceptual thinking. A theory of conversation (Pask, 1975) sets forth the basic idea that learning occurs through conversations about a subject matter that serve to make knowledge explicit. Tharp and Gallimore (1988) note that conversation can be instructional in intent and designed to promote learning or be natural and spontaneous, free from didactic characteristics.

To hold quality instructional conversations, educators first focus on the instructional goal or objective that will be *uncovered and explored* through the social dialogue of the students and teacher. Second, the teacher must be skillful in conducting interactions that promote thinking. We can encourage student thinking and the way they engage in it through our questions and by the way we respond to their ideas (Costa, 1991; Dantonio, 1990; Dantonio and Paradise, 1988).

Through our questions and responses to student comments, we can help them focus consciously on how particular kinds of cognitive operations function and assist students in how to carry out the operations, enhancing the quality of their thinking. To question effectively and productively during instructional conversations, educators must possess talent in questioning that cues and leads students through the procedures of particular kinds of thinking operations. We must also provide students enough guided practice in thinking so that students can understand, apply, and adopt the cognitive procedures in other appropriate thinking contexts (Beyer, 1997; Dantonio, 1990).

EFFECTIVE QUESTIONING

An ubiquitous statement that is prolific in the literature on effective questioning is *"In order for questions to be effective, they must be directed toward instructional goals."* An equally nondescript notion is *"Teachers must be flexible and sensitive to student needs and interests when asking questions."* Although obvious, surely, there must be more discriminating information available to classroom practitioners for the construction of effective questioning practices.

In the literature on student thinking, Sternberg and Spear-Swerling (1996) advocate the use of a dialogical approach. This approach is based on dialogues between teacher and student and student and student. It requires that the teacher act as a guide or facilitator, asking students to process, or think through, their responses. The dialogical approach encourages students to critically think through their responses rather than simply spit back what they think the teacher wants to hear. Sternberg and Spear-Swerling (1996) caution us about the way we have traditionally thought about classroom interactions and offer a new vision for the teaching of thinking:

> *We teachers tend to think about class discussion in the same way that we think about the processes of thinking. That is, we consider processes as means to an end. But in teaching thinking, the processes of thought and their expression in class discussions are legitimate and important ends in their own right. (p. 119)*

To heed their wisdom, we must be sure that our questions stimulate, guide, and embellish the thinking of our students.

Wilen (1987) provides nine suggestions as the basis for effective teacher questioning practices. They are:

- Plan key questions to provide lesson structure and direction.
- Phrase questions clearly and specifically.
- Adapt questions to student ability level.
- Ask questions logically and sequentially.

- Ask questions at a variety of levels.
- Follow-up on student responses.
- Give students time to think when responding.
- Use questions that encourage wide student participation.
- Encourage student questions (p. 11).

To his list, we add:

- *Listen carefully to the student response, using it to point the way in asking questions to uncover student thinking.*

QUESTIONING SEQUENCE

Many researchers have been advocating the use of questioning sequences as a means for uncovering the depth of student thinking and knowledge. While taxonomies such as Bloom's (1956) and question classification systems like Aschner and Gallagher's Question System (1965) have frequently been used by researchers to classify the cognitive level of questions and may serve to increase classroom practitioners' awareness of varying types of questions, the use of taxonomies and classification systems, alone, will not improve the quality of teacher questions (Brophy, 1986; Reigle, 1976). Nor is there evidence that they improve the quality of student responses.

Teacher questioning, viewed from a window open to exploring the issues related to generating student responses, and qualifying those responses into meaningful understandings through productive questioning practices, is supported by a rich source of professional literature. It furnishes the classroom practitioner with sensible guidelines for making important instructional decisions on how to question and how to work with student responses.

Consistently, the literature on effective questioning practices has insisted that questioning sequences are far more effective in promoting student understanding than any one type of question (Beyer, 1997; Costa & Lowery, 1989; Dantonio, 1990; Gall, 1970; Gall et al., 1978; Klinzing & Klinzing-Eurich, 1987; Riley, 1981; Wilen, 1991; Wright & Nuthall, 1970). Gall (1970), in his early review of teacher questioning practices, stated two advantages of teachers asking a sequence of questions. First, he mentions that question sequences provide a more accurate view of what constitutes effective questioning practices; and second, he points out that questioning sequences are more useful than question classifications in developing teachers' abilities to improve the quality of student responses and classroom interaction patterns.

Questioning sequences are a sequential series of cognitively focused questions combined with questions that assist students in clarifying, verifying, supporting, and redirecting their responses (Dantonio, 1990). They have the potential for engaging students in instructional conversations that brighten and deepen students' understandings of curricular concepts. Such questioning sequences are characteristic of productive questioning practices.

The responses students give to our questions divulge their way of connecting things up for themselves. They share, through conversation, what they know and don't know. Smith (1998) reminds us that to understand something means "that you are connecting what is new to what you know already" (p. 88). *Our role as questioners is to facilitate students in making such connections.* As Duckworth (1996) informs us:

> *Meaning is not given to us in our encounters, but is given* by *us—constructed by us, each in* our *own way, according to how our understanding is currently organized. As teachers, we need to respect the meaning our students are giving to the events that we share. In the interest of making connections between their understanding and ours, we must adopt an insider's view. . . . (p. 112)*

Paying attention to student responses obligates teachers to view learning from the student's perspective.

Productive question practices can assist classroom practitioners in gaining entrance into students' perspectives and can support them in making connections between a student's mental constructs and the curricular content they are being taught. To be considered an effective, productive questioning practice, questions must actively engage learners in composing responses that involve them in a learning process (Beyer, 1997; Borich, 1992; Dantonio, 1990; Gall; 1970; Good & Brophy, 1987; Orlich et al., 1996; Ornstein, 1988; Sternberg and Spear-Swerling, 1996; Wilen, 1991). When students are meaningfully engaged in their own learning processes, they are better learners and they learn more (Caine & Caine, 1994; Smith, 1998). *Process is the heart of teaching for understanding.* Effective questioning is the lifeline.

Focusing Thinking: Core Questions

In order to create a productive question sequence, there are two functions for questioning. *One is to focus thought. The other is to facilitate the procedures of thought through conversation.* We will first explore questions that focus, guide, and direct the initial efforts of student thinking. In thought-focused questions, the precise language of the cognitive operation is used to cue students as to the kind of thinking they must perform (Beyer, 1997; Dantonio, 1990). Beyer (1997) states, "Using the precise language of thinking is important because the word *think* means so many things (believe, wonder, guess, hypothesize, know, decide, predict, etc.) that it fails to communicate clearly *specific* kind of thinking, thinking product, or mental state" (p. 71).

Beyer (1997), in his book, *Improving Student Thinking,* refers to such questions as "process-structured questions." He defines process-structured questions as "clusters or sets of questions that lead students sequentially through the essential mental steps of *a specific thinking* operation" (p. 179). (emphasis in original) (Once again, the literature abounds with buzzwords for questions focusing, guiding, and directing thinking operations. A thesaurus is a dangerous weapon in the hands of an education writer.) Questions that focus, guide, and direct thinking have been called:

"Focus questions" by Taba et al. (1964) and Taba (1966)
"Focused questions" by Kelly (1989)
"Focusing questions" by Moore (1992)
"Process-structure questions" by Beyer (1997)
"Cognitive domain questions" by Hunkins (1989)

and

"Initial and core questions" by Dantonio (1990), and Beisenherz & Dantonio (1996)

Again, to be consistent with our other writings on questioning, we will use the term *core questions.*

Core questions focus and direct the content and cognitive operation for classroom discourse (Dantonio, 1990). The use of core questions during classroom discourse requires that classroom practitioners think about learning as a process, not simply a content to be memorized. Core questions do not require students to memorize information. They signal and cue particular kinds of cognitive operations, and students use them to guide them in recalling and performing the operations (Beyer, 1997). Their intent is to guide student thinking about content during classroom interactions.

When developing and asking core questions, teachers must be critically conscious of and proficient in crafting questions that are clear, focused on thinking and content identified in learning objectives. The phrasing of the question is critical. The question should be open, which means that students will use words and sentences to answer the questions rather than "yes" or "no" responses. Questions that begin with "Wh" words—what, why, and so on—produce longer and more varied responses from students (Dantonio, 1990; Kubota, 1989), as well as provide windows for asking subsequent processing questions to refine student ideas and cognitive operations.

Placing verbal cues within core questions provides students with insights for making judicial decisions when answering the questions. In designing them, teachers must carefully choose action verbs that connote cognitive operations, such as recalling, comparing, and determining causes and effects

(Costa & Lowery, 1989; Dantonio, 1988, 1990; Orlich, 1996). Dantonio (1990) points out that clearly phrased core questions:

> *(1) contain words that are easily understood by learners;*
> *(2) are stated simply, without cluttering the question with additional questions or explanations;*
> *(3) focus the student on the content and*
> *(4) identify the individual thinking operation students are to use in answering the question. (p. 14)*

Once the thinking operation is placed securely into an instructional question, these questions can be sequenced together to create opportunities for constructing concepts and other forms of thinking systems. In this book, we are focusing on conceptualization. In the next section, we will discuss how to sequence core questions to produce questioning patterns that, in a sense, are stepping-stones that assist students' movement from one thinking operation to another, connecting isolated facts into patterns and relationships that form concepts.

QUESTIONING PATTERNS

Scaffolding—developing a sequential framework of core questions that guide student thinking from one type of cognitive operation to a different type of cognitive operation until the cognitive operation is completed—creates question patterns. Scaffolds make a skill-using procedure explicit, like a blueprint. The scaffolds in building question patterns are the syntactical structure of the core questions that signal each change in a cognitive operation so that students can follow the steps in a cognitive operation.

Taba and associates (1964) and Taba (1966) developed and documented the effectiveness of instructional questioning strategies that were focused on the productive development of student thinking. Her strategies, concept development, interpretation of data, and application of a generalization detailed a sequence of core questions that focused students on particular kinds of thinking operations. She believed that

> *The role of questions becomes crucial and the way of asking questions by far the most influential single teaching act. . . . Questions can . . . be arranged to create stepping stones for transitions from one mode of thinking to another or for the formation of new conceptual schemes. . . . The impact of teaching lies not alone in its single acts but in the manner in which these acts are combined into a pattern. (pp. 53–55)*

For example, if we want students to discriminate the critical characteristic between two forms of literature, the epic poem and the Shakespearean sonnet, the core question pattern or scaffold might look like:

Observing:	What do you notice about the epic poem (the Shakespearean sonnet)?
Recalling:	What do you recall about the critical characteristics of each?
Comparing:	How are they alike?
Contrasting:	In what ways are they different?

In this instance, we sequence the thought processes of observing, recalling, comparing, and contrasting in order to guide the students through the thinking they need to do in order to discriminate between the two forms of literature. We begin with *observing*, in order for students to use their sense of sight to gather critical information that will inform them about the critical characteristics of each form of poetry. Next, we ask students to *recall* information they know about the forms of poetry that may not be available to them based solely on their observations.

Third, we ask the students to *compare* the forms of poetry in order to qualify their understanding that both types of poems contain the critical characteristics necessary for a poem to be a poem. Finally, because our goal was for students to be able to distinguish between the epic poem and the Shakespearean sonnet, we ask them to determine the *differences*. If we wanted students to form the concept of poetry rather than to distinguish between two different forms of poetry, we would have reversed the comparing and contrasting core questions.

In our attempt to initiate and guide thoughtful classroom discourse, we must be certain that the action words selected for our core questions clearly cue or trigger for our students individual kinds of cognitive operation. To do so, teachers must be keenly aware of the kinds of cognitive operation they want students to use in answering core questions. Likewise, in listening to student responses, we must discern if students have used the designated cognitive operation cued by our core question and then use their responses to guide our probes of their thinking and ideas.

Qualities of Student Responses

Once students have responded to our core question, we must realize that their responses may require additional questions in order to assist them in generating quality responses that deepen their understanding of concepts.

Clues for asking additional questions can be found in student responses. In a sense, student responses are the windows of learning through which teachers can enter into students' minds. Our entrance into these windows of learning can enlighten us as to what students know, how well they know it, and how they think about ideas. As we peer into students' understandings, we are afforded opportunities to guide them in the construction of quality responses, enabling them to better understand their ideas.

Quality student responses have several characteristics. Gall (1973) set forth a list of seven attributes that can be used to assess the quality of student responses. The attributes or criteria for assessing learner responses are:

> Clarity: The learner answers in understandable English without mumbling, failing to finish, or confusing his/her thoughts.
>
> Accuracy: The learner's answer contains no factual errors and is based on accurate information.
>
> Appropriateness: The learner answers the question that was asked.
>
> Specificity: The learner clearly identifies who and what s/he is talking about.
>
> Support: The learner gives reasons, facts, or examples to support his/her statement, or s/he explains the criteria or assumptions on which s/he bases his/her opinion.
>
> Complexity: The learner's answer shows that s/he is aware that there are many ways of looking at the problem being discussed, and that s/he must consider the options before a valid judgment can be reached.
>
> Originality: The learner draws upon current knowledge and past experiences to create or discover ideas that are new. (pp. 3–4)

In classroom discourse, teachers must constantly assess each student's response. On-the-spot decisions must be made to determine how well each student understands what he or she is saying. Using the seven criteria for responses as a guide for determining the qualitative aspects of student responses, teachers can make better decisions about the kinds of additional questions needed to shape students' answers into quality responses.

Following Up on Student Responses: Processing Questions

Actively listening to student responses and using their responses in asking timely, thoughtful follow-up questions foster occasions for teachers to delve into student thinking and promote instructional conversation. Follow-up questions ask students to rethink their original responses in order to clarify, to verify, to support, or to personalize what they are saying. In doing so, students are more likely to find meaning in curricular content. Follow-up questions have been called a variety of names in the educational literature. (It amazes us that education writers are prolific in generating buzzwords and are never at a loss for concocting new terms, and in doing so, often confuse simple ideas. We, too, are among the education writers who are guilty of this practice.) For purposes of guiding our readers through the maze of labels assigned to follow-up questions, we offer the following list of labels:

"Probing questions" by Borg et al. (1970) and Hunkins (1989)

"Metacognitive questions" by Beyer (1997)

"Probes" by Borich (1992)

"Probing" and "follow-up questions" by Gall (1970, 1984, 1987); Gall et al. (1978); and Gillett (1980)

"Follow-through questions" by Taba et al. (1964); Taba (1966); and Ehrenberg and Ehrenberg (1978)

"Facilitative," "metacognitive," and "processing questions" by Dantonio (1990); Dantonio and Paradise (1988); and Beisenherz and Dantonio (1996)

In order to be consistent with our previous work in questioning, we will continue to call follow-up questions *processing questions.*

We define processing questions as questions that "help learners think though their original responses so that learners understand the thinking behind what they have said" (Dantonio, 1990, p. 13). Processing questions are asked to engage students in developing a more complete understanding of content and cognitive operation. Processing questions—such as "What do you mean by that?" "How do you know that?" "What makes you say that?" "Explain that in a different way." "What examples do you have to support your idea?" "How did you arrive at your understanding?"—provide classroom practitioners information as to what and how students are thinking. They also launch new and exciting ways of extending student ideas (Dantonio, 1990; Duckworth, 1996). *It is the student response, not the teacher question, that illuminates the breadth and depth of student knowledge. Their responses unveil how they think about things and monitor their thinking operations.* This is called metacognition by cognitive psychologists.

METACOGNITION

Metacognition is the process of thinking about thinking while engaged in the act of thinking. Flavell (1976) described it as follows: "Metacognition refers to one's knowledge concerning one's own cognitive processes or anything related to them, e.g., the learning-relevant properties of information or data. For example, I am engaging in metacognition if I notice that I am having more trouble learning A than B; if it strikes me that I should double check C before accepting it as fact" (p. 232). Cognitive psychologists refer to metacognition as consisting of three types of knowledge: declarative, procedural, and conditional.

Declarative knowledge is our overt understanding of something. It is what rises to the top of our minds and is the information or knowledge that we share. Sometimes it is referred to as the "whatness" of knowledge—the facts, the rules, or other knowledge that efficiently communicate ideas. *Procedural* knowledge is the mental steps, processes, or phases that represent how we arrive at information, or the details of how a cognitive operation is carried out. *Conditional* knowledge determines appropriateness. It relays the conditions under which something is to be done or applied.

Metacognition engages learners in the active monitoring and regulation of their cognitive operations while they are involved in instructional conversations. It represents the control students possess through their knowledge. When we ask the processing questions, especially if we ask them as prompted by the students' response, we sponsor students' metacognitive thinking. *When students understand what they think, how they arrived at their ideas, and when it is appropriate to use particular thinking operations, we empower their learning.* Such productive questioning becomes tools for students' self-generation of thoughts and independent learning.

Beyer (1997) presents the concept of metacognitive reflection and distinguishes it from metacognitive processing. He believes that metacognition is thinking about thinking as one is performing the thought act. Metacognitive reflection, on the other hand, is students' abilities to explain their cognitive operation once they have performed it.

> *Metacognitive reflection in the classroom to improve student thinking requires doing more than simply having students reflect on their own thinking. It also involves getting them to articulate as precisely as possible how they carried out that thinking, sharing the results with others who have engaged in the same thinking operations, and considering critically the procedures and cognitive knowledge revealed or implied. (p. 107)*

To produce quality in terms of conceptual thinking students, and for students to apply productive questioning practices to their learning strategies, they must be able to understand what, how, and under which conditions they need to use particular thinking operations. They must be able to analyze and explain their thinking to others. The processing questions, used systematically, repetitiously, and appropriately during cognitively focused, instructional conversations provide students the modeling needed to assist them in their future learning efforts.

PRODUCTIVE QUESTIONING PRACTICES

By weaving together core questions with appropriate processing questions based on student responses, productive questioning practices are formed. The authors of this book have put together a series of productive questioning practices designed to guide students in thinking about concepts through the use of individual and combined thinking operations. The learning/questioning strategies are called Qu:Est: Questioning for understanding: Empowering student thinking.

The use of these productive questioning practices in classroom discourse creates opportunities for students to refine their ideas and thinking. "In developing and refining learners' cognitive processing, the structuring of the answer and the subsequent teacher questioning may be more important than asking the initial question" (Dantonio & Paradise, 1988, p. 75). The embedding of thoughtful processing questions that follow student responses to core questions provides students a way to engage in meaningful conversations with the teacher and other students. Productive questioning practices can have powerful effects on learning, eliciting more quality responses from students and providing the foundation for students to use productive questions as a guide for their own learning.

The intent of productive questioning practices is twofold: First, they assist students in creating precise, mental pictures that can be internalized and used in making connections with other learnings; and second, they compel students to develop and refine their thinking. Dantonio (1990) asserts that thinking is a skill, and like other skills, it improves through effective practice. To provide students effective practice in thinking, or what Taba et al. (1964) and Taba (1966) refer to as "thinking experiences," teachers must be conscious of their questions and the quality of thinking they expect in student answers.

Using competently phrased core questions with thoughtfully sequenced processing questions furnishes opportunities for teachers to ascertain astute insights into how students think about issues. By eliciting and capturing more quality responses from our students, they are rewarded by understanding their ideas more vividly and deeply. Concomitantly, students grow in their awareness of how productive questioning practices can be a resource to direct and to support future learning.

SUMMARY

Teaching for understanding is a process for learning. As classroom practitioners' understanding of learning as a process matures, productive questioning practices will play a pivotal role in the development of students' reasoning abilities and in their making sense of complex, sophisticated ideas.

Students not only need to internalize knowledge (Gardner, 1991; Perkins, 1993; Perrone, 1998), they must encounter powerful, invigorating learning strategies to break though years of dull instruction—which was focused on memorizing—that dimly lit, if not extinguished, their desire to learn. For students to be excited about learning, instruction must ignite them to think critically and creatively. Their classrooms must glow with meaningful conversations. This glow, this light, can only grow more brightly, appear more frequently, and blaze more intensely as teachers gently nudge open the responses of students through careful, thoughtful questioning.

REFERENCES

Aschner, M. J., & Gallagher, J. J. (1965). *A system for classifying thought processes in the context of classroom verbal interaction*. Urbana, IL: Institute for Research on Exceptional Children, University of Illinois.

Ausubel, D. P. (1960). The use of advance organizers in the learning and retention of meaningful verbal material. *Journal of Educational Psychology, 51*, 267–272.

Ausubel, D. P. (1968). *Educational psychology: A cognitive view*. New York: Holt, Reinhart, and Winston.

Beisenherz, P. C., & Dantonio, M. (1996). *Using the learning cycle to teach physical science*. Portsmouth, NH: Heinemann.

Beyer, B. K. (1997). *Improving student thinking*. Boston: Allyn & Bacon.

Bloom, B. S. (Ed.). (1956). *Taxonomy of educational objectives, Handbook I: Cognitive domain*. New York: David McKay.

Borg, W., et al. (1970). *The mini course: A microteaching approach to teacher education*. Beverly Hills, CA: Collier-Macmillan.

Borich, G. D. (1992). *Effective teaching methods*. (2nd edition). New York: Merrill.

Brooks, J. G., & Brooks, M. G. (1993). *The case for constructivistic classrooms*. Alexandria, VA: Association for Supervision and Instruction.

Brophy, J. E. (1986). *Synthesizing the results of research linking teaching behavior to student achievement*. Paper presented at the annual meeting of the American Educational Research Association, San Francisco. (ERIS Document Reproduction Service No. ED 293 914).

Bruner, J. (1960). *The process of education*. Cambridge, MA: Harvard University Press.

Bruner, J. (1966). *Toward a theory of instruction*. Cambridge, MA: Harvard University Press.

Bruner, J. (1986). *Actual minds, possible worlds*. Cambridge, MA: Harvard University Press.

Bruner, J. (1990). *Acts of meaning*. Cambridge, MA: Harvard University Press.

Bruner, J., Goodnow, J. J., & Austin, G. A. (1956). *A study of thinking*. New York: Science Editions, Inc.

Bruner, J. (1996). *The culture of education*. Cambridge, MA: Harvard University Press.

Costa, A. L. (1991). *The school as a home for the mind*. Palatine, IL: Skylight Publications.

Costa, A., & Lowery, L. (1989). *Techniques for teaching thinking*. Pacific Grove, CA: Midwest Publications.

Dantonio, M. (1990). *How can we create thinkers? Questioning strategies that work for teachers.* Bloomington, IN: National Education Service.

Dantonio, M., & Paradise, L. V. (1988). Teacher question-answer strategy and the cognitive correspondence between teacher questions and learner responses. *Journal of Research and Development in Education, 21*, 71–76.

Dewey, J. (1910). *How we think.* Boston: D.C. Heath.

Dewey, J. (1938). *Experience and education.* New York: Macmillan.

Duckworth, E. (1996). *"The having of wonderful ideas" and other essays on teaching and learning.* New York: Teachers College Press.

Ehrenberg, S. D., & Ehrenberg, L. M. (1978). *Building and applying strategies for intellectual competencies in students.* Miami, FL: Institute for Curriculum and Instruction.

Ennis, R. H. (1989). Critical thinking and subject specificity: Clarification and needed research. *Educational Researcher, 18* (3), p. 5.

Flavell, J. H. (1976). Metacognitive aspects of problem solving. In L. B. Resnick (Ed.), *The nature of intelligence*. Hillsdale, NJ: Erlbaum.

Gall, M. D. (1970). The use of questions in teaching. *Review of Educational Research, 40*, 707–721.

Gall, M. D. (1973, February). *What effects do teacher's questions have on students?* Paper presented at the Annual Meeting of the American Educational Research Association, New Orleans, LA.

Gall, M. D. (1984). Synthesis of research on teachers' questioning. *Educational Leadership, 42*, 40–47.

Gall, M.D., & Gillett, M. (1980). "The Discussion Method in Classroom Teaching, *Theory into Practice 19*, 98–102.

Gall, M. D., & Rhody, T. (1987). Review of research on questioning techniques. In W. W. Wilen (Ed.), *Questions, questioning techniques, and effective teaching* (pp. 23–43).Washington, D C: National Education Association.

Gall, M. D., et al. (1978). Effects of questioning techniques and recitation on students' learning. *American Educational Research Journal, 40*, 175–199.

Gardner, H. (1991). *The unschooled mind.* New York: Basic Books.

Good, T. L., & Brophy, J. E. (1987). *Looking into classrooms* (4th Ed.). New York: Harper and Row.

Hunkins, F. P. (1989). *Teaching thinking through effective questioning.* Needham Heights, MA: Christopher Gordon Press.

Kelly, T. E. (1989). Leading class discussion of controversial issues. *Social Education, 53*, 368–370.

Klinzing, H. G., & Klinzing-Eurich, G. (1987). Question responses and reaction. In J. D. Dillon (Ed.), *Questioning and discussion: A multidisciplinary study.* Norwood, NJ: Ablex.

Kubota, M. (1989). *Question-answering behaviors in ESL and EFL classrooms: Similarities and differences.* (ERIC Document Reproductive Service No. ED 313 913).

Moore, K. D. (1992). *Classroom teaching skills* (2nd ed.). New York: Random House.

Nickerson, R. (1988–89). On improving thinking through instruction. In E. Z. Rothkopf (Ed.), *Review of research in education, 15*, 31. Washington, DC: American Educational Research Association.

Orlich, D. C., et al. (1996). *Teaching strategies* (4th Ed.). Lexington, MA: D. C. Heath and Company.

Ornstein, A. C. (1988). Questioning: The essence of good teaching—part 2. *NASSP Bulletin, 72* (505), 72–78.

Pask, G. (1975). *Conversation, cognition, and learning.* New York: Elsevier.

Perkins, D. (1993). Teaching for understanding. *American Educator: The Professional Journal of the American Federation of Teachers. 17,* 3, 8, 28–35.

Perkins, D. (1998). What Is Understanding? M. S. Wiske (Ed.), In *Teaching for understanding.* pp. 39–58. San Francisco: Jossey-Bass.

Perrone, V. (1998). Why do we need a pedagogy of understanding? In M. S. Wiske (Ed.), *Teaching for understanding* (pp. 13–38). San Francisco, Jossey-Bass.

Prawat, R. S. (1991). The value of ideas: The immersion approach to the development of thinking. *Educational Researcher, 70,* (2), 3–30.

Reigle, R. P. (1976). Classifying classroom questions. *Journal of Teacher Education 27,* 156–161.

Riley, J. P. (1981). The effects of preservice teachers' cognitive questioning level and redirecting on student science achievement. *Journal of Research in Science Teaching, 18,* 303–309.

Rowe, M. B. (1987). Using wait-time to stimulate inquiry. In W. W. Wilen (Ed.), *Questions, questioning techniques, and effective teaching* (pp. 95–106). Washington, DC: National Education Association.

Smith, F. (1998). *The book of learning and forgetting.* New York: Teachers College Press.

Sternberg, R. J., & Spear-Swerling. (1996). *Teaching for thinking.* Washington, DC: American Psychological Association.

Swartz, R. (1991). How to infuse thinking. *Cogitare, 3,* 1–7.

Taba, H. (1966). *Teaching strategies and cognitive function in elementary school children.* (U.S. Office of Education Cooperative Research Project No. 2402). San Francisco: U.S. Office of Education.

Taba, H., Levine, S., and Elzey, F. F. (1964). *Thinking in elementary school children.* (U.S. Office of Education Cooperative Research Project No. 1574). San Francisco: U.S. Office of Education.

Tharp, R. G., & Gallimore, R. (1988). Rousing schools to life. *American Educator, 13,* (2), 20–25, 46–52.

Wilen, W. W. (1987). Effective questions and questioning: A classroom application. In W. W. Wilen (Ed.), *Questions, questioning techniques, and effective teaching.* Washington, DC: National Education Association.

Wilen, W. W. (1991). *Questioning skills for teachers.* Washington, DC: National Education Association.

Wright, C. J., & Nuthall, G. (1970). Relationships between teacher behaviors and pupil achievement in three experimental elementary science lessons. *American Educational Research Journal 7,* 477–491.

▶ Part III

Learning to Question

Teaching for thinking has emerged as one of the primary aims of a quality education. During the past two decades, national commissions on school and teacher development reforms have advocated instruction that includes the teaching and learning for understanding—students are provided instruction that assists them in the internalization of concepts and other learnings that can be used under different circumstances in and out of classroom studies. Such learning is the basis for continued lifelong learning. Linda Darling-Hammond, in her book *The Right to Learn* (1997), cites:

> *Students taught for understanding can evaluate and defend ideas with careful reasoning and evidence, independently inquire into a problem using a productive research strategy, produce a high-quality piece of work, and understand the standards that indicate good performance. They demonstrate what they understand by using what they have learned to solve problems they have not encountered before. (p. 96)*

In the following chapters, we describe a design for instructional questioning strategies, Questioning for understanding: Empowering student thinking (Qu:Est), that addresses the agenda for these reform statements. We focus the teaching for understanding, in this book, on conceptual learning. While teaching for understanding is more than conceptual learning, we have limited our work at the present time to conceptualization because we find that knowledge of concepts is fundamental to most school curricula. Additionally, the literature of classroom observation points out that instruction tends to be recitation-based, where students are memorizing specific facts without conceptual understanding of how knowledge fits together to form concepts. For the most part, in our personal observations of classroom instruction, we find students engaged in the memorization of concepts rather than involved in the active construction of conceptual understanding.

Conceptual understanding requires that students engage in thinking operations that allow them to collect specific facts, arrange the facts to create patterns, determine the reasons for the patterns, and name appropriately and precisely the critical characteristics of the constructed patterns in order to efficiently communicate the concept. This is important if students are to not only recognize and use concepts in productive, meaningful ways, but also understand the thinking necessary for forming and extending concepts.

REFERENCES

Darling-Hammond, L. (1997). *The right to learn*. San Francisco: Jossey-Bass.

National Commission on Excellence in Education. (1983). *A nation at risk*. Washington, DC: U.S. Department of Education.

National Commission on Teaching and America's Future (NCTAF). (1996). *What matters most: Teaching and America's future*. New York: Author.

National Council of Teachers of Mathematics. (1989). *Curriculum and evaluation standards for school mathematics*. Reston, VA: Author.

National Council on Education Standards and Testing (NCEST). (1992). *Raising standards for American education*. Washington, DC: U.S. Government Printing Office.

National Foundation for the Improvement of Education (NFIE). (1995). *Touching the future*. Washington, DC: Author.

National Foundation for the Improvement of Education (NFIE). (1996) *Teachers take charge of their learning: Transforming professional development for student success*. Washington, DC: Author.

National Governor's Association. (1986). *Time for results: The governor's 1991 report on education*. Washington, DC: Author.

Renaissance Group (1991). *Teachers for the new world*. Cedar Falls, IA: University of Northern Iowa.

▶ 5

Questioning for Understanding: Empowering Student Thinking

FACILITATIVE SET

Questioning for understanding: Empowering student thinking (Qu:Est) is a design for planning and conducting instructional strategies composed of productive questioning practices. The instructional strategies focus on individual thinking operations necessary for constructing concepts. Qu:Est Instructional Strategies are designed to assist teachers in asking productive questions that facilitate learners' conceptual awareness and understanding.

Qu:Est Instructional Strategies promote learning as a process. In order for students to attain a firm understanding of concepts and the thinking operations necessary to construct conceptual understandings, they must share their ideas with each other. Success in facilitating or mediating instructional talk relies on a teacher's firm understanding of the nature and function of productive questions as tools in planning, delivering, and assessing instruction. Qu:Est strategies assist students and their teacher to participate in instructional conversations by engaging them in thinking experiences that expose and refine student knowledge of content. *Instructional conversations are opportunities for teachers and students to dialogue about important concepts using informed and focused thinking operations.*

Qu:Est was developed using principles of learning derived from the literature on effective questioning practices, teaching for understanding, and how children learn. The design is based on the following premises:

> Memorizing is not equivalent to learning. Learning is the result of students consciously thinking through their ideas to construct deep and broad understandings as they personalize and use the information in meaningful, relevant ways.

> Learning requires students to possess a heightened awareness of various types of thinking operations and to be conscious of the role various types of thinking operations play in the conceptualization process.

> Development, refinement, and monitoring of one's thinking abilities evolve as students talk through their ideas and share their understandings in conversation with each other guided by teachers.

> To empower student cognitive operation, teachers and students must engage in the deliberate practice of thinking operations with content familiar to students. In doing so, students are able to concentrate and reflect on the purpose and structure of the various thinking operations.

> As students gain confidence in their knowledge of thinking operations and become adept in their abilities to use various types of thinking in informed ways, content knowledge is enhanced.

In other words, learning requires our full attention on both *how* we think about things and *what* we are thinking about. We must be fully awake or conscious of our learning processes in order to construct deep, broad, meaningful, and relevant understandings of content.

Learning relies on our abilities to actively engage in experiences that sharpen our perceptions, refine our thinking, and connect the unknown to the known. This means, as educators, we must come to grips with how thinking operations inform our understandings and how our understandings demand that we refine our thinking abilities. In order for students to develop and refine their thinking abilities, instruction must focus on familiar content. For students to develop enriched understandings of content, they must engage skillfully in the use and monitoring of their thinking operations. Carefully framed questions promote the development and refinement of student thinking operations and awaken students' understandings of ideas.

CONCEPTUAL UNDERSTANDING

Conceptualizing demands that learners become active participants in their learning process. As passive learners, students may memorize information that does not possess any meaning for them. It's like putting information into a recording device that has not been programmed to understand the information. Therefore, nothing happens when one goes to retrieve the information. To "re-call," "re-cite," "re-view," "re-state," "re-member," or "re-collect," something must be put in place, first, before the action of "re" or "doing again" can be operationalized. When we teach for memorization, we may be requiring learners to input ideas that possess no innate learning program.

Active conceptual learning, on the other hand, requires that learners collect specific information pertinent to concepts for themselves. They must acquire and process the information for meaning. Following the collection of understood information, learners must sort through the information they gathered to discover relationships or patterns among the isolated facts. Once learners discover and understand the relationships, they communicate the relationships in words or phrases that mean something to the learner and that also represent the critical characteristics of the concept. These words or phrases are *concept labels.*

Concept labels are the capstones of conceptual understanding—not the nitty-gritty critical characteristics needed for understanding. To simply require students to memorize concept labels and concept definitions is not the same as forming the concept and applying names that mean something to students. Likewise, having students classify new examples of concepts to concept labels does not guarantee that students understand the critical characteristic or *concept attributes.* For example, the concept label, *verb,* means nothing to young students. However, "words that show action or words that tell what someone or something is doing" (concept attribute) is where the meaning is.

Classifying new examples of the concept is a matter of matching the critical characteristics of the known concept with the attributes of a new situation or example. To classify meaningfully new *concept examples* requires students to analyze the new example's characteristics to determine if it meets the critical characteristics or attributes of a concept. Using *verb* as an illustration again: When a student says "runs" is the *verb* (concept label) of the sentence "Lon runs down the street" (concept example), the student must understand the meaning of "runs," understand how the word is used in the sentence, and then compare it to the critical attributes of the concept to determine if it meets the concept attributes. *Conceptualizing demands that students be in full charge of their thinking and be able to monitor their learning in this manner.*

QU:EST INSTRUCTIONAL STRATEGIES

Qu:Est Instructional Strategies are process-centered lesson designs that incorporate productive questioning practices for carrying out instructional conversations to develop and refine students' cognitive abilities as they engage in instructional conversations about curricula. Each lesson design focuses on individual thinking operations that are embodied in the conceptualization process. The instructional strategies combine thought questions with follow-up questions that assist students in thinking through their responses so that they are aware of how they arrived at and can monitor their answers.

The Instructional Strategies are organized in the following manner:

COLLECTING STRATEGIES
Observing
Recalling

BRIDGING STRATEGIES
Comparing
Contrasting
Grouping

ANCHORING STRATEGIES
Labeling
Classifying

The strategies, while described as discrete cognitive operations, can be conducted separately or can be sequenced to form an initial understanding of a concept, to distinguish between like concepts, or to extend students' initial understandings to include related subconcepts.

The Collecting Strategies

Collecting Strategies are the foundation for building concepts. The cognitive operations classified as Collecting Strategies are Observing and Recalling. Used independently, they sharpen students' abilities to gather specific details from their experiences and recollections, as well as from printed and audiovisual media sources. In terms of forming concepts, they are the primary ways in which students garner specific information that will be used to identify and distinguish the critical characteristics or attributes of concepts.

The Observing lesson design will focus instructional conversation on the collection of specific physical information that students can pick up through their senses. Conducting these lessons with students sharpens their ability to perceive valuable information from their personal experiences, concrete examples, or their manipulation of something. The Recalling lesson design will assist students in retrieving accurate, reliable information. In a sense, it is a research strategy that requires students to verify their responses from multiple sources—for example, personal experience, text material, authorities, or generalizations. Possessing reliable, meaningful facts is essential to forming well-constructed concepts.

The Bridging Strategies

However, conceptualization requires more than just collecting and recollecting specific pieces of information. Learners must also play around with the information they gather in order to construct meaningful relationships.

The thinking operations of Comparing, Contrasting, and Grouping are integral to building and creating concepts. When learners discover relationships among previously isolated facts, putting together the specific information to form larger ideas, connecting the bits and pieces of one example to the characteristics of a similar example, or grouping similar objects or ideas together because they all possess similar characteristics, they are identifying the critical characteristics, attributes, or patterns of a concept.

In the Qu:Est Instructional Strategies, the thinking operations of Comparing, Contrasting, and Grouping have been categorized as **Bridging Strategies.** "Bridging," for us, is a metaphor that explains how learners move from the gathering of isolated facts to connect up, to transition toward, or to create a passageway into establishing relationships among information that forms the critical characteristics of a concept. The Bridging Strategies are designed to assist teachers in asking productive questions that provide opportunities for students to connect isolated facts to form critical attributes or characteristics that are the basis of a concept. The relationships are based on the mental connections learners have made through their experiences with the information.

The Bridging Strategies are the means by which students sort and organize information to form relationships and to create patterns of ideas that are conceptual in nature, not isolated facts. By providing learners with opportunities to practice Comparing, Contrasting, and Grouping, they will better understand the individual thinking operations and become more aware of the types of questions they need to ask when engaged in various forms of conceptual thinking.

The Anchoring Strategies

Anchoring Strategies are designed to assist teachers in asking questions that facilitate the cognitive operations of Labeling and Classifying. These strategies are used once students have constructed concept definitions, using the Bridging Strategies, and students now need to name the concept or determine if new examples fit the critical characteristics of the concepts or related subconcepts. These two thinking operations are instrumental in communicating and categorizing concepts formed by students.

The Labeling lesson design provides a means for efficient communication of concept attributes. By engaging in conversations using the Labeling lesson design, students learn to appreciate the value of vocabulary building and how precise wording is important in conveying ideas. The Classifying lesson design provides students with opportunities to use their constructed knowledge of concepts to analyze new or unknown information or examples. The Anchoring Strategies formalize the construction of concepts, securing that students have established a meaningful link between specific facts and information and the naming of their discovered patterns.

Sequencing Qu:Est Instructional Strategies

The Qu:Est Instructional Strategies, while they need to be studied and practiced alone to attain competence in their use, are most powerful when sequenced to build concepts. The objective of the lesson determines the sequence of the strategies. The independent strategies can be organized to form an initial concept, to distinguish between two like concepts, or to distinguish between two related subconcepts. If three or more related subconcepts are indicated by the objective, a third sequence is used.

To plan the strategies for conceptual understanding, first teachers must plan the conceptual content plan. Every concept or related subconcept to be built by students should possess concept examples, concept attributes, and at least one appropriate concept label. For example, *The Wizard of Oz, Alice in Wonderland,* and *The Mouse and His Child* are all concept examples of the concept label "fantasy literature." Fantasy literature is the concept label that efficiently communicates the concept attributes of the examples. The concept attributes, or critical characteristics, may be described as "literature that portrays characters in conflict situations in which the characters or the situations are altered to create an illusion of life that intensifies a message."

In this situation, students will be forming an initial concept, Fantasy literature, presuming that they already understand the concept of literature. An initial concept sequence is developed when the objective calls for students to have a foundational understanding of a concept before they can distinguish or extend the concept. To illustrate this, before students can understand the concept of fantasy literature, they must first understand the concept of literature. Fantasy literature may have many related subconcepts—for example, children's stories, epic poems, science fiction, and others—each possessing a unique attribute that distinguishes it from the other.

Forming an Initial Concept Sequence

The sequence for forming an initial concept using the Qu:Est Instructional Strategies is:

- *Observing* and *Recalling* information from each example. The collected information must include both critical characteristics of the concept and noncritical information.
- *Contrasting* the information from each example to sort out differences that are not the critical characteristics of the concept. Using the examples from fantasy literature, each story has different characters, different settings, different messages, and so forth.
- *Comparing* the information from each example to determine the essential common issues of the concept. These are the ideas that form the concept attributes, critical characteristics, properties, or concept definition. In this case, "literature that portrays characters in conflict situations in which the characters or the situations are altered to create an illusion of life that intensifies a message."
- To complete the sequence, *Labeling* is used so that students can find or create a name that communicates meaningfully to them the idea represented in the concept. Students create and support their own names for the concept before the teacher provides the term that will be used by the class. In this way, students can associate a term that possesses meaning for them with one that may not.
- *Classifying* can be used to determine if students can identify and analyze an example not used in the concept formation sequence as representing the concept.

Distinguishing between Concepts

The sequence for differentiating between two similar concepts or two related subconcepts is as follows.

- *Observing* and *recalling* the specific details of each example of the two concepts or related subconcepts.
- *Comparing* to determine the commonalities that are not essential for discriminating one concept from the other.
- *Contrasting* to determine the essential, critical difference between the concepts or related subconcepts.
- *Labeling* each subconcept for efficiency in communicating the concept.
- *Classifying* other examples of both concepts to assess students' understanding of each concept and their ability to analyze new examples using the criteria established.

Extending Concepts to Related Subconcepts

Often the objectives of lessons require that students understand many related subconcepts. In this case, a concept map should be created in the planning process. For example:

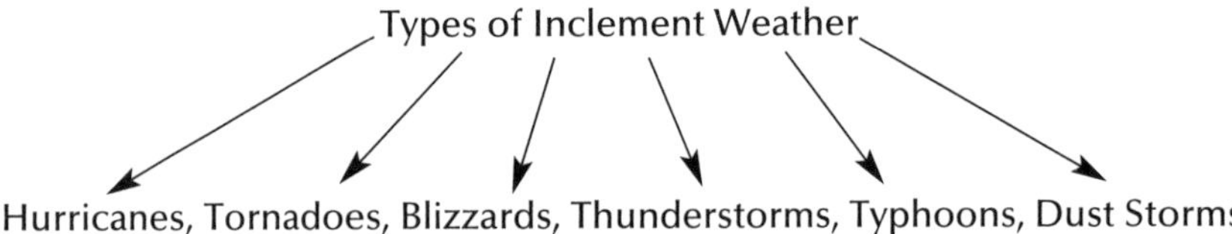

Each concept label needs to be defined by concept attributes and illustrated with concept examples. The sequence for carrying out the process of extending concepts to related subconcepts using Qu:Est follows:

- *Observing* and *Recalling* specific information about each of the subconcepts.
- *Grouping* the information or examples because they are alike in some way. Students must also establish a reason for each grouping that distinguishes it from the other groups.
- *Labeling* the groups with meaningful, relevant words or phrases that communicate the critical characteristics, attributes, or properties of the groupings.
- *Classifying* new examples into groups or under labels and supporting the new example to the concept attributes of the grouping or label.

INQUIRY SUGGESTIONS AND QUESTIONS

- What objectives or content do you teach that could be used as material for an individual Qu:Est Instructional Strategy?
- What concepts are most important in your subject area or gradelevel?
- Which of the concept sequences could you use to assist students in developing a meaningful understanding of your selected concepts?

6

The Nature and Function of Productive Questions

FACILITATIVE SET

The study of productive questioning is serious business, yet when done well, looks effortless. If we want our students to think creatively, thoughtfully, and productively, we must understand our students' struggle to develop and refine their responses, which deepen and broaden their understandings. As teachers, we use questioning for many purposes. We use questions to stimulate student thinking, to raise issues, to explore content, and to find out what students remember or don't remember. Qu:Est is designed to enable teachers to use productive questioning practices to assess, prior to instruction, student thinking and content understanding; to carry out instructional conversations that develop and refine student thinking operations and content knowledge; and to assess, following instruction, students' newly developed conceptions. For both teacher and students, the productive questioning practices of Qu:Est provide a means for engaging in thoughtful instructional conversations and regulating the dialogue.

Productive questioning is a pivotal instructional tool, for it focuses learning on the process of thinking while attending to the study of content. Additionally, productive questioning involves listening carefully to what students are saying in order to follow up on the way that they think, encouraging depth and breadth of ideas. To question effectively requires that we understand the nature and function of our questions and the impact productive questioning has on learners and the curriculum under study. It means that we must not only be responsible for carefully crafting our questions, but we must also be eminently conscious of the subtle nonverbal cues that we must play out during instruction in order to be effective in eliciting responses from students.

To better understand the nature and function of productive questioning practices, we present:

1. A vignette in which teachers are engaged in a dialogue with us about the teaching of thinking. Throughout the vignette we model the kinds of questioning practices exposed by Qu:Est;
2. Our reflections about the teachers' reactions to the productive questioning practices;
3. A self-study discussion that explains the nature and function of productive questioning practices; and
4. A series of inquiry suggestions and questions to assist our readers in investigating the use of core and processing questions.

Vignette: This Thinking Stuff Is Serious Business

The teachers are talking noisily as I enter the room. When it quiets down, I ask the teachers to arrange the desks into a horseshoe design. I position myself in the middle of the horseshoe, close to the students. I begin the lesson by asking, "How many of you believe that you teach kids to think in your lessons?" I eye each person in the room as I ask the question. All hands go up. I am well aware that the teachers who sign up for this class do so because of their keen interest in the teaching of thinking.

"OK, I'd like you to think about how you approach teaching kids to think in your classrooms. Please jot down some examples of things you do that promote thinking." I provide about five minutes for the group to collect their thoughts. This "think time," called "wait-time" in the literature, is important for generating a quality response, and the act of writing down responses offers the teachers a reference to aid them in their conversation about teaching for thinking.

"Now that you have had an opportunity to think about your classroom instruction, let me focus our interactions. What are some of the qualities of thinking?" I ask as I move to the overhead to record their answers.

This question receives a number of responses. The responses teachers give are types of thinking, rather than qualities of thinking. They cite the following types of thinking: creative thinking, critical thinking, analytical thinking, problem solving, decision making, remembering, inductive thinking, deductive thinking, conceptualizing.

It is obvious to me that they have read articles and books on the subject and have sincere thoughts about the importance of teaching for thinking. After most of the teachers have had an opportunity to share their answers, I refocus their thinking by saying: "You are giving me types of thinking, but not the characteristics of thinking. How do you know when someone is thinking?"

"Well, we assume someone is thinking when they answer questions," Jill offers.

"What do you mean by 'thinking'?" I ask the group as I sit in a vacant chair near the middle of the horseshoe.

Jim responds, "Well, it means using your mind."

I smile at Jim and slowly look at the rest of the class. "Hmm, who else has a definition for teaching thinking?"

"It's when you ask questions that get students to analyze something," Sharon responds.

"You are giving me an example. I would like a definition. So what do you mean by the term 'thinking'?" I ask Sharon.

"Analysis," she says.

Jody adds, "Yes, analysis is a part of thinking critically about something."

John joins in before I can ask Jody to clarify 'critically.' "It is when you are holding a discussion and students are coming up with their own ideas."

I get up from the desk and move to the door at the front of the class, some distance from the teachers.

"Again," I say to John, "you are giving me an example of teaching for thinking. I asked for the qualities associated with thinking—so what are some attributes of thinking?"

"Thinking is creating new ideas or exploring old ideas," he offers.

"Yes," Chris joins in, "it's thinking though ideas."

"Thinking through?" I query. "What does 'thinking through' mean?"

"You know," he says.

"No, I don't know. You are using 'thinking' to define 'thinking.' What does 'thinking' mean?"

"Let's see—it means interpreting."

"Chris," I say, suspecting that he's picking words out of the air, "give me an example of interpreting."

I notice that students are shifting nervously in their chairs. I quietly walk over to a desk next to Chris and sit.

Chris makes an attempt to answer: "Well, for example, when you asked what we do in our class to promote thinking, I wrote that during discussions, I want students to tell me *why* something happened the way it did. (He stresses the word "why.") In history, there are always many reasons for events occurring, and I want students to connect the events with the causes for the events. When they do that, I know that they are beginning to see history as a series of connecting stories rather than something occurring randomly and having no supporting reasons."

I nod and look around. The class is silent. Focusing back on Chris, I ask, "In what way is 'connecting' events to their causes 'interpreting'?" I am well aware that I am pushing, and I sense frustration from the group.

"Because it shows that students find a relationship between two events in history. They are inferring that one event led to the next," Chris says emphatically.

I smile, turn to face the other teachers in the class, and address my question to them. "Who else has a definition for 'interpreting'?" I query.

There is silence in the room. I wait. The room is tense. Thirty seconds pass.

Finally, Sharon says, "Analysis is interpreting?"

Knowing that she, like others, is sensitive to Chris's experience, I query nonchalantly, "Hmm, give me an example of analysis." I look out the window.

"Like when you ask students to compare and contrast two characters in a story," she offers.

"How is comparing two characters in a story helping them analyze or interpret?" I venture.

"Well, it is. They have to know about each of the characters and how they are alike and different. You know, they have to know the content and go from there," she stammers.

I smile. "What makes you think that by the students knowing or remembering the content that they are analyzing it?"

"I don't know. They just are. And it's not the remembering, but the inferences that they make about the characters that is interpreting." Sharon's intonation tells me that she has had it with my questioning. I move toward Sharon and stand behind her so that she cannot see me.

"Who else has an example of teaching kids to think?" I say, redirecting the question to the entire group.

Bill, seated directly across the room from Sharon, replies: "I use brainteasers—stories that have more than one answer."

Jane, sitting to Bill's right, says, "I have them tell me *why* all the time."

"Let's go back to Bill's response," I say as I nod affirmatively to Jane. Bill's face becomes taut.

"What is there about the stories having more than one answer that makes you think that you are teaching them to think?"

"Well, it's their opinions," he proffers.

"And what do you recall that you do to help shape their opinions? I am curious."

He says, "I make sure everyone has a chance to talk."

"Well, you said that the stories have more than one answer. How do you know that the answer a student gives you is a result of analyzing the story or brainteaser and not what they recall someone else said?"

"I don't, I guess. I just thought that if I get different students to say different things that it would make them realize that everyone sees things differently."

"Jane," I say.

Jane stiffens and says, "Oh, no, I wish I hadn't said anything. I know you're going to ask me something."

"Yes. What makes you think that asking students 'why' is helping them think?" I wait—five seconds, ten seconds, fifteen seconds. Jane looks down.

The teachers are all looking down. No one is making eye contact. I wait twenty seconds. I move from my position next to Chris and stand behind Jane, sitting three seats away. Finally, after what was a very uncomfortable period of time, Evelyn, from across the room, says, 'Why' questions make students reason through their ideas."

"By 'reasoning through,' what do you mean?" I ask and look toward the other teachers. Their eyes tell me that they are trying to think of a response to help Jane out of this situation.

"Oh, boy," Evelyn says, rolling her eyes up. "Think about," she declares.

"Jane." She shudders again and buries her head in her arms crossed on her desk. I cross the room again, standing in front of Evelyn's desk. I look at Jane. "Give me an example of a 'why' question that you would ask students."

Five seconds, ten seconds pass. Her facial expression tells me that she is searching for an answer.

"Yesterday, I taught a lesson about pollution. I wanted to know *why* students thought pollution was contributing to the decline of life," she says, hesitantly.

"OK." I nod and turn away, surveying the rest of the class. Relief floods Jane's face. "In what way does that question cause students to think about pollution?" Standing in the middle of the horseshoe, I direct the question to the entire group.

Five seconds, ten seconds pass. Finally Jerry answers in a frustrated voice. "Because it makes students think about the types of pollution and what it does to the earth."

"How do you know that?" I pitch back.

"Oh, now," Jerry says, "ask Jane. She's the one who asks that question." All eyes drift sympathetically toward Jane. Jane begins to laugh. The entire group laughs nervously.

Once the teachers regain their composure, Judy says, "I guess what you're doing is making us examine our answers, and we're not used to doing that. And if the truth were known, we don't really know why we think we're teaching thinking. It's pretty sad. Here we are all telling you that we teach thinking, and we can't explain why we think we teach it."

I sit, again, next to Chris, listening to the teachers' interactions.

"Yes," Jane says, "I'm stumped. I was always told to ask 'why' questions, but I never thought about what was happening to students when I asked them "why." Sometimes, I don't even know what I looking for by asking them 'why'.

"I know," Sharon agrees. "It's like there's this little voice in the back of my mind and when I ask 'why,' the discussion seems to go all over the place. I have a lot of learning to do."

"And unlearning," I add.

Sharon smiles brightly, cocking her head to the right and, in jest, asks the caveat: "And, just what do *you* mean by 'unlearning'?"

We all laugh, knowing that this will be a spirited undertaking that will challenge us all.

Reflection on Teacher Learning

The teachers in this scenario experience firsthand how difficult it is to answer questions that direct their thinking and that encourage them to rethink their initial responses. The teachers, as will their students, experience the most difficulty with answering questions that require them to qualify their responses by clarifying words they use or by relating an example to the meaning of their words. Perhaps this is because we assume that we all know what we mean. Maybe we have difficulty qualifying our responses because we view the questioning of them as a challenge. Or it just might be that we use words in answering questions that we find the most comfort in using even though we have not thought very seriously about their meaning.

Whatever the reason, teachers soon learn that to teach for thinking is not a snap, especially if we want students to understand *not only what they think but also how they arrived at their understandings*. We must search deeply for understandings, and we must concentrate on constructing responses that make sense to others and to us. We simply cannot infer that because someone is able to answer a question that focuses the learning dialogue that the person has depth of understanding; nor can we assume that others listening and engaging in the dialogue understand the speaker.

Productive questioning practices, used wisely during instructional conversations, increase opportunities for exploring student responses and sharpening students' understanding of how they think and why it is important to engage in instructional conversations that prod their ideas. Qu:Est provides a framework for planning and conducting lessons that engages teachers and students in strategies for thinking about thinking.

SELF-STUDY DISCUSSION

Qu:Est consists of four key concepts: (1) posing thought-focused questions, (2) using student responses as a basis for further questioning, (3) pacing and sequencing additional questions to guide the thinking experiences of students, and (4) providing "think time" combined with appropriate nonverbal gestures and use of the classroom space to invite thoughtful responses. The central issue of Qu:Est is not simply the asking of questions, but understanding the nature and function of our questions. Likewise, Qu:Est is designed to assist teachers in discovering how students think, determining what students can and cannot perform given a particular kind of cognitive operation, and discerning the information or concepts that hold meaning for students. For students, Qu:Est strategies become learning tools they can use to structure their thinking about concepts.

Nature of Questioning

The *nature of questioning* refers to what we intend from our instructional questions. Our intention for classroom discourse is shaped and directed by the goals and objectives for the instruction. Issues such as how we phrase questions, the content we want students to focus on, and the cognitive operation we want students to use in order to explore the content are sensitive to the nature of our questions. Likewise, the pacing of our questions and our patience in waiting for well-reasoned responses depend on our understandings of question structure and the subtle, productive use of classroom space.

In order to determine the kinds of questions we want to use during instruction, we must attend to the goals and objectives of the lesson. We must answer questions about the purpose of the lesson and the outcome(s) for instruction before we can develop appropriate questions for instruction.

Questions that deal with the nature of thinking, the sequence or patterns of thought questions, and the shaping of quality responses from students are central to conducting successful, thoughtful instructional conversations. The nature of questioning turns our attention toward the purpose and outcome of our lessons, the structuring of question patterns, and how we foster student interactions.

Nature of Questioning

Determining the Purpose and Outcome

What are the kinds of thinking students must do to accomplish the objective(s) of the lesson?

What kinds of responses am I seeking from students to drive the lesson?

What will the answer sound like if students answered the question(s) appropriately?

What will the answer sound like if they don't answer the question(s) appropriately?

What should I do with either kind of response?

Questioning Patterns

If there are multiple cognitive operations to accomplish the objectives, how should I sequence additional questions in order for students to achieve the purpose of the lesson?

If there are multiple thought processes needed to accomplish the lesson's purpose, how will I know when to change the kind of thinking students are doing to achieve the purpose of the lesson?

How do I determine the sequence of questions for following up on student responses?

Shaping Quality Student Responses

What do I do with the responses I expect?

What do I do with responses I didn't expect?

What questions do I need to clarify student responses and help them understand the ideas they are exploring?

What questions do I need to personalize the content for students?

What kinds of questions will students need in order to sustain their focus on the content and cognitive operation called for by the objective(s) of the lesson?

What questions do I need to explore the depth and breadth of the content?

Question Function

Question function refers to how we intend students to respond to our question, what we do with their responses or how we guide their thinking, and how we assist them in understanding using productive questioning practices as tools for learning. Function also relates to how we, as questioners, conduct ourselves as we ask students questions. To be effective in asking questions, we must know how we expect students to answer our questions. To be skillful in our attempts to guide and refine student thinking, we must listen carefully to what students have to say and use their responses in asking our next questions to shape their ideas and understanding about their thinking. The more conscious we are about the questions we ask and the ways we follow up on student responses, the greater the impact we will have on what students think and how they think.

Wait-time (Rowe, 1987) is a pivotal issue for carrying out instruction conversations. If we expect our students to form well-reasoned responses, then we must wait patiently for their responses. Answering our own questions or posing questions on top of previously asked questions interferes with the learning process. Silence during classroom discourse is an opportunity for students to think about issues. We must be sure not to cloud their thinking with our talking.

Once students are directed to answer a question, then appropriate time must be given in order for students to feel the responsibility for answering the question. Research reminds us that by employing a longer wait-time after our questions and before we allow students to respond to each other, we increase student responses and the quality of their responses. If a question is important enough to be asked, then our patience in waiting for students to respond is equally important. For it is the student who must do the thinking and learning about the content. We, as teachers, must learn how to create better classroom conditions for learning to take place.

In conducting Qu:Est strategies, we have found that how we respond both orally and nonverbally to student responses is critical in guiding their thinking. It is another aspect of the concept of question function. The phrasing of our questions and the manner in which we deliver our questions are crucial aspects of engaging students in instructional conversations. Our questions can be phrased to invite responses or to intimidate students. Likewise, our body language, classroom position, and gestures can encourage or discourage responses from students.

We have constant decisions to make about how we conduct ourselves during classroom discourse. The impact of how we position ourselves in the setting, the interaction patterns we create among students, and our personal gesturing must be orchestrated to promote productive conversations and must be synchronized with the questions we ask. How we sharpen our talent to conduct productive instructional conversations can be refined only by continual practice of productive questioning and reflection on our practices. In order to facilitate productive instructional conversations among our students, we must make deliberate decisions about how we set up our learning environments and how our demeanor will affect student dialogue.

Question Function

Positioning Issues

Where should I stand in asking my initial questions?

Where should I stand when listening to student responses?

In what way does my physical position in the classroom encourage or hinder student responses?

How does my physical position in the classroom encourage or hinder student-to-student dialogue?

Interaction Patterns

To whom should the students direct their responses?

How do I encourage students to talk to each other rather than to the teacher?

How much time should I give students to think about questions before answering them?

How much time should I allow following a student response before asking another question or permitting other students to respond?

What kinds of seating arrangements do I need to promote productive instructional conversations?

How shall I determine the pace of the instructional conversation?

When should I slow down or increase the pace of the lesson?

How do I keep the conversation moving?

What kind of grouping patterns promote the best responses?

What do students need to do to generate responses?

Gestures

What intonation should my questions possess?

What should I do when students are not responding?

What should I do to encourage shy or unresponsive students?

How do I signal a student that he or she is doing too much of the talking?

Through what gestures can I moderate the flow of ideas during the instructional conversation?

What facial expressions engender student responses and what facial expressions deter students from responding?

INQUIRY SUGGESTIONS AND QUESTIONS

To further probe your understanding of the Qu:Est Instructional Strategies, reflect on the following questions concerning the nature and function of productive questioning.

- What questions in the narrative initiated a particular kind of thinking operation?
- What do you notice about the phrasing of the initial thought questions?
- What questions in the narrative probed student ideas?
- What relationships are there between the student response and subsequent teacher questions?
- What do you notice about the phrasing of the questions following a student response?
- What happened when the instructor realized that the students were not answering the initial thought question?
- What did the instructor do to personalize, support, or enhance student responses?
- What practices were used to stimulate ideas?
- In what way does the management of classroom space inspire or detract from the instructional conversation?
- How does the instructor use movement and space to encourage instructional dialogue?
- In what ways do wait-time and pacing of the questions and responses contribute or not contribute to the lesson?
- How did the instructor use intonation in asking questions?

REFERENCE

Rowe, M. B. (1987). Using wait-time to stimulate inquiry. In W. W. Wilen (Ed.), Questions, questioning techniques, and effective teaching, pp. 95–106. Washington, DC: National Education Association.

▶ 7

Collecting Strategies

FACILITATIVE SET

The Collecting Strategies provide opportunities for students to sharpen their thinking experiences using the cognitive operations of Observing and Recalling. These mental operations are the basis for identifying and retrieving relevant information for conceptualizing. Observing and Recalling lessons are not memorizing techniques. Rather, they are strategies for comprehending and personalizing specific information that will be used in the students' active participation in constructing concepts. The outcome of the Collecting Strategies is for students to gather isolated facts that they understand and can relate to their life experiences. Observing and Recalling are necessary first steps in forming, differentiating, and extending concepts.

OBSERVING AND RECALLING STRATEGIES

Through use of the Collecting Strategies, learners gather critical information from relevant examples about the concepts to be constructed. It is in their active processing of collected information that learners establish or create meaning for themselves. Careful observing and accurate retrieval of the critical characteristics of concept examples are necessary in order for learners to eventually sort and distinguish relevant information from irrelevant information or to generate concept attributes and labels appropriate for the concepts.

The thinking generated by learners through the use and practice of the Collecting Strategies provides the foundation for learners to form concepts and to differentiate between and among similar concepts, as well as to extend concepts to subconcepts. By providing learners with opportunities to practice Observing and Recalling, they will better understand the thinking operations and become more aware of the types of questions they need to ask of themselves when encountering situations that call for gathering and retaining information.

Qu: Est's Collecting Strategies will sharpen learners' understanding of situations requiring their use of Observing and Recalling. Concomitantly, learners will learn how and when to use these thinking operations when reviewing their work. The following sections will facilitate readers' understanding of how to conduct the Qu:Est Collecting Strategies of Observing and Recalling. The coding used for possible student responses and processing questions are identified on the coding symbols which follow the lesson (p. 122).

- Questioning Strategy Chart
- Sample Lesson Design
- Self-Study Discussion
- Curriculum Applications
- Essential Issues of Analysis
- Coding Symbols
- Sample Transcript
- Coded Transcript
- Reflections on the Coding

The following content has been previously published by National Educational Service, 1990 and revised for this publication.

OBSERVING QUESTIONING STRATEGY CHART

Purpose of the Process:

To be used in situations requiring learners to perceive and collect characteristics related to the five senses for future processing as well as to sharpen their perceptual skills

Nature of the Questions

Focusing the senses to gather information about the physical characteristics of an object, event, or situation

How the Questions Function

Specific details gathered through the senses are clarified and verified for precision and accuracy of perception

Learner Response

Describing through language or demonstration specific, verifiable details by seeing, hearing, tasting, smelling, and/or touching

SAMPLE OBSERVING LESSON DESIGN

PURPOSE: Provide learners with opportunities to gather the physical properties of a flower through observation

OUTCOME: Students identify, explain, and verify information about the critical characteristics of a flower gathered by using their five senses

REASON: Prerequisite to developing the concept of flower or practice in using one's senses to gather information

CONTENT CHARACTERISTICS: Petals, stem, stamens, pistils, color, shape, leaves

RESOURCES: Each student or small group of students has a rose, a tulip, or other flower (conduct lesson with one type of flower at a time); paper; pencil; board; diagrams

CORE QUESTION: Observing

- Using your senses, what do you notice about the (rose)?

Possible Student Responses

- It's pretty.—RF
- It's not fully bloomed.—VR
- Lots of petals.—CL/VR/RD
- It's red.—OB
- The leaves are alternating.—CL/VR
- My mother grows them.—RF
- It's yellow in the middle.—CL/VR/NF
- The yellow comes off on my hands.—VR/RL

Processing Question Stems for Observing

RF (Refocusing off-focus response to observing)

- What are you noticing that makes you say the rose is pretty?
- You're telling me about your mother's roses—what do you notice about this rose?

CL (Defining and using additional or more precise language)

- What do you mean by lots of?
- What are you referring to when you say the leaves are alternating?

VR (Verifying details)

- How do you know it's not fully bloomed?
- Draw the leaves coming one after the other.
- Show me the yellow part.

NF (Narrowing the focus of the critical characteristics)

- Tell me more about the middle part.
- What do you notice about the stem?

RD (Attaining more student participation)

- What else can you tell me about the petals?
- Who else notices this yellow?

SELF-STUDY DISCUSSION OF THE OBSERVING STRATEGY

Observing is a thinking operation whereby individuals perceive and collect physical characteristics about an object, event, or situation through their senses (sight, sound, taste, smell, and touch). The Observing thinking operation is the primary way in which we make sense of reality and of our experiences and environment. It begins formally when we are born. Through exploring the world through their senses, infants begin to collect information that is later used to compare and contrast, identify concepts, and classify and label the formed concepts.

Situations, that require the Observing thinking operation must be real or representational. One cannot observe the symbolic. For example, when it is important to gather the physical characteristics of a piece of fruit, the fruit must be present in order to ascertain the size, shape, color, position of seed, taste, pulp, stem, remains of the blossom, and smell. If a picture of the fruit is presented, then only a limited amount of information can be picked up by the senses. Specifically, only the sense of sight can be used. If a model of a piece of fruit is used, then other sensory information can be gathered through touch. However, if the word *orange* is written on the board and students are asked to observe, then the only information available for observation is the position of the letters, the number of letters, vowels, consonants, and the shape of the letters. Whatever sensory information learners provide must be done through recalling experiences with oranges—not through direct observation.

By focusing instruction on the Observing Instructional Strategy, teachers can assist learners in sharpening their perception. Through structured lessons in observing, the physical characteristics of things can be attended to with more detail. By discerning the physical characteristics, teachers can guide students to distinguish between the critical and noncritical characteristics of concepts. Using our senses to gather information means attending to size, shape, color, texture, and so on.

Often, when we observe something, we miss the finer details that may interfere with our understanding or meaning-making. Structured experiences in "how to observe," however, teach learners to move beyond the obvious to gather a rich source of information, which in turn enables them to use the process as a strategy for gathering critical information important in the discovery of their environment and to make meaning of their experiences.

Direct teaching of the Observing Strategy requires that teachers initially use instructional devices that focus on the content to be observed and use words that cue the observing operation. "What do you notice about the orange?" is a well-focused core question. The syntax of the question can be analyzed as follows. The noun, "orange," identifies the object of the observation. The verb phrase, "do you notice," structures the type of thinking learners are to do if they are to gather the information.

A poorly structured core question would be, "What can you tell me about the orange?" It is poorly structured because there are no words in the question that identify the thinking operation students are to use. As a result, students may recall information about oranges, they may evaluate the oranges, or they may compare and contrast it to other oranges they have experienced.

The focusing on observing in the question by using words that cue the thinking operation is especially important in gathering information through observing. The reason for this is that so often, when individuals are asked to observe something, they immediately provide an inference for the observation. For example, when asked, "What do you notice about the boy in this picture?" a common answer is, "He is smart" or "He is studious." Both answers are inferences based on observed data. Because the boy may be holding a book or be seated at a school desk looking at the teacher, the observer has jumped to a conclusion about the physical information picked up through looking at what the boy is doing. It becomes the teacher's role to guide students in collecting the physical attributes of the picture that formed the inference response by attending to the observable details and then linking the details to the inference made by students.

Guiding and directing Observing go beyond asking the core question. Teachers must listen carefully to the answers given by learners in order to ascertain how learners arrived at their information. The literature of education refers to this process as metacognition. By asking additional follow-through questions or processing questions such as clarification, verification, refocus, and narrow focus questions, teachers will assist learners in understanding and refining their original responses.

If a learner provides an inference answer to a focused Observing question, the teacher must help the learner gather the physical information that resulted in the inference. By clarifying, verifying, and narrowing the content to be observed, learners have opportunities to rethink their original responses and see them from other perspectives. This broadens their perceptions and conceptions of their experiences and environment.

CURRICULUM APPLICATIONS

- Pieces of fruit: apples, oranges, peanuts, pears, bananas, tomato
- Money: coins, bills
- Maps: the world, country, states
- Letters: positions, structure, shapes
- Pictures: color, texture, style, objects, settings
- Sentences: word placement, punctuation, capitalization
- Events: a car accident, peace rally, and so on

ANALYZING LESSONS: OBSERVING (OB)

During the analysis of the lesson, information is gathered and reflected on, identifying the manner in which the lesson was conducted by the teacher and the impact that it has had on students. A coding system is used to facilitate data collection of both teacher questions and learner responses. This data in turn provides the substance for identifying, forming patterns, and correcting critical aspects of the instructional strategy in order to assist learners in their development and refinement of thinking operations.

This section is divided into five parts: (1) the learner response; (2) the coding symbols; (3) a sample transcript; (4) the coding of the transcript; and (5) reflections on the coding.

The Learner Response: On-Focus and Off-Focus Responses

Observing, like the other Qu:Est Instructional Strategies, has both on-focus and off-focus learner responses. On-focus responses are answers that identify the critical attributes of an object, event, or situation picked up through one's senses. Reporting the information is in language that communicates the physical attributes that can be verified by sight, hearing, taste, smell, or touch. Off-focus responses are answers that go beyond information picked up by our sensory experiences. These responses are based on the senses but are translated by the learner into other thinking operations. These responses need refocusing before clarifying or verifying, because they may establish a pattern of off-focus responses that does not attend to the Observing operation.

For example, if an apple is the object of an Observing lesson, on-focus responses would be "it's red," "it has a lot of liquid in it," "the inside is white," "the seeds are in the center and hard." All of this information is sensory information and can be verified by our senses. If learners provide responses such as "it's a Macintosh," "it's good," "eating them is good for your health," "it's rotten," then these responses must be refocused to the sensory information that resulted in learners making such comments about the apple. The off-focus learner responses during an Observing lesson usually entail learners providing labels that classify objects, or making inferences about the observation, and/or stating personal opinions.

Teachers must immediately refocus such responses because they tend to set a pattern for other learner responses. Additionally, learners will have a great deal of difficulty distinguishing between true observations and interpreted observations. The refocus practice "You're telling me the apple is rotten" or "What are you noticing about the apple that makes you say that it is rotten?" will enable the learner to attend to the sensory information that led him or her to the inference of "rotten." The learner may have produced the response because he or she noticed soft brown spots on the apple's surface. Once the response is refocused to Observing, the teacher may proceed with clarifying, "What do you mean by soft?" and verifying, "How do you know that it is soft?" In this manner, the observed response assists learners in understanding how they arrived at the observation.

Coding Symbols

Coding the questions and responses in a lesson is a way to understand the patterns of teacher questions, learner responses, and the relationships that exist between teacher questions and learner responses. Coding establishes objective information that can be used for discussion of the attributes of the Observing Strategy. To code an Observing lesson, the following symbols may be used:

Teacher Questions

OB	Observing core question
	Closed Observing core question (elicits a yes/no response)
0	Core question lacks process or content
CL	Clarifying question
VR	Verifying question
RF	Refocusing question
RD	Redirecting question
NF	Narrow focusing question

Learner Responses

+	On-focus response
–	Off-focus response
CL	Clarifies response
VR	Verifies response
?	Student question

Sample Transcript of an Observing Lesson

T. What do you notice about the apple?

S. It's red.

S. It's round.

T. What do you mean by round?

T. Draw me the shape of the apple.

S. (Draws apple shape on the board)

S. It's more like a heart.

T. What else can you tell me about the apple?

S. It's rotten.

T. What are you noticing that makes you say that it is rotten?

S. It has soft brown spots that sink.

T. What do you mean by spots that sink?

S. When you look at the apple the spots are lower than the rest.

T. How do you know that other than by looking?

S. When you touch the brown spots, they are mushy.

Coding of the Sample Transcript

T:	OB	CL		VR		RD	RF	CL	VR
S:	+	+	CL	VR	–	–	+	VR	VR

Reflections on the Coding

The teacher's first Observing core question was focused in terms of content and process and was open. This resulted in two on-focus student responses, one of which was clarified and verified. The clarifying and verifying questions elicited appropriate responses from learners as well as extended learners' understanding of their initial observations. When the teacher redirected the core question, the question lacked words that cued learners for observing. The learner responded with an off-focus inference. The teacher appropriately refocused the response, enabling the learner to cite his or her observations that resulted in the inference. Through the clarifying and verifying questions, the student revealed the sensory information that was the basis for the inference.

Again, with permission from the National Educational Service, copyright 1990, the following context has been adapted for inclusion in this book

RECALLING QUESTIONING STRATEGY CHART

Purpose of the Process:

To be used in situations requiring learners to retrieve information gathered through past experience, reading, viewing, or listening

Nature of the Questions:

Retrieving information previously gathered and committed to memory from past experiences, reading materials, and/or audio-visual media

How the Questions Function:

Specific details about information gathered through various media are clarified and verified for precision and accuracy of recollection

Learner Response:

Reciting specific information stored in memory that can be verified by the source

SAMPLE RECALLING LESSON DESIGN

PURPOSE: Provide learners with opportunities to recall specific details from a written passage identified by the teacher

OUTCOME: Students identify specific information from source verifying information for accuracy.

REASON: Prerequisite skill for selecting appropriate passages needed when citing evidence for a research topic

CONTENT CHARACTERISTICS: Specific reasons for teaching thinking identified in the literature on questioning, specific issues related to teacher-student interactions, and types of questions that elicit particular thinking operations

RESOURCES: Read "A Stone of Light Through Yonder Window Breaks" in this book

CORE QUESTION: Recalling

- From your reading, what do you recall about the implications of teacher questions?

Possible Student Responses

- Most questions are recall.—CL
- There is little relationship between teacher questions and student responses.—CL
- Metacognition is important.—RF/CL
- Listening for the student response is most important.—VR

Processing Question Stems for Recalling

RF (Refocusing off-focus response)

- What are you recalling that makes you say metacognition is important?
- You're telling me a reaction you have to what you read. What do you recall that leads you to say questioning for thinking is hard?

CL (Defining and using additional or more precise language)

- What do you mean by metacognition?
- What are you referring to when you say recall?
- Draw a diagram that illustrates the relationship between teacher question/student response.

VR (Verifying for accuracy)

- Where in the passage did you find teachers asking recall questions? Read the passage.
- What other writers have pointed out this fact?
- From your own experience, how do you know there is little relationship between teacher questions and student responses?

NF (Narrowing the focus of the critical characteristics)

- Tell me more about the idea of metacognition.
- What do you recall about the literature raising more questions than it answers?

RD (Attaining more student participation)

- Who else can cite a reference for this?
- What other information is stated as to the reasons for asking recall questions?

SELF-STUDY DISCUSSION OF THE RECALLING STRATEGY

Recalling is a thinking operation whereby individuals retrieve specific details derived from their past experiences, from written passages, or by viewing or listening to media productions. The Recalling thinking operation is the primary means of collecting and storing information. Although memorization is highly relied on by teachers for assuring that students have "learned" material presented in formal lectures and other types of classroom instruction, memorization must be distinguished from the Recalling thinking operation. In memorization, students commit to memory information, paying little attention to the process used in memorizing.

The end product in memorization is that students "recite," "remember," or "recollect" specific facts provided by some other source. Often students may repeat answers without knowing what they are talking about. They simply cite what was given to them. In the Qu:Est Recalling Instructional Strategy, the emphasis is on process. It focuses on how well students understand information and the relationships they can make between things they know and the new information they are studying. The Recalling Strategy, used as a Collecting thinking operation, requires that learners comprehend factual information so that the information becomes relevant and useful. Recalling is a learning tool that can be used to collect information, to verify specific facts, and to form concepts.

The depth and breadth of specific and accurate information collected during the Recalling Instructional Strategy, and how we go about validating our ideas, lends credibility to our lives and work. Situations that require Recalling are derived from our life and schooling experiences. Typically, teachers have learners recall specific details from reading materials or lectures. Often, teachers are satisfied if learners are able to use the labels as cited in texts or other forms of classroom instruction. This is only a limited use of the thinking operation. If learners are to understand or comprehend what they have read, heard, or viewed, then teachers must attend to learners' recalled responses by probing for further information.

By probing learners' initial recalled response, teachers will obtain an assessment as to the extent of learner comprehension of facts and ideas. Questions such as "What is meant by (certain terms)?" or "Where did you find the information?" or "How do you know the information is true?" will provide insightful data that reveal the extent of the students' knowledge. Teachers must focus their core recall questions with words that cue recollection. This may, at first, appear trivial or unnecessary; however, by using cueing words, the teacher assists learners in understanding how they gathered the content. It prevents "educated guessing" and enables learners to become confident in their abilities to provide sound, verifiable responses.

For example, if a teacher says, "Tell me about the short story you read last night," the learners can say how they felt about the story, talk about other stories they read like it, or recall specific details of the story. By using "signal words" for recalling such as "recall," "remember," and "find out," students are focused on the thinking operation, and teachers have a means for guiding and developing rich student understandings. For example, by using the signal word *recall* in the question, "What do you recall about last night's reading?" the learner is more apt to speak directly to the details of the story read the previous night.

Guiding and directing Qu: Est's Recalling Instructional Strategy goes beyond asking the core question. Teachers must listen carefully to the answers given by the learners in order to help them process their understandings of the facts. By asking processing questions to help students clarify meanings, refocus responses, verify information, personalize their understandings to known information, and cite more specific information about the details, teachers empower the learner's comprehension.

CURRICULUM APPLICATIONS

- Objectives calling for the retention of specific facts
- Recollection of events of field trips
- Vocabulary development
- Remembering lines from plays
- Citing details from a commonly viewed movie
- Recalling steps in solving a problem
- Reciting a poem
- Retrieving specific details of prior Observing lessons
- Citing facts for building concepts
- Gathering evidence for a topic sentence
- Reciting rules or procedures
- Recalling taxonomies
- Recalling similar situations or experiences
- Gathering facts for story plot graphs

ANALYZING LESSONS: RECALLING (RL)

During the analysis of the lesson, information is gathered and reflected on, identifying the manner in which the lesson was conducted by the teacher and the impact that it has had on students. A coding system is used to facilitate data collection of both teacher questions and learner responses. This data in turn provides the substance for identifying, forming patterns, and correcting critical aspects of the instructional strategy in order to assist learners in their development and refinement of thinking operations.

This section is divided as follows: (1) the learner response; (2) the coding symbols; (3) a sample transcript; (4) the coding of the transcript; and (5) reflections on the coding.

The Learner Response: On-Focus and Off-Focus Responses

Recalling, like other Qu:Est Strategies, has both on-focus and off-focus responses. On-focus responses are answers that identify and specify details of experience, printed material, and audiovisual material. The reporting of the specific details must be in language that learners understand—not labels that are memorized or that have vague meanings.

Off-focus responses are answers that go beyond information picked up and stored in memory as fact. Inferences and personal opinions are not facts but must be verified and supported by sources. Usually, when learners provide inferences or personal opinions in order to recall questions, they are interpreting the information and do not realize that what they have said cannot be directly indicated in the source. These responses need refocusing before clarifying or verifying because they may establish a pattern of off-focus responses that do not ascertain the facts of the content.

Additionally, verification is especially critical in the Recalling lesson. Verification is gathered both as a part of the primary material and outside of the material in the form of past experiences, principles and generalizations, and authorities that connect prior learning to what students are currently studying. By using the verification process with the sources, learners are taught how to identify citations from the source that lends credibility to facts and to use the citations as evidence for their thinking. Verifying information through personal experiences instills relevance. Verifying through principles, generalizations, and authorities further extends learners' research skills by building additional evidence to support facts. For example, when discussing specific facts of a story, the teacher should ask the following kinds of verifying questions so that learners are enlightened by their understanding of the facts. The questions are:

Verification using the source:

- Where did you find that in the story?
- Read that passage.
- How do you know this is true?

Verification using personal experience:

- Tell me about a situation you had like the one in the story.
- Where have you seen this before?

Verification using principles or generalizations:

- Is there a moral you know that exemplifies this?
- What rule do you recall that says this happens over and over?

Verification using authorities:

- Who says that?
- Name some other authors using the same ideas.

Coding Symbols

Coding the questions and responses in a lesson is a way to understand the patterns of teacher questions, learner responses, and the relationships that exist between them. Coding establishes objective information needed for discussion of the critical attributes of Qu: Est's Recalling Instructional Strategy. To code a Recalling lesson, the following symbols may be used:

Teacher Questions		Learner Responses	
RL	Recalling core question	+	On-focus response
	Closed Recalling core question (elicits a yes/no response)	–	Off-focus response
0	Core question lacks process or content	CL	Clarifies response
CL	Clarifying question	VR	Verifies response
VR	Verifying question	?	Student question
RF	Refocusing question		
RD	Redirecting question		
NF	Narrow focusing question		

Sample Transcript of a Recalling Lesson

T. In the death scene of Romeo and Juliet, what do you recall are the events?

S. Both die.

S. Romeo is misguided by what he sees.

T. In what way is Romeo misguided?

S. He thinks Juliet is dead.

T. How do we know this is not true?

S. The friar has given her a poison to make her look dead.

T. What other details do you recall about Juliet's fake death?

S. She no longer has the will to live.

T. Where does it say that in the story?

S. Well, it doesn't; I just thought that she doesn't want to live without Romeo.

T. Can you recall something about her fake death scene that led you to believe that she doesn't want to live without Romeo?

S. She tells the friar to fake her death.

S. She talks about awakening to see Romeo.

S. Her lines are desperate.

T. What do you mean when you say her lines are desperate?

S. You know, frightened.

T. Give me an example of what someone would say if they were frightened.

Coding of the Sample Transcript

T:	RL		RF	VR	RD		RF			CL	VR
S:	O	O	RL	VR	O	O	CL	CL	–	CL	

Reflections on the Coding

The teacher's first Recalling core question was focused in terms of content and process. The questions are open, requiring that students explain their answers. The questions resulted, however, in two off-focus learner responses, one of which was refocused and verified. The verifying questions elicited appropriate responses from several learners that revealed their understanding of the death scenario, as well as contributed to their understanding of Juliet's state of mind. However, one verification question is closed and elicits an off-focus response. As a result of the teacher not refocusing the first two off-focus responses, a pattern of inferential responses is given by the learners. This limited the depth of the recitations and learners' interaction with each other's responses because the teacher had to attend to refocusing, clarifying, and verifying inferences rather than eliciting a broad base of specific, verifiable factual information.

▶ 8

Bridging Strategies

FACILITATIVE SET

The Bridging Strategies include the cognitive operations of Comparing, Contrasting, and Grouping. Each of these strategies is the means through which students sort and organize information to form relationships and to create patterns of ideas that are conceptual in nature, not isolated facts. In this chapter, we first describe Comparing and Contrasting Strategies because they are generally used together to form concepts and to distinguish between two similar ideas or related subconcepts. Following the discussions on the Comparing and Contrasting Strategies, we will present the Grouping Strategy. The Grouping Strategy has a slightly different questioning format. The Grouping Strategy is used when there are three or more related subconcepts to be developed by students.

COMPARING AND CONTRASTING STRATEGIES

The Bridging Strategies, Comparing and Contrasting, require learners to distinguish among the characteristics of items, examples, or situations and to determine the similarities and differences that exist in the critical characteristics of the information gathered. For example, in forming the concept of *noun*, learners must encounter various forms of nouns and recognize that regardless of the form or how it is used, the word represents the name of a person, place, thing, or idea. It is not simply the memorization of the rule or label that establishes the conceptual understanding. It is the learners' careful attention to how their collected information about different nouns fits together to form a pattern that characterizes the essential attributes of words that indicate persons, places, things, or ideas. By using the cognitive operations of similarities and differences, learners connect or bridge individual examples of the concept or disconnected information.

In distinguishing between subconcepts, again learners must compare and contrast the critical characteristics of the subconcepts to understand the distinct qualities that make something like the main concept, yet different enough to have its own classification. Sticking with the example of grammar, simple sentences and compound sentences are subconcepts of the larger concept of sentence. All subconcepts of sentence contain the critical characteristics of the concept of sentence; however, because they are subconcepts, learners must distinguish the critical characteristics that make a simple sentence simple and a compound sentence compound.

For meaningful conceptualization to occur, learners must be actively involved in using the thinking operations of Comparing and Contrasting to analyze various examples of the related subconcepts. By collecting the critical characteristics of each and distinguishing between them, learners create the patterns necessary for appropriate concept recognition. Simply memorizing the differences between simple and compound sentences will not build an understanding of why or how simple sentences are simple and compound sentences are compound.

The following sections will facilitate readers' understanding of how to conduct the Qu:Est Bridging Strategies.

- Questioning Strategy Chart
- Sample Lesson Design
- Self-Study Discussion
- Curriculum Applications
- Analyzing Lessons
- Coding Symbols
- Sample Transcript
- Coded Transcript
- Reflections on the Coding

With permission from the National Educational Service copyright 1990, the following material has been adapted for this publication.

COMPARING AND CONTRASTING QUESTIONING STRATEGY CHART

Purpose of the Process:

To be used in situations requiring learners to identify and distinguish similarities and differences between or among items

Nature of the Questions:

Noting the similarities and differences of objects, events, situations, and/or phenomena

How the Questions Function:

Similarities and differences are distinguished and/or sorted, then clarified and verified

Learner Response:

Articulates the noted similarities and differences identified between or among objects, events, situations, and/or phenomena

SAMPLE CONTRASTING LESSON DESIGN

PURPOSE: Provide learners with opportunities to contrast the attributes of the U.S. twentieth-century's space exploration and the fifteenth-century global explorations

OUTCOME: Students will identify, explain, and verify information that distinguishes America's twentieth-century's space program from the fifteenth-century global explorations.

REASON: Distinguishes reasons for exploration and the technology of the times or to provide practice in the contrasting thinking operation

CONTENT CHARACTERISTICS: Reasons for expansion of territory; quest for products; exploration of the unknown; changes in traveling vessels and equipment; special needs, philosophy, and interests of times; and so on.

RESOURCES: Library materials and notes on fifteenth-century explorers; library materials and notes on the twentieth-century space program; paper, pencil, overhead projector

CORE QUESTIONS: Contrasting

- From your readings, what differences are there between today's exploration of space and the fifteenth-century exploration of the New World?

Possible Student Responses

- We have advanced technology guiding our spaceships, but they only had crude instruments.—CL/VR
- They didn't know where they were going.—RF/CL/VR
- One's in the air, the other is in water.—VR

Processing Question Stems for Contrasting

RF (Refocusing response to Contrasting core question)

- You have told me about the fifteenth-century explorers' not knowing where they were going. How is that different from today's explorations?

CL (Defining and using additional or more precise language)

- What do you mean by crude instruments?
- What are you referring to when you say they didn't know where they were going?

VR (Verifying details)

- How do you know the instruments were less technical?
- Where did you find _______ information?
- How do you know the fifteenth-century explorers didn't know where they were going?

NF (Narrowing the focus of the critical characteristics)

- Tell me more about the advanced technology of America's twentieth-century space explorations and how it differs from the technology of the fifteenth century.

RD (Attaining more student participation)

- Who else has information about people's desire to explore the unknown?
- What other information have you found regarding the differences between the two exploration times?

SAMPLE COMPARING LESSON DESIGN

PURPOSE: Provide learners with opportunities to compare the attributes of America's twentieth-century space exploration and the fifteenth-century global explorations

OUTCOME: Students will find the similarities, explain, and verify the accuracy of information that is similar between the twentieth-century space explorations and the fifteenth-century global explorations

REASON: Extends students' understanding of the attributes, relationships, and reasons for people's exploration of new worlds

CONTENT CHARACTERISTICS: People's curiosity, expansion of territory, exploration of the unknown, uses of traveling devices and equipment, reasons for exploring, philosophy, goods, and so on

RESOURCES: Library materials and notes on fifteenth-century explorers; library materials and notes on the twentieth-century space program; paper, pencil, overhead projector

Core Questions: Comparing

- From your reading, what similarities are there between America's twentieth-century exploration of space and the fifteenth-century exploration of the New Worlds?

Possible Student Responses

- They were trying to discover unknown territory.—CL/VR
- Both traveled in ships.—CL/VR
- Both were venturesome.—CL/VR
- The fifteenth-century explorers were traveling for monarchies.—RF/CL

Processing Question Stems for Comparing

RF (Refocusing response to Comparison core question)

- You said that the fifteenth-century explorers traveled for their countries. How is that like America's twentieth-century space explorations?

CL (Defining and using additional or more precise language)

- What do you mean by venturesome?
- What are you referring to when you say unknown territory?

VR (Verifying details)

- How do you know both groups of explorers are venturesome?
- Where did you find _______ information?
- How do you know both groups traveled in the name of their countries?

NF (Narrowing the focus of the critical characteristics)

- Tell me more about the technology of the times and how the uses of it are similar.

RD (Attaining more student participation)

- Who else has information about people's desire to explore the unknown?
- What other information have you found regarding the similarities between the two exploration times?

SELF-STUDY DISCUSSION OF THE COMPARING/CONTRASTING STRATEGIES

Comparing and Contrasting are two thinking operations that provide opportunities for learners to sort information previously observed and/or recalled. Although they are separate cognitive operations, teachers often use them in combination. Even though this is a common instructional practice, for the purpose of teaching learners the thinking involved in each of the operations, they must be addressed separately. In this way, learners can better comprehend the kind of information signaled by the core question and be able to communicate the specific prompted characteristics.

Comparing requires learners to sort through information to discover the similarities between and among examples of a concept. Through this thinking operation, learners are provided with the foundation needed for conceptualizing. The similar characteristics often become the critical distinguishing characteristics of a concept. For example, in studying about culture, by using the Comparing Instructional Strategy with different types of cultures, learners discover that there are particular critical attributes or characteristics that make up anything that can be classified as a culture.

While different people in different parts of the world may appear different in ways that things are done or what they believe, or how they look or dress, commonalities do exist. All cultures have, for example, rites of passage, other rituals, life-sustaining issues, and so forth. It is important for learners to note comparisons, as this cognitive operation helps them to understand that specific pieces of information and facts can be related to form greater and deeper understandings. Understanding commonalities is the basis through which we bond with our experiences and establish meaningful patterns of seemingly nonmeaningful, isolated facts.

Contrasting requires learners to sort through information to discover the discrepancies between items. Contrasting is the primary means for distinguishing related subconcepts from major concepts and from each other. For example, in the study of the concept of the sentence, learners must be able to distinguish simple sentences from compound sentences and compound sentences from complex sentences. By noting the differences in sentence structure and the function of words in each sentence type, learners will be more apt to discern the critical characteristics that make each sentence type distinct from the others. These distinctions among sentence types become the critical characteristics of the subconcepts of sentence. The importance of the contrasting thinking operation cannot be understated, for it is central to decision making and to discovering the uniqueness of entities in our life experiences.

Of these two Bridging Strategies, Contrasting is the more difficult for learners to learn and the most demanding for teachers to use when conducting instructional conversations. The discrimination that must be made is the identification of discrete, specific critical characteristics that separate items or concepts from each other while often possessing qualities of a larger concept.

Stating a difference requires that learners be able to make *conditional statements.* A *conditional statement* usually incorporates a conjunction that discriminates between characteristics of two items. For example, conditional statements would be: a basketball is round *but* a football is oblong; an inverted fraction has the large number on top; *however*, a regular fraction has the smaller number on top.

To facilitate this type of distinction in learner responses, the teacher must rely heavily on the refocusing question. Often, learners elicit half of the difference and assume that everyone knows the other part. Thus, the teacher is constantly refocusing the response: "You said the basketball is round; how is it different from the football?" "You pointed out that the simple sentence has one subject and one verb; in what way is the compound sentence different?" The object of refocusing the response is for the learner, not the teacher, to state the difference. In no way should the teacher assume that the difference is noted if it is not stated by learners.

In assisting learners to understand and use the Comparing and Contrasting Instructional Strategies, additional processing questions must be asked once the focus of the response is clear. The processing questions, addressing the issues of clarification, verification, and narrow focus, will help learners better understand the similarities and differences they report. These questions also provide depth for the discussion. Teachers must be cognizant that the more examples learners have to compare and contrast, the more difficult the processing becomes. Therefore, it is necessary to begin the sorting of information with two examples for Comparing and Contrasting, then add on additional examples.

CURRICULUM APPLICATIONS

- Distinguishing between governments
- Analyzing types of poetry
- Discovering relationships among animals
- Distinguishing between political candidates
- Identifying similarities and differences in mathematical operations
- Comparing synonyms
- Discovering qualities of habitats
- Finding relationships in letter formations
- Using a process or skill appropriately
- Distinguishing between coins from different countries

ANALYZING LESSONS: COMPARING (CM) AND CONTRASTING (CT)

During the analysis of the lesson, information is gathered and reflected on, identifying the manner in which the lesson was conducted by the teacher and the impact that it has had on students. A coding system is used to facilitate data collection of both teacher questions and learner responses. This data in turn provides the substance for identifying, forming patterns, and correcting critical aspects of the instructional strategy in order to assist learners in their development and refinement of thinking operations.

This section is divided as follows: (1) the learner response; (2) the coding symbols; (3) a sample transcript; (4) the coding of the transcript; and (5) reflections on the coding.

The Learner Response: On-Focus and Off-Focus Responses

Comparing and Contrasting possess both on-focus and off-focus responses. On-focus responses are answers that identify and sort information according to the initiated/cued thinking operation. If Comparing is to be elicited by the core question, then learners must state similarities; if Contrasting is focused, then learners need to discriminate the characteristics of examples. At any given point in the lesson, learners may become confused and begin reporting the opposite of the cognitive operation initiated. It is at this time that the teacher must begin to refocus learner responses so that learners can attend to the thinking operation signaled by the core question.

Reporting either comparisons or distinctions must be specific. Too often, learners report general characteristics of items without discriminating the finer details. Thus, what appears to be a similarity is actually a difference. For example, in a lesson comparing and contrasting pieces of fruit, learners may report that a banana and an apple both have skins. Another learner may say, "No, because the banana's skin is called a peel and it cannot be eaten unless you take the peel off." Although both responses are true, the second learner's response is more distinguishing. As a result, what first appeared to be a likeness becomes a difference.

As stated before, refocusing is the critical instructional tool in conducting the Bridging Strategies. Refocusing is necessary in order for learners to state more aptly both similarities and differences. The refocusing question for Comparing is: "You're telling me a difference; I asked for a similarity." In Contrasting, learners will often report a likeness as a difference. The following question helps learners discover the difference they are attempting to address: "You've told me that during Mardi Gras and Halloween, people wear costumes. That appears to be a likeness. In what ways are the costumes different?" To further extend learners' understanding of Comparing and Contrasting, once a focused response has been given, the teacher can use the additional processing questions, of clarifying, verifying, narrow focusing, and redirecting to pace the lesson and to add depth and quality to learner responses.

Coding Symbols

Coding the questions and responses of a lesson is a way to understand the patterns of teacher questions, learner responses, and the relationships that exist between teacher questions and learner responses. Coding establishes objective information for providing a basis for discussing the Qu:Est Comparing and Contrasting Strategies.

To code Comparing and Contrasting lessons, the following symbols may be used:

Teacher Questions

CM Comparing core question
CT Contrasting core question
½ Core question lacks process or content
Closed Comparing core question (elicits a yes/no response)
Closed Contrasting core question (elicits a yes/no response)
CL Clarifying question
VR Verifying question
RF Refocusing question
RD Redirects any question
NF Narrow focusing question

Learner Responses

+ On-focus response
– Off-focus response
CL Clarifies response
VR Verifies response
½ Part of response missing
? Student question

Sample Transcript of a Contrasting Lesson

T. In what way is Mardi Gras different from Halloween?

S. Different times of year.

S. They have different purposes.

T. What distinctions do you find in their purposes?

S. Mardi Gras signals the beginning of Lent; Halloween is just a holiday.

S. During Mardi Gras, people dress to be royal; on Halloween, people dress to scare each other.

T. What other purposes are there?

S. To have fun.

S. To get things.

T. How is having fun different in the two holidays?

S. Only people in New Orleans have fun on Mardi Gras.

T. How is that different from Halloween?

S. Everyone has fun.

T. Put those two ideas together so that we can tell the difference in having fun.

S. Well, in New Orleans people goof off all day long and the rest of us work and go to school, but on Halloween everybody can dress up and scare people.

Coding of the Sample Transcript

T:	CT		NF		RD		NF	NF	RF
S:	½	½	+	+	–	–	½	½	+

Reflections on the Coding

The teacher's first Contrasting question was clear, open, and focused on content and process, but learners provided only half of their thinking. The teacher asked a narrow focusing question of the second learner's response rather than refocusing the response to elicit a conditional statement. Even though two additional responses contained conditional statements of differences, the teacher made no attempt to clarify the differences between the conditional responses and the half-answered responses. This sets up a pattern of off-focus and half-answered responses. It is only after the teacher refocused the final response that he or she received a clear difference statement. Because of the need to continually refocus student responses, the teacher could neither clarify nor verify the differences elicited by the learners, which resulted in a shallow lesson.

Sample Transcript of a Comparing Lesson

T. Let's compare Mardi Gras with Halloween.

S. OK.

T. How are they alike?

S. They both are fun.

T. How do you know this?

S. Well, I have fun on Halloween, and my mom says that Mardi Gras is a big party.

T. How are they alike in purpose?

S. People dress up.

T. How do they dress up?

S. One is scary and the other is funny.

T. You appear to be stating a difference; in what way is the dress alike?

S. They wear masks.

S. They wear costumes.

T. What do you mean by costumes?

S. It's a disguise.

Coding of the Sample Transcript

T:	CM	CM	VR	NF	CL	RF		CL
S:	–	+	VR	+	–	+	+	+

Reflections on the Coding

The teacher's first comment does not instruct the learners to answer, just to accept the idea. They do. He or she then asks for similarities, and a learner states a similarity that is further processed by the teacher's verification question. Although the narrow focusing question is appropriate, a learner begins to see a difference in the original response; therefore, he or she reports a difference in "dressing." The teacher refocuses the response and receives two on-focus responses that can then be clarified to further illustrate the learner's concept of "dressing up."

GROUPING QUESTIONING STRATEGY FACILITATIVE SET

Grouping is the third cognitive operation of the Bridging Strategies. Grouping is a fun thinking operation that has powerful implications for learning. It is used when three or more concepts or related subconcepts are to be constructed. For example, using the concept label of sentence again, with the Grouping Strategy subconcepts can be extended to include declarative, interrogative, exclamatory, imperative, and complex sentences.

There are three important aspects to concepts and subconcepts. All concepts and subconcepts have *concept labels,* names that communicate the essential idea of the concept—for example, "interrogative sentence"; all possess *concept attributes,* the critical characteristics that make up the idea and distinguish it from everything else (sometimes called the definition or properties)—

for example, "sentences that ask a question"; and all have explicit *concept examples,* specific exemplars that are illustrative of the concept attribute—for example, "Where are the missing books?" Using the Grouping Strategy enables learners to group examples of concepts based on particular reasons. It is the reason for the grouping that results in establishing the concept attributes.

Grouping is an inductive strategy that allows learners to collect their own information, sort it, find relationships among it, and organize meaningful groups based on their own discoveries. These discoveries enable individuals to identify common attributes among information or examples of concepts and to facilitate students' conceptual understanding of the critical characteristics of concepts and extend students' understanding to include related subconcepts. For example, the concept label *forms of government* has many subconcept labels including *democracy, socialism, communism,* and others.

In order to group, students must have a firm grasp of the thinking operations of Comparing and Contrasting. These thinking operations are subsumed in the Grouping thinking operation. In order to form groups, students must compare and contrast information or examples of concepts and related subconcepts. Groupings can be formed based on the following criteria: description—such as color, size, volume, time, location, function—things used together or operating together; or classifications—things belonging to the same category. Again, the following format will be used to describe the Grouping Strategy:

- Questioning Strategy Chart
- Sample Lesson Design
- Self-Study Discussion
- Curriculum Applications
- Analyzing Lessons
- Coding Symbols
- Sample Transcript
- Coded Transcript
- Reflections on the Coding

GROUPING QUESTIONING STRATEGY CHART

Purpose of the Process:

To be used in situations requiring learners to group information of specific examples based on noted commonalities or patterns

Nature of the Questions:

Sorting information to find characteristics of items that appear similar and placing the information or items in groups for specified reasons

How the Questions Function:

Information or items are placed together based on reasons that are clarified and verified. Groupings are supported.

Learner Response:

Stating that specific information or items go together for specific reasons based on common attributes, properties, or critical qualities. Citing the reasons for the grouping establishing the critical attributes.

SAMPLE GROUPING LESSON DESIGN

PURPOSE: Provide learners with opportunities to group animals for various reasons, including physical characteristics, habitat, eating patterns, location, species, and so forth.

OUTCOME: Students will form subconcepts from the grouping of animals and explain the critical attributes of their concepts.

REASON: Develop an understanding of various ways in which things are eventually classified as well as build an understanding that the same things can be grouped for different reasons.

CONTENT CHARACTERISTICS: Groupings based on physical features, eating habits, environmental conditions, and other factors.

RESOURCES: List of unsorted animals and pictures of the animals

American eagle	rabbit	lion	deer
cocker spaniel	black bear	caribou	lark
tiger	horse	snowy owl	robin
mockingbird	cougar	lemming	polar bear
Persian cat	white alligator	cow	ox
pig	elk	chicken	crab
elephant	swan	frog	bull
cardinal	kangaroo	lizard	snake

CORE QUESTION: Grouping

- From what you know about each of these animals, which of them go together for some reason?

Possible Student Responses

Group 1	Group 2	Group 3	Group 4
mockingbird	cougar	caribou	cocker spaniel
cardinal	black bear	lemming	Persian cat
robin	elk	polar bear	rabbit
Group 5	**Group 6**	**Group 7**	**Group 8**
lark	horse	caribou	horse
muskrat	cow	white alligator	husky
deer	chicken	American eagle	ox

Processing Question Stems for Grouping

RF (Refocusing response to Grouping core question)

- You are telling me the reason for your group. What are the specific items in your group?
- You are giving me a label for the group. Which of the animals have you put together?

SP (Citing the reasons for the groupings)

- Thinking about the animals that you have placed together, what are your reasons for thinking they go together?
- On what basis did you put the horse, husky, and ox together?

Possible Student Responses

Group 1: They all fly.	Group 2: They live in the mountains.
Group 3: They like cold climates.	Group 4: They make good pets.
Group 5: They eat in meadows.	Group 6: They belong on a farm.
Group 7: They are endangered.	Group 8: They pull things.

CL (Defining and using additional or more precise language)

- What do you mean by "endangered"?
- What are you referring to when you say "make good pets"?

VR (Verifying details)

- How do you know the animals in Group 3 all like cold climates?
- Give me an example of what a husky pulls.

NF (Narrowing the focus of the critical characteristics)

- Which of the animals go together because they are found on farms?
- Which of the animals go together because they eat the same food?

RD (Attaining more student participation)

- Who has another group for different reasons?
- Who has the same group for different reasons?

CURRICULUM APPLICATIONS

To construct any concept such as

- System of the body
- Classification of leaves
- Means of transportation
- Types of sentences
- Forms of literature
- Shapes
- Letters grouped for form; shape
- Attributes of countries
- Forms of government

SELF-STUDY DISCUSSION OF THE GROUPING STRATEGY

Grouping is one of the primary ways in which concepts are elaborated and extended into related subconcepts. The reason for the grouped examples or information eventually becomes the concept(s) attributes (qualities, critical characteristics, and properties). It is a powerful Bridging Strategy, because learners themselves devise the critical characteristics for grouped information or examples rather than just memorizing rules or principles. For example, in the study of nutrition, by grouping various examples of food items, learners begin to see relationships among food groups, nutritional values, types of storage, deficiencies, uses, food preparations, effect on metabolism, and so on.

Grouping also provides opportunities for learners to develop diversity in their understanding of information. Information can be grouped for attributes of time, place, description, category, function, or cause-effect relationships.

Given a list of items and asked to group them, learners begin to understand that different people group things for different reasons. Thus, the Grouping Strategy aids in the understanding of different viewpoints.

Direct teaching of Grouping requires that teachers are willing to spend time in allowing learners to play around with connecting or organizing information for themselves. By focusing instruction on the Grouping Instructional Strategy, teachers can assist learners in developing flexibility in their thinking patterns. Through structured lessons using the Grouping process, teachers can provide students practice in sorting and discriminating among vast amounts of details in order to discover patterns in the content that make sense to the learners.

ANALYZING LESSONS: GROUPING (GR)

During the analysis of the lesson, information is gathered and reflected on, identifying the manner in which the lesson was conducted by the teacher and the impact that it has had on students. A coding system is used to facilitate data collection of both teacher questions and learner responses. This data in turn provides the substance for identifying, forming patterns, and correcting critical aspects of the instructional strategy in order to assist learners in their development and refinement of thinking operations.

This section is divided as follows: (1) the learner response; (2) the coding symbols; (3) a sample transcript; (4) the coding of the transcript; and (5) reflections on the coding.

The Learner Response: On-Focus and Off-Focus Responses

Grouping, like other Qu:Est Strategies, has both on-focus and off-focus responses. On-focus responses are answers that place items together for noted relationships. Two issues are involved. Both the grouped items and the reasons for the grouping must be stated. First, the items of the group must be stated. When learners are asked to place items together for some reason, this should result in learners listing the items together. To state the reason for the group is an off-focus answer for the core Grouping question because no group has been created. The teacher must refocus the response in order to elicit the items in the group.

Second, once groups have been elicited, learners must then state the relationships or noted patterns for placing the items together. On-focus responses illustrate the relationships that caused learners to put the items together. The same items can be grouped for different reasons. The processing question that cues learners to state the relationships is called a *supporting question*.

The question is designed to discover the critical attributes of the grouped items. These attributes may identify time, location, descriptive, functional, or categorical relationships. The purpose of the supporting question is for learners to *"hook up"* the individual characteristics found in each member of the group with the reason for grouping the items. The reason or basis for the group is the critical characteristics of the grouped information or examples.

For example, if a bottle of Coke, a bottle of milk, and a bottle of juice are grouped together as a result of determining that they are all in glass containers, the support response for the grouping must identify that attribute. When asked, "What makes you say all these items go together?" the learner response might be, "They are all things held by something made of glass." If the relationship noted was that the liquid inside has no specific shape, then the response to the supporting question should be, "The contents take the shape of the thing that holds it." Both are on-focus responses because the reason stated identifies the attributes of the grouping and can be verified by the items in the group.

Off-focus responses to the supporting question are answers that do not specify the relationship for the grouping. There are two types of off-focus responses for the Grouping supporting question: reasons that clearly do not signal the characteristics for the grouping, and labels that name the group. Labels are not the relationships for the grouped items. Labels are names or terms that economically synthesize and communicate the relationship or an anchor that can be used in recalling the category for the grouped items.

The refocusing question or clarifying question must be used to assist learners in determining the critical characteristics of the grouping when a label is given for the grouping. This is important because the reasons for the group often are the critical characteristics or definitions of concepts. For learners to name something prior to understanding its critical characteristics, they will have difficulty in conceptualizing. For example, they may say that $\frac{9}{4}$ is an example of an improper fraction but not be able to explain the critical aspects of the example that make it an improper fraction.

Once the items of a group have been identified and reasons given for the relationships, teachers need to ask for clarification of terms to enhance learners' understanding of the relationships. Next, the reasons for the groups should be verified for accuracy in order to make sure that all the items of the group have the same characteristic that is specified by the reason for the group. Redirecting for more groups and narrowing the reasons for specific types of groups are important if teachers have specific conceptual information that they want learners to attain from the Grouping lesson.

Coding Symbols

Coding the questions and responses in a Grouping lesson is a way to understand the patterns of teacher questions, learner responses, and the relationships that exist between teacher questions and learner responses. Coding establishes objective information for discussing the lesson. To code a Grouping lesson, the following symbols may be used:

Teacher Questions		**Learner Responses**	
GR	Grouping core question	+	On-focus response
	Closed Grouping core question (elicits a yes/no response)	–	Off-focus response
		CL	Clarifies response
SP	Supporting question	VR	Verifies response
CL	Clarifying question	SP	States relationship
VR	Verifying question	½	Part of response missing
RF	Refocusing question	?	Student question
ED	Redirecting question		
NF	Eliciting specific groups		

Sample Transcript of a Grouping Lesson

T. We've been studying a number of countries all over the globe this term. Let's see how we can group these countries based on what we know about them. After talking with your pair partner, determine which countries go together and for which reasons.

S. Spain, Bolivia, and Mexico.

S. England, Australia, and India.

S. Spain, Italy, and Germany.

T. Okay, I'm sure you have more grouping, but let's deal with these groups first. Why did you group Spain, Bolivia, and Mexico?

S. They all speak Spanish.

T. How do you know this is true?

S. Because when we learned about these countries, we found out that the people all used Spanish words.

T. How about England, Australia, and India?

S. They speak English.

S. They all have English customs.

T. I hear two reasons for this group. When you say they all have English customs, what do you mean?

S. English people went to these countries and many of the habits of the people are like the English.

T. Give me an example of English habits in India.

S. The English people have tea at 4:00 in the afternoon.

T. Why did you group Spain, Italy, and Germany together?

S. They are all a part of Europe.

T. What do you mean by Europe?

S. They are countries located on the European continent.

Coding of the Sample Transcript

T:	GR			SP	VR	½		CL	VR	SP	CL
S:	+	+	+	SP	VR	SP	SP	CL	VR	SP	CL

Reflections on the Coding

The teacher organized learners well for this lesson, and the focusing Grouping question was clear and focused on content and process. It elicited three groups that were then supported by the students. The teacher, following the support for the groups, clarified and verified responses. Although this is appropriate, the teacher needs to redirect the supporting, clarifying, and verifying questions in order to gather greater details about the countries before moving on to subsequent groupings. This procedure would provide opportunities for more learners to share information that may have resulted in other reasons for grouping the same countries. This is important because learners would have been able to discover relationships other than those of language and customs related to founding countries.

▶ 9

Anchoring Strategies

FACILITATIVE SET

The Anchoring Strategies engage students in instructional conversations focusing on Labeling and Classifying. These cognitive operations provide opportunities to fasten concept attributes to appropriate names and new examples for ease in communication, retrieval, and categorization. They are performed subsequent to students' meaningful understanding of the concept attributes. The Labeling and Classifying Strategies are not memorization techniques. Students must reason through names and analyze unfamiliar examples by connecting concept attributes to the name or example. By providing students with opportunities to practice the Labeling and Classifying Strategies, they will better understand the individual thinking operations and how they contribute to the conceptualization process.

LABELING AND CLASSIFYING STRATEGIES

The Anchoring Strategies of Labeling and Classifying require learners to find ways of communicating and categorizing concepts for facilitating the accessibility of the learned concepts. To label, students must use the concept attributes to create or find appropriate and succinct names that precisely fit the critical characteristics that are a part of the concept definition.

For example, in our previous Grouping lesson, students may create a grouping of animals that go together "because the animals breed by laying eggs." In the Labeling instructional conversation, they may name this group *egg-laying animals*, *egg-sitting creatures*, *incubating animals*, or more creatively, *laygo-eggo animals.* Whatever the name, the name must be defined and then the definition of the word or phrase must be analyzed in terms of its appropriateness to the concept attributes.

In the Classifying Strategy, students use both the newly constructed labels and unfamiliar examples and nonexamples of the concepts to decide if the newly presented examples fit the critical characteristics of the concept attributes. Again, for illustration purpose, we will use the reason for the grouping of animals "They breed young by laying eggs." We will also assume that the name students assigned to the group is *egg-bearers.*

To classify, we must have examples and nonexamples of the concept (label and attributes) not currently classified in order for the students to determine if an animal currently unassigned to the concept has the appropriate characteristics to be a part of the *egg-bearers.* If the students' grouping has only birds in the "breed young by laying eggs" reason, and we want them to analyze an alligator to determine if it meets the critical characteristics of *egg-bearers,* then they must compare the critical attributes of the concept and the attributes of the new example, alligator, to determine if the alligator rightly belongs in the group.

Through focused and structured lessons using the Anchoring Strategies, learners will sharpen their understanding of situations requiring Labeling and Classifying. They will learn how and when to use these thinking operations so that they can communicate concepts efficiently and effectively. Learners also will become cognizant of why the Anchoring processes are important in communicating, retaining, and accessing knowledge. As a result, the cognitive operations of Labeling and Classifying will become part of the learners' repertoire of study and learning tools.

The study of the Anchoring Strategies will be organized in the following manner:

- Questioning Strategy Chart
- Sample Lesson Design
- Self-Study Discussion
- Curriculum Applications
- Analyzing Lessons
- Coding Symbols
- Sample Transcript
- Coded Transcript
- Reflections on the Coding

Once again, the following section has been graciously permitted for use in this text by the National Educational Service, copyright 1990.

LABELING QUESTIONING STRATEGY CHART

Purpose of the Process:

To be used in situations requiring learners to generate names, terms, or phrases for the critical characteristics or attributes of a concept

Nature of the Questions:

Generating or finding appropriate terms, names, phrases, and so forth which facilitate the efficient communication of a set of critical characteristics or attributes

How the Questions Function:

Names, terms, or phrases are assigned to an item, group, or set of characteristics; the names are clarified and supported

Learner Response:

Specifying and supporting labels that appropriately communicate the critical attributes of a concept or subconcept

SAMPLE LABELING LESSON DESIGN

PURPOSE: Provide learners with opportunities to generate names for animals grouped for various reasons, including the physical characteristics, habitat, eating patterns, location, species, and so forth.

OUTCOME: Students will be able to find or create names that appropriately communicate the critical attributes of the formed concepts.

REASON: Facilitate the communication of a set of characteristics assigned to grouped animals, as well as extend vocabulary development

CONTENT CHARACTERISTICS: Groups of animals based on physical features, eating patterns, habitats, environmental locations, and so on, which become the critical attributes of the concepts and the labels that communicate the critical attributes—for example, carnivorous animals, woodland animals, savanna animals, African animals, and others

RESOURCES: Groupings of animals (see previous Grouping lesson)

CORE QUESTION: Labeling

- Based on the reasons given for grouping the animals, what would be an appropriate name for the groups? (Do one group at a time.)

Possible Student Responses

- Group 1: Flying animals, birds, winged animals
- Croup 2: Mountain animals, high-altitude animals
- Group 3: Tundra animals, frigid animals
- Group 4: Pets, household animals
- Group 5: Meadow-lurking animals, grazing animals

Processing Question Stems for Labeling

RF (Refocusing response for labeling)

- You are giving me a reason for the group. What would be an appropriate name for the group?

CL (Defining and using additional, or more precise, language)

- What do you mean by "high altitude"? What are you referring to when you say "lurking"? Describe "tundra."

SP (Citing the reasons for the labels)

- Why do you think _______ is an appropriate name for Group 1?
- What is there about Group 2 that makes you say "high altitude" is an appropriate name for this group?

Possible Student Responses

- Group 1: Because animals have to have wings to fly.
- Group 2: All these animals are found high in the mountains.
- Group 3: These animals are found in areas of snow and ice.
- Group 4: People keep these animals in their homes.
- Group 5: Because they find their food in grassy places.

VR (Verifying details)

- How do you know that the animals in Group 3 are found in these areas?
- Give me an example of what Group 5 animals would eat.

RD (Attaining more student participation)

- Who has another appropriate name for Group 1?

SELF-STUDY DISCUSSION OF THE LABELING STRATEGY

Labeling is a process whereby names, terms, or phrases are generated in order to communicate economically the critical characteristics of formed concepts. It is an inductive process that allows learners to collect their own information, synthesize it, and determine the best name for the attributes of the set of items, characteristics, or ideas. This requires that learners know the critical characteristics of a concept and choose names that appropriately fit the critical characteristics of a concept. Through the thinking operation of Labeling, learners begin to realize that what something is called results from its attributes, that the names must aptly relate to these attributes, and that the label must precisely communicate the essential idea.

For example, in naming pets, people first collect information about the animal, they form the distinguishing characteristics, and then they name the animal based on the distinguishing characteristics. A black cat may be named *Blacky* or *Midnight*. A bronze cocker spaniel may be named *Buffy* or *Dusty*. If its loving nature is the most distinguishing characteristic of the animal, it may be named *Lovey*. A rabbit may be called *Nibble* because of the way it eats food. The point is that this is an instantaneous process and we rarely think about how it happens. When we focus on the thinking operation, we realize that naming or labeling is a sophisticated cognitive operation that requires many steps.

Labels are used to communicate concepts. It is commonly assumed that if learners know the label for a concept example, they also know the critical characteristics of the concept. This is a poor assumption. For learners to comprehend concepts, they must know the critical characteristics of the concept and that the label is simply a term to communicate these characteristics. This is not easy.

For example, if learners are given illustrations of triangles, they may be able to call them triangles, but they may not be able to state the critical attributes of a triangle, which is the conceptual learning. Unless learners can state the critical characteristics, attributes, or properties of an example of a concept, as well as the reason why the label is appropriate for the critical characteristics or the example of the concept, then they have simply memorized the name. They have not constructed a deep, meaningful understanding of the concept. Many people use words without understanding the meanings. Others use words without precision. The strength of the Labeling Strategy is to facilitate students' understanding of the power of words in communicating their thoughts.

Vocabulary development can be enhanced through the Labeling Strategy. Generating various names for the same concept will encourage learners to use words as tools for the precise communication of ideas. An illustration can be understood using the concept of "fracture." Other words for fracture can be "break," "split," "crack," "cleft," "disjunction," "rupture," and others. The best synonym for fracture will be based on how the word is to be used to communicate the concept. Additionally, generating a variety of labels for any given concept will assist learners in associating words that they know to words that they don't know, thus solidifying conceptualization rather than memorization. Generating labels and studying the relationship of the label to an idea will increase learners' abilities to use words appropriately, concisely, and precisely.

Teaching using the Labeling Strategy requires a willingness on the part of teachers to allow learners to play around with language. Labeling requires patience on the part of teachers and creative thinking on the part of students. Well-conceived names require students to synthesize information in order to devise quality responses. It is a difficult thinking operation, requiring extended wait-time in order for learners to generate appropriate, meaningful labels. To facilitate learners' thinking, teachers should ask learners to jot down names for the labels before reporting on them orally.

Learners should be encouraged to devise as many labels as they can for specific items, groups, or concepts without fear that they are not using the "right" or "correct" labels. Teachers must remember that the labels learners assign to describe or to name something will have more meaning for the learner than the technical label given by the teacher or textbook. Technical labels can be provided by the teacher once learners have generated meaningful names for themselves. By focusing instruction on the Labeling Strategy, teachers can provide students opportunities to increase their vocabularies while discovering that words are tools for communicating ideas. As a result, students will be more precise in the words they choose to anchor concepts.

Like other Qu:Est Instructional Strategies, the cognitive operation of Labeling must be focused and facilitated. The core question "What are some appropriate names for this?" must possess words that cue both the content and the process. The on-focus response to a Labeling core question should be the name or term that aptly denotes the critical characteristics of the concept. Once elicited, labels are clarified, verified, and supported in order to assist learners in understanding the meaning of their labels and how the generated labels fit the critical characteristics of the concept named. Like the Grouping Strategy, the Labeling questioning process requires a supporting question to ascertain the reason(s) for the label. The supporting question is: "What makes you think _______ is an appropriate name for _______?"

The supporting question elicits the relationship between the critical characteristics noted about the concept and the meaning of the label. Therefore, prior to asking the supporting question, teachers should clarify the labels: "What do you mean by endangered species?" The definition of "endangered species" is then the information that must be used in determining whether the labels fit the critical characteristics of a concept. The supporting question permits opportunities for the learner to rethink the definition of the label as well as to match the critical characteristics of a concept to label in communicating the idea.

CURRICULUM APPLICATIONS

- Naming types of literature
- Naming poetic devices
- Naming scientific concepts and processes
- Devising titles for things
- Generating names for inventions
- Naming periods in history
- Naming characters
- Naming grammatical concepts
- Naming songs
- Naming essays or research projects
- Creating synonyms

ANALYZING LESSONS: LABELING (LB)

During the analysis of the lesson, information is gathered and reflected on, identifying the manner in which the lesson was conducted by the teacher and the impact that it has had on students. A coding system is used to facilitate data collection of both teacher questions and learner responses. This data in turn provides the substance for identifying, forming patterns, and correcting critical aspects of the instructional strategy in order to assist learners in their development and refinement of thinking operations.

This section is divided as follows: (1) the learner response; (2) the coding symbols; (3) a sample transcript; (4) the coding of the transcript; and (5) reflections on the coding.

The Learner Response: On-Focus and Off-Focus Responses

Labeling, like other Qu:Est Strategies, has both on-focus and off-focus responses. On-focus responses are answers that name items, concepts, or relationships noted. Two issues are involved. Both the name and the reasons for the label or name must be stated. When learners are asked to generate appropriate labels, this should result in learners listing as many appropriate terms as possible.

On-focus responses illustrate the relationship between the defined label and the group or concept. If learners give a reason for the generation of a label, the reason for the label is an off-focus answer, because no name has been given. The teacher must refocus the response in order to elicit labels. Second, once labels have been elicited, learners must then state the relationship between the definition of the label and the critical characteristics of the group or concept they are naming.

Off-focus responses to the supporting question are answers that do not specify the relationship between the defined label and the critical attributes of the group or concept. In other words, learners simply define the label without "hooking up" the critical characteristics noted about group or concept. The refocusing question or a supporting question must be used to assist learners in determining the critical characteristics of both the group and/or concept and the meaning of the label. This is important because it helps learners view language as a tool for communicating ideas specifically and accurately.

The issue of wait-time is especially important when asking learners to label. At first, the generation of labels will be slow because labeling requires learners to synthesize information and communicate often complicated ideas in a concise and appropriate word or phrase. Once learners produce the labels, the names may be trite or mundane. Redirecting the Labeling core question will provide the opportunity for learners to rethink the names, terms, or phrases for communicating the critical attributes of the concept in more creative ways. The more labels that can be generated, clarified, and supported, the deeper students' understanding will become. Teachers must not hurry the process.

Coding Symbols

Coding the questions and responses in a lesson is a way to understand the patterns of teacher questions, learner responses, and the relationships that exist between teacher questions and learner responses. Coding establishes objective information for discussing the critical aspects of the performed lesson. To code a Labeling lesson, the following symbols may be used:

Teacher Questions		**Learner Responses**	
LB	Labeling core question Closed Labeling core question	+	On-focus response
		–	Off-focus response
CL	Clarifying question	?	Learner question
VR	Verifying question	CL	Clarifying response
SP	Supporting question	VR	Verifying response
RD	Redirecting question	SP	Support response
NF	Narrow focusing question		

Sample Transcript of a Labeling Lesson

T. We have been discussing ways in which people pollute the environment. Based on our discussion, what would be a good name to communicate the ideas we've talked about?

S. Polluters.

T. What do you mean by polluters?

S. People who throw things on the ground instead of putting waste in bins.

T. What is there about people throwing waste on the ground that makes you say that polluters is a good name for our discussion?

S. Well, we said that when people drive, they throw cups and paper out the windows. They are polluting our highways.

T. What are some other appropriate names for our discussion?

S. Environment inhibitors.

S. Nonecology minded.

S. Environment killers.

T. What makes you say that environment killers is an appropriate name to communicate the idea of polluting the environment?

S. By throwing stuff into the environment, we destroy the natural development of plants and animals.

S. Yes, that makes them die.

T. Does inhibit mean die?

S. No, just not grow right.

T: What about the term "environment inhibitors" makes you say it is an effective name for polluting the environment?

Coding of the Sample Transcript

T:	LB	CL	SP	RD			SP		CL	SP
S:	+	CL	SP	+	+	+	SP	CL	CL	

Reflections on the Coding

The teacher's initial question is well focused and clearly stated for the lesson. Several students responded with on-focus answers. The teacher takes the second generated label and asks the supporting question instead of asking for clarification. This leads the learner to use the term "inhibit" to define "inhibitors," which does not clearly distinguish the meaning of the label as it applies to the critical characteristics of the discussion. As a result, the teacher must focus attention on the meaning of the word "inhibit" before "hooking up" the label to the discussion.

CLASSIFYING QUESTIONING STRATEGY CHART

Purpose of the Process:

To be used in situations requiring learners to categorize items and/or examples based on the known critical attributes of a concept or related subconcept

Nature of the Questions:

Placing specific items or examples of concepts into known categories that exemplify critical characteristics of the item or example

How the Questions Function:

Specific examples or items are placed into known categories or concepts and are supported based on specific critical characteristics central to both the examples and the concept definition

Learner Response:

Selects an appropriate category for an example based on the critical characteristics of both the example and the critical characteristics of the concept

SAMPLE CLASSIFYING LESSON DESIGN

PURPOSE: Provide learners with opportunities to collect information about examples of a sentence to determine the appropriate sentence category and the reason for the sentence classification

OUTCOME: Learners will be able to identify, select, create new examples of a concept given a concept label, and explain the critical attributes of the new example that fits the critical characteristics of the concept attributes.

REASON: Facilitate learners' comprehension and retention of concepts

CONTENT CHARACTERISTICS: Sentence structure to include three subconcepts of sentences:

Concept Definition	**Concept Label**
(Sentences with one subject and one predicate containing a complete idea)	*Simple Sentence*

Concept Example: Bill Lee ran down the street.

(Sentences with two complete subjects and two complete predicates joined by a conjunction.)	*Compound Sentence*

Concept Example: Joan found the book, and she returned it to the library.

(Sentences with an independent and dependent clause hooked together to support each other.)	*Complex Sentence*

Concept Example: When Sherry realized that she was late, she ran home.

RESOURCES: An overhead projector, a written list of the following sentences projected, and a copy for each student

- Christopher awakened early this morning.
- Paul and John were best friends and played together often.
- Sherry went home with Jane, and they played all night.
- Following the strange trail home, the boys got lost.
- After school let out for the year, Alex moved away.
- When I fix dinner, I am always sure to set a place for my friends.

CORE QUESTION: Classifying: *There are four types of core Classifying questions. Type 1 is the least difficult. Type 4 is the most difficult.*

- CF (1) Is sentence _______ an example of a (simple, compound, complex) sentence? (Do one concept at a time.)
- CF (2) Circle all the simple sentences, underline the compound sentences, and place an * next to the complex sentences. (Do one sentence type at a time.)
- CF (3) Find or create an example of a simple, compound, and complex sentence. (Again, do one concept at a time.)
- CF (4) How can we change this example of a _______ sentence into an example of a _______ sentence? (Again, do one concept at a time.)

Possible Student Responses

- CF (1) Yes or no. Supporting question needed to elicit reason
- CF (2) Numbers 1, 2, and 4 are simple sentences. *Supporting question needed to elicit critical attributes*

- CF (3) My sentence is an example of a ______. *Supporting question needed to elicit attributes*
- CF (4) To change sentence 2 into a compound sentence, you would have to add "they." *Supporting question needed to elicit the procedures.*

Processing Question Stems for Classifying

SP (Citing the reasons for classifying)

- CF (1) What makes you say sentence 1 is an example of a simple sentence?
- CF (2) What makes you say that sentences 1, 2, 4, and 5 are examples of simple sentences?
- CF (3) What makes you say that the sentence you found or created is a simple sentence?
- CF (4) What did you have to do to sentence 2 to make it a compound sentence?

VR (Verifying details)

- How do you know that there are not two complete sentences in sentence 2?
- Give me an example of a sentence with two complete thoughts.

CL (Defining and using additional or more precise language)

- What do you mean by "has more than one subject"?
- What are you referring to when you say that "When I fix dinner" is a dependent clause?

RD (Attaining more student participation)

- Who else thinks sentence 4 is a compound sentence, and what makes you think that it is?
- Who doesn't think sentence 4 is a compound sentence, and what makes you say that it is not?

SELF-STUDY DISCUSSION OF THE CLASSIFYING STRATEGY

Classifying is a cognitive operation whereby new examples of concepts are placed or grouped into *known categories or labels of concepts*. It is typically used as an assessment tool for concept formation or differentiation, or it can be an instructional process for assisting learners in the development and refinement of concepts as they extend to new examples. Classifying involves knowing the critical characteristics or attributes of a concept or group, noting the critical attributes of a new example, and determining whether the new example fits the critical characteristics of the concept or group.

The Classifying Strategy is the inversion of the Grouping Qu:Est Instructional Strategy as defined in this book. In the Grouping Strategy, learners place items together to create or generate groups based on common critical characteristics of the items. In Classifying, as defined here, learners are taking new examples and matching them with *known* groupings or concepts, or concept labels. Usually, the Classifying core question identifies the label of the group or concept and asks the learners to determine if the new example is a part of the identified concept or group. This means that the learners must understand both the critical characteristics of the concept or group and the label used to communicate it.

Direct teaching of Classifying assumes that learners know the label and critical characteristics of a concept. Classifying requires that learners identify the critical characteristics of the new example of the category or concept and explain why the new example fits into the known category or concept. There are several ways of conducting Classifying lessons. Four such types are: (1) asking learners whether or not a new item is, or is not, an example of a concept or category; (2) listing examples and nonexamples of a concept or category and asking learners to determine which of the items are examples of the concept or category; (3) asking learners to generate or find an example of a concept or category; and (4) asking learners to change a nonexample of a concept into an example of a concept.

Obviously, the first type of Classifying is the simplest. If learners cannot identify a given example as part of a concept or category, then they most likely will not be able to distinguish nonexamples from examples, nor generate or find one of their own. Like the other thinking operations in Qu:Est, the Classifying thinking operation must be focused and facilitated by the teacher. The core questions are: (1) Is this an example of the (concept label)? (2) Which of the items in the list are examples of the (concept label)? (3) Find or create an example of the (concept label). (4) How can we turn this nonexample of the (concept label) into an example of the concept?

The core question must signal to the students that the Classifying thinking operation is to be used in responding to the question. The response to the core question is the identification of the critical characteristics of the new example and matching the identified characteristics with the critical characteristics of the concept attributes. Like the Grouping and Labeling Strategies, the Classifying Strategy requires that teachers ask supporting questions to assist learners in identifying and matching the critical characteristics of the new example with the critical characteristics of the concept. The supporting question for Classifying is: "What is there about this (example) that makes you say that it is an example of the (concept label)?" Unless learners can match the identified characteristics of the new example with the critical characteristics of the concept, they have not performed the Classifying thinking operation. They simply have made a guess about the new example without being able to reason through the connection.

CURRICULUM APPLICATIONS

- Grammar concepts: examples of nouns, verbs, adjectives, adverbs
- Mathematical concepts: examples of fractions, shapes, decimals, borrowing, and so forth.
- Science concepts
- Examples of types of government
- Examples of constitutional amendments
- Examples of various bacteria
- Examples of types of diseases

ANALYZING LESSONS: CLASSIFYING (CF)

During the analysis of the lesson, information is gathered and reflected on, identifying the manner in which the lesson was conducted by the teacher and the impact that it has had on students. A coding system is used to facilitate data collection of both teacher questions and learner responses. This data in turn provides the substance for identifying, forming patterns, and correcting critical aspects of the instructional strategy in order to assist learners in their development and refinement of thinking operations.

This section is divided as follows: (1) the learner response; (2) the coding symbols; (3) a sample transcript; (4) the coding of the transcript; and (5) reflections on the coding.

The Learner Response: On-Focus and Off-Focus Responses

Classifying, as do the other strategies, has both on-focus and off-focus responses. On-focus responses are answers that appropriately categorize a new example to a known concept label. Two issues are involved. Both the placement of the new example into the known concept label, and the reasons for placement, must be consistent with the concept's critical attributes. Asking learners to determine the placement of a new example into specific concept labels should result in learners indicating that the critical characteristics of the new example match the critical characteristics of the concept. For example, when asked if "Mary," in the sentence "Mary carried the ball," is the subject of the sentence, learners must state, "Yes, Mary is the subject because it is a noun that tells who is doing the action."

Off-focus responses to the supporting question for Classifying are answers that do not specify the relationship between the critical attributes of the new example and the critical attributes of the known concept. In other words, learners simply place the new example into a category without "hooking up" the critical characteristics. The supporting question must be used to assist learners in determining the critical characteristics of both the new example and the category. This is important because it helps learners understand that examples are specific items of a larger idea or concept.

Coding Symbols

Coding the questions and responses in a lesson is a way to understand the patterns of teacher questions, learner responses, and the relationships that exist between them. Coding establishes objective information for discussing the critical attributes of a Classifying lesson.

To code a classifying lesson, the following symbols may be used:

Teacher Questions

CF	Classifying core question Closed Classifying core question (elicits a yes/no response)
SP	Supporting question
CL	Clarifying question
VR	Verifying question
RF	Refocusing question
RD	Redirecting question
NF	Narrow focusing question

Learner Responses

+	On-focus response
–	Off-focus response
CL	Clarifying response
VR	Verifying response
SP	States relationship for grouping
?	Student question

Sample Transcript of a Classifying Lesson

T. Which of the drawings shown belong to invertebrates?

S. The jellyfish.

T. What makes you determine that the jellyfish is an example of an invertebrate?

S. It has tentacles and is not a solid mass.

S. Its body is filled with liquid.

T. How do you know that the jellyfish doesn't have a solid mass?

S. It has a hollow body cavity.

T. Point to it.

S. (Learner does.)

T. What are some other examples of invertebrates?

S. The sponge because it has no skeleton.

S. Snails.

T. What is there about the snail that makes you say it is an invertebrate?

S. It's soft and spongy.

Coding of the Sample Transcript

T:	CF	SP		VR	RD/VR	SP	
S:	+	SP	SP	VR	VR	+	+

Reflections on the Coding

The teacher's initial question establishes the category for classification through the label "invertebrates." The question elicits several on-focus responses that are both supported and verified. Several learners respond with on-focus answers. After the first learner responds and the teacher attempts to hook up the response with the supporting question, the next learner to answer provides both the example and the reason for the example belonging to the invertebrate phylum. This is especially desirable. It is an indication that the learner both knows the characteristics of the example and perceives the relationship between the example's characteristics and the critical attributes of the concept.

▶ Part IV

Questioning to Learn

Carrying out instructional conversations is not an easy task. It means that, as educators, we must be mindful of our curricular goals while underscoring the importance of student ideas and students' ability to process their understandings. We must be good active listeners and skillful in our abilities to question productively.

In the following five chapters, we present situations and critical issues involved in conducting instruction through conversation aimed at the development and refinement of student thinking. Chapter 10 is a narrative illustrating the experience of a teacher attempting to use Qu:Est Strategies for the first time. It exemplifies the problems that surface and the decisions the teacher makes as she gains confidence in the use of the strategies. The following chapters explore the critical issues involved in successfully implementing the Qu:Est Strategies. The issues are: opening closed questions, structuring and phrasing core questions, using processing questions to shape quality student responses, and managing student responses to both develop conceptual ideas and to understand the cognitive operations students use.

The chapters have been written to provide our readers with an analysis of the critical issues involved in productive questioning using the Qu:Est Instructional Strategies. The chapters are organized as follows: A Facilitative Set is provided to introduce the critical issue. Following the Facilitative Set, a vignette, designed to illustrate the critical issue in a learning context, is presented. The vignette is explored in two ways. First, a reflection on the learning that is taking place is written by the teacher conducting the lesson. Second, a self-study discussion describes the critical issue. In the last part of each chapter, we pose inquiry questions and suggestions to guide you in your investigation of the critical issues.

We believe that through continued, conscious study of productive questioning practices to discern the relationships between teaching and learning, we can effect more vigorous and appropriate instruction for students. We heighten our awareness and ability to conduct meaningful instructional conversations that contribute to students' understanding of concepts. Likewise, we create meaningful and relevant opportunities for students to inquire into how they can use productive questioning as tools to learn and to monitor their future learning experiences.

▶ 10

Everything I Really Needed to Know about Life I Learned by Asking Questions

BY CINDY YBOS

FIRST TRY

Core question? What's my core question? OK, I remember now. Ask it. *"What do you observe about this copy of an Escher drawing?"*

Now listen to their responses. What responses? Oh, no. They're not answering. Why aren't they answering? They're just sitting there looking at me. They're looking at the picture, and then they're looking at me.

It wasn't like this in class last week. Marylou made it look so easy. She asked the question and we all answered. There were so many answers. How did she handle that?

Oh, wait. Someone is answering. Wait-time. That's what I needed. It's offered timidly, but it's an answer. Focus on the answer.

Now what do I do? Clarify? Verify? Think about the answer. I just want the floor to open up and swallow me. Maybe I could just end the lesson right here and now. They won't know. I didn't tell them I was trying anything new. They won't know. I will know, though. Besides, I have to have something to share with the other graduate students who are taking this class. My students are still waiting for me to say something. Redirect. That's what I'll do.

"OK, who else has an answer?"

That sounds lame. I don't want an answer anyway. I want an observation.

Take a few mental breaths and think about the answer that the student gives you. How long has this been going on? Less than a minute! I'll never make it through this. Another answer.

"OK, what do you mean by that?"

That was better. It sounded as if I was in control. Look at the student's face. Is that panic or surprise? They think I have lost my mind. I have dashed their expectations about "class discussions." They don't know how to handle this. I wonder if I look as panic-stricken as they do.

Now the answers are coming more quickly. How did Marylou handle multiple answers to a question?

"Let me listen to this one first, and then I'll listen to yours."

That felt good. I need to change my questions—what did she call those questions? Support questions? Probing questions?

I have a headache and I'm tired. Only two minutes. She says I have to do this for five minutes. It's been an eternity, and I'm not even halfway through.

My old way of teaching is so much easier. Why do I do this to myself? Why can't I just be happy with the way things are?

I can't think about this now. I have to focus on the answers. I can't let my mind wander. Verify. How do I do verification questions? I promise this is the last class I'll ever take like this. I should have known. It all sounded too good to be true. No memorization exams. No, there are no reams of materials to read and memorize, but this is worse. You actually have to perform. Is it perform or jump through the hoops? It doesn't matter. I know that if I get out of this course alive, I'll never fall for this trap again.

"Give me an example of repeating patterns."

Repeating patterns? I hadn't thought about that when I wrote my "lesson plan." How can you know what follow-up question to ask when you can't anticipate the answer the student will give you? None of this makes any sense to me right now.

Three minutes. Oh, good. The answers are coming much faster now. Where do I go with this? What good does it do to ask these questions if I can't close the lesson? Darn her. I got it going now, and I just can't stop. How many times can you clarify, verify, or redirect? Narrow focus. That was another one. Let me try that one for a while.

"Tell me more about the animals you observe in the picture."

This isn't making any sense to these students. It doesn't make any sense to me. They look like mice who are afraid that if they give the wrong answers the cat will devour them. They don't know that the cat has no idea what the right answers are. The cat is more afraid of the mice than they realize.

"What do you mean when you say angular?"

Four minutes. All right, enough is enough. I don't care that it's not five minutes. I quit. I'm tired and frustrated. Besides, I have many other things I need to be doing with these students. They have materials and procedures to learn. Why am I wasting my time with this? I'll never use it after I'm finished with this course.

"Very good. Now let's use these manipulatives to explore some math concepts."

Now on to the really important part of class.

SECOND TRY

So everyone else had problems doing this too. I felt better after Marylou's class last week. I heard many of my own questions, complaints, and arguments from other people's mouths the whole class period. Marylou seemed to expect these comments and was very reassuring. I'm still nervous about doing this.

My students haven't made any comments, though. They just look at me with those trusting but fearful eyes during class.

"What do you recall about your reading assignment on assessing children's understanding of mathematics concepts?"

What process—no, thinking skill—whatever it's called am I supposed to be using? Here we go again. The answers are flowing more smoothly now, though. I've gotten that clarify and verify thing down, but I need other kinds of questions too. I could also redirect. What's it called when they don't do the thinking process and you want to bring them back?

"You're telling me how you think others might feel in that situation. I would like for you to tell me what you remember from your reading assignment."

Stupid! It's not remember. It's recall. You want them to recall. The students don't know. What difference does it make? How can you say that? You want an "A" in this course, don't you? Of course it makes a difference. When the professor passes final judgment on your "performance," it will make a big difference. By the way, when is she going to tell us what we have to do for an "A"? Can't think about that now. Have to pay attention to the students' answers.

"Who else recalls what you read?"

Was that right? Was that an instructional mistake or a grammatical mistake? The tape recorder will catch it all, and then I'll share it all in my graduate class. The good thing about making such mistakes is that I have something to discuss in class. The good thing about class is that everyone else is having just as many problems as I am. The good thing about that is that we all can't fail. Maybe we can. How do you grade a performance, anyway?

In that class, I usually feel frustrated. I'm not an auditory learner, and I have to "listen" to these lessons and record what type of question and response is given. As if that's not enough, she actually expects us to give advice to one another on how to improve our questioning skills. What does she think we are? Gifted? I know I can do it, but it just takes me longer to think through all of this than it does anyone else.

"Tell me more about that."

Clarify, verify, redirect, narrow focus, refocus—it's becoming a litany that I say under my breath each time I listen to a student's answer. There has to be more to this than the smorgasbord approach I'm taking. How does she know which to use? Make a note to ask her in class. Why bother? She doesn't give you straight answers anyway.

"How did the author of the article suggest you mitigate the shortcomings of that kind of assessment?"

The students don't seem as afraid to answer the questions now. Have they figured out that I don't know what I'm doing, or are they catching on to this little game? Maybe they're more comfortable with reading than with looking at pictures. Reading is more "college-like" than looking at absurd drawings.

"What do mean by formative evaluation?"

Anticipating student responses to this seems easier also. Maybe this recall thing is more concrete than the observation. Will the rest of the processes be more or less concrete than this one?

Maybe my problem is that I'm trying for too much at one time here. Maybe I should just work on one type of question at a time and ask it whenever I get a chance in class. That would solve one problem I have. I still don't know how to stop this thing. My ending is abrupt and lacks style. That's something else to ask in class next time.

"OK, using the information from the articles, I want you to form groups and create at least two kinds of assessment tools for your group lesson."

Amazing. I used this stuff for the whole five minutes this time. The students seemed to enjoy it also. They are truly looking forward to creating assessments. That's a first. Students have never had that reaction before. Now all I have to do is listen to the tape and critique it.

THIRD TRY

The students are wising up. When I ask "What do you mean by _______?" or "How do you know that?" they're rolling their eyes now. The jig is up. They realize I have no idea what I'm doing, but they're willing to play along for the grade. They even giggle a little when I ask those questions. That helps. Being relaxed makes the mistakes easier to accept.

"What similarities are there among these three lesson plans?"

This questioning stuff is really messing up my lesson plans. I usually have a specific, logical order in which I present all of this information, but I'm having to juggle topics around so that I can keep up with my assignments in class. The students are getting this information in such a jumbled up order. They don't seem to mind, though. How can they ever make any sense of this? If I were a student in this class, I would be going crazy right now because everything is so out of order.

"What do you mean when you say they all have objectives?"

I have discovered that the students know more than they think they do. They also know more than I thought they did. Using questioning has helped bring their knowledge to the surface. As they articulate their thoughts, I think they clarify them as well. This increases their confidence and willingness to take risks.

I don't know if I want them to be so willing to take risks. They are feistier when they have confidence, and do I really want them to be feisty?

The students seem to be more comfortable with comparing and contrasting information than with observing because it seems familiar to them. I would have never thought to have students look at lesson plans this way before, though. In the past when I "taught" lesson planning, I always gave the students an outline of what each type of lesson should be like and what I wanted them to do. Then they did it and I graded it. Simple.

Now they are going to have to tell me the attributes of each lesson and then . . . then what? Where am I going with these lessons? How could I have learned so much but still feel so stupid? I'm not sure what to do with "this stuff." Intuitively, I think the students should apply their knowledge and insights to a product that will be useful to them, but I'm not sure that's what Marylou wants me to do.

What was that? A student asks another student a verification question! Amazing! Why did that happen? They're talking and questioning one another. Wait a minute. I'm the teacher here. What do these students think they are doing? I'm supposed to lead this discussion. Does this mean I'm losing control of this class?

Is it a bad thing to "lose" control of the class? Did I ever really have control of it anyway? College students are very good at "playing the game" to get "the grade." What kind of game is questioning? How do students know what I'm going for when most of the time I have no idea what I'm doing? How does that affect my relationship with these students? I would think that the students would be more comfortable. I know I'm more comfortable because I feel a great deal of pressure has been removed from my shoulders. I no longer have to be the supreme giver of knowledge and the judge of the quality of knowledge students give to me. The students are responsible for their own learning, and how much they get out of this process depends on how much they put into it.

Oops. They're wandering too far off the topic of the day. How do I bring them back without dampening their enthusiasm?

"How do your experiences apply to the lesson plans we're discussing today?"

There, I did it and they didn't even know it. Hey, this is kind of fun. Since there's no right or wrong, I can't make mistakes, right? Well, maybe I can make mistakes but are they that critical?

"How do you know that?"

That just popped out of my mouth without my even thinking about it.

"What do you mean by that?"

There goes another one. Maybe this is starting to sink in. I still have many issues to resolve in "mastering" these techniques. How often do I use the questioning processes? In what order do these processes have to be used in classes? How do these questioning processes relate to other instructional strategies I have been using? Do I have to do a whole questioning lesson each time, or can I sprinkle a little here and there as I think the class needs it? Do I really have to think out each student response and plan follow-up questions?

Wait a minute. We've been doing this for ten minutes now. There goes my schedule for today. I hadn't planned on spending so much time "discussing" lesson plans. How am I going to make up this time?

"Now how are these lesson plans different?"

To me, this is the real meat of the lesson. Should I have done this first? I wish I could remember what Marylou did in class. Maybe I should video the classes and review them several times before attempting these lessons in my own class. What would I video anyway? She does a quick lesson, and then we try it on our own. Most of the time, the class is like the blind leading the blind because we have to give each other comments on our performance.

"What do you mean when you say that one is a discovery lesson?"

Personal concepts—I wonder if educators look at the concepts we teach as personal. I know I never have. What I have had to teach has always been something "out there" that "others" thought was important. These questioning techniques, however, make everything up close and personal.

"Where have you experienced that before?"

See, it's personal. The students have to build personal understanding. Really, it's more than personal; it's intimate. I've always been uncomfortable with that word—intimate. I wonder if my students feel as if questioning is an intrusion of their space. Maybe that's why it's so frightening to them when the nutty teacher starts doing questioning such as this. They have to expose themselves.

What have their previous experiences been in answering questions? They always knew there was a right and a wrong and the teacher would determine which answer is which.

These questioning lessons are different. I never tell them that their answers are right or wrong. I respond to their questions with other questions.

Usually, if they have made an error in thinking, they can self-correct when I ask the processing question. I never tell them that they are right or wrong. When a student has to self-correct, however, there's always a moment of embarrassment. Is that embarrassment useful or detrimental? That's another question for Marylou.

"What differences do you notice about the assessment in each lesson plan?"

Assessment is something I haven't thought much about in Marylou's class lately. Everything seems to be "evolving" naturally. The midterm seems straightforward enough. I'm still skeptical, however, that she's really going to let us critique one another and that we will do so much self-evaluating for the grade. I guess it makes sense, though. If nothing else, she's consistent—that is, consistently unpredictable in a structured sort of way.

How would the students in this class react if I said they were going to evaluate one another and their own work? They would really think I had lost it then. If they didn't think I was crazy, they would probably think I was lazy. After all, isn't a teacher supposed to work hard, mark many papers, and justify all the evaluations that are handed out at the end of the semester?

The key to making self-evaluation and peer evaluation successful is trust. How many of these students really trust one another or me?

"Now that you have examined the similarities and differences among these three kinds of lessons, in your groups, choose two kinds of lessons that you will create using the materials and resources we have discussed in previous classes. You will have the rest of this class period and all of next class period to work in your groups."

The good thing about using these questioning lessons is that I'm so mentally exhausted after them that I don't feel guilty about letting the students work in groups afterward. I have noticed a change in the students' attitudes toward cooperative learning since I've started doing the questioning first rather than lecture. They seem more enthusiastic about working on the projects. I wonder if there is a connection. Maybe the students are thankful that they don't have to answer any more of those "hard" questions. Maybe they understand the concepts more thoroughly and can more readily see how to apply them. That's something to think about.

FOURTH TRY

Amazing. Here I think I'm the best teacher since Aristotle, and now she tells us that we have just scratched the surface! What the hell is she talking about now? My students are excited and discussing these topics with an energy that I've never seen before, and she tells us that there's even more to learn.

I'm just getting the hang of how to do the first few lessons, and she's gone on to two other lessons. I can't keep up with this. She just demonstrates the lesson in class, and then we do it. When are we going to get down to what's going to be on the final? She just has us practice in class and then try out these lessons in our classrooms. The following week we discuss and ask questions. This is too weird for me.

What am I doing this week? Do I have to do labeling or grouping? What's the difference, anyway? How can you create a group without labeling it? Why would you create a group without labeling it, anyway? I'll just do an observation or a recall lesson and say I forgot. No, that's not going to do me any good. Besides, she might have us do this on our final exam. Then where will I be?

"Can you . . ."

There I go again. I have to stop that. Why can't I just ask the question without saying "Can you . . . ?" I know, I'll get the students to help me.

"Let me say something before we start today's lesson."

A quick explanation and then we'll get on with the lesson. If I tell the students to refuse to answer any questions that begin with "Can you . . . " I know I'll break that habit very quick. The students like to catch the teacher making a mistake. Besides, I have my pride at stake now. Is it my pride, or am I still worried about my grade? I still don't know what I have to do to get an "A," but lately that doesn't seem as important.

"Look at these shapes. Group them in a way that makes sense to you."

It's a good thing I'm teaching a topic that lends itself to this type of question. What about all those other poor people who are really having to go out of their way to make these fit their lessons? What does that mean? Are these people teaching what they should be teaching, or do these techniques just lend themselves more easily to certain subjects than others? What about kindergarten teachers? How are those little kids going to do all of this? Well, that's one struggle that I don't have to worry about.

"What was it about these items that made you put them in this group?"

That doesn't sound right to me. Am I asking the question correctly? What is the pattern to these questions? Wait a minute. Isn't that a thinking process? Now that I think about it, I have been using these thinking processes as part of my teaching all along, but I just didn't have a structure to it. What do people at the university call it—a framework? Is that what this is supposed to be? A framework that allows me to organize what I have been doing with teaching?

"How do you know that all the angles of those shapes add up to 360°?"

Three minutes into the lesson, and I'm rolling along. I'm still tired when I finish. I still have a headache. I still say OK to stall while I think about the next question to ask. I still don't know how to end this . . . what do I call this? Is it a lesson? Is it a technique? What made me think I knew so much about doing this? Maybe she's right. Maybe I have only scratched the surface.

Getting the terminology down is difficult. I wish all of this made more sense to me. I wonder if preservice teachers could handle any of this information. I have more than ten years of teaching experience, and I'm having trouble keeping up with all of this. How are all those "new" teachers in our class keeping up? Maybe they haven't picked up as many bad habits as I have, so they have less to unlearn.

"Who has another group for a different reason?"

I wonder if the students in this class could handle learning these questioning strategies. These students are struggling with so many new concepts. Would it be fair to pile more on them? Especially something that is so foreign to them. It's one thing to have a teacher who will use these techniques on you in class, but it's quite another to have to try it yourself. I know my personal experiences have not been the bed of roses I thought they were going to be when I started this course.

I wonder what would happen if in 50 years all elementary and high school teachers were using these questioning techniques? What would a methods course for preservice teachers look like? Would questioning be a routine part of the curriculum? Would it even be a big deal, or would these preservice teachers have internalized it so much that they would do it automatically? So much of what I see these students doing in their lesson plans is the "traditional" dole-out-the-information type of lesson, and I am concerned. What would it take to change their perception of teaching? What is more important, how can *I* change the teachers who are sitting right here in my class today? Someone once said that to teach is to touch the future. It's frightening to me sometimes that these teachers will walk out of this class using the tools that I have provided. What kind of tools have I provided for them? Until I took this course, I was very confident that I was providing them with practical, proven tools that would make each the best teacher each could be. Now I'm not so sure. I'm learning that there are ways of teaching "out there" that I have never imagined. It's ironic that as my students become more confident in this class, I am becoming less confident in my own work.

I have also noticed that I'm asking more questions now than I used to in the past.

"In what group would this object belong?"

Although I'm asking more questions, I am also making more connections between what I have experienced or heard in the past and what I am experiencing and hearing now. For example, there are points in the course textbook that remind me of things my undergraduate teachers tried to "tell" me but that just didn't make any sense at the time.

Take concepts, for instance. As an undergraduate, I read what Bruner had to say about concepts and I just said, "OK, big deal." I have heard of Hilda Taba, but her "stuff" seemed so far removed from anything I have ever experienced that I never gave it much thought. Now that I have to create a lesson for students to identify how things are alike or different, I suddenly realize that concepts are a functional way of thinking. I am suddenly aware that I "classify" things all the time in my life and that "classification" becomes the basis for my behavior. For example, I have a "now and later" approach to the tasks that I have to do. I mentally classify each task on my list as something I have to do immediately or something that can wait. By classifying those tasks, I can decide what I have to do, what materials I need, and how to use my time efficiently. "Now and later" are my own personal concepts.

This is the first time in my teaching career that I can recall being given a systematic approach to teaching "concepts." I think I have always had the feeling that something was missing in my teaching but could never quite put my finger on it before.

Yes, this way of teaching feels better, but I can't say that it feels right. Maybe it's because I don't feel that I'm working hard enough to help these students learn.

Grouping is something that is less familiar than the other processes. That doesn't make sense. I know I have recalled, observed, and classified before, but surely I have grouped items in a class at some point in my life. Maybe I haven't. Maybe the groups were always given to me, and I just accepted them.

How many other things in my life have I just accepted without questioning? How many of these students accept things without questioning them? How many times are we encouraged to "build knowledge" from scratch? I know that many people say that building your own knowledge is too time-consuming.

"What name would you give this group?"

The students are responding quite favorably to these types of questions. I've noticed them using these questions in other situations also. They're questioning me when I give them new information. That feels good. I wonder if others feel that it is good for students to ask so many questions.

FIFTH TRY

The lesson plans for these lessons are horrendous. I feel as if I'm being unnecessarily redundant and tedious with them. Then when I face the class, the lesson plan seems useless. Sometimes the students provide answers that I have anticipated, but most of the time, they don't. I wonder if I do this with the next class, if I could anticipate the answers more accurately. Maybe that's the true secret to asking effective questions. Maybe it's that you have to know your students as well as you know yourself.

"Which of these lesson plans is an example of a concept development approach to teaching fractions?"

Reflection

What have I learned in this class? I started this class just wanting to be a better teacher. I have gotten so much more than that. I have learned things that have given me a broader perspective on teaching and learning:

1. Impact and control are not the same thing.
2. We are what we think about our experiences. Learning to question students teaches us to question everything else in our lives.
3. To really teach and learn means to get personal.
4. Learning anything new ebbs and flows like tides. Teaching yourself is as important as teaching students. Students will grow with you when you grow.
5. We have a long way to go in truly understanding the learning process.

▶ 11

Closed Questions: Do You Understand?

FACILITATIVE SET

Learning to question productively and consciously during classroom dialogue requires that teachers unlearn behaviors that have been a part of their school learning experiences. When we observe teachers who have not encountered Qu:Est, one persistent questioning practice permeates their question asking—asking closed questions. The abundant use of closed questions that can be answered simply by the students responding with a "yes" or "no," when the teacher really wants a well-reasoned response, can interfere with students' confidence about their knowledge, and often results in instructional conversations that are dead-ended.

This behavior, starting questions with "can," "do," or "will," while unconscious for many teachers, is a habit learned from a teacher's own learning experiences and solidified through sloppy habits in question asking. Asking closed questions is a barrier to effective, productive questioning that engages students in meaningful classroom discourse. By becoming aware of the instructional and learning barriers these questions impose on instructional conversations and student learning, teachers can become more conscious about the use of open-ended questions that provide rich opportunities for student dialogue.

At this point, we will present the following activities to assist our readers in understanding the differences between asking closed and open questions during classroom interactions:

1. A vignette of teachers focusing on the study of open and closed questions;
2. Our reflections about the process of studying open and closed questions;

3. A Self-study discussion that analyzes open and closed questions;
4. Inquiry questions and suggestions to assist our readers in investigating the use of open and closed questions.

Vignette: Opening Closed Questions

"Can you tell me what 2 + 2 is?" I ask the group.

"4," a teacher responds.

I glance at the other teachers and shake my head "no." "Do you know what 2 + 2 is?"

"4," another teacher says, emphatically.

I redirect the question. "Who else can tell me what 2 + 2 is."

"It depends on what base you're in. If it is a base of 10, then the answer is 4. If it's any other base, the answer is not 4," the teacher offers bravely.

"All wrong," I say. The teachers are flustered and agitated. They squirm in their seats. I proceed to another teacher and ask "What do you recall is the answer to 2 + 2?"

She is unsure as she sighs heavily and whispers, "I remember it to be 4."

"Right!" I exclaim.

Confusion abounds. The group of teachers is murmuring, shaking their heads.

Then I ask, "What are the differences among the questions I asked you?"

Silence.

I write the questions on the board.

Can you tell me what 2 + 2 is?

Do you know what 2 + 2 is?

Who else can tell me what 2 + 2 is?

What do you recall is the answer to 2 + 2?

Enduring the uncomfortable silence, differences apparently dawn on several teachers as they raise their hands.

Barry says, "The 'can you' and 'do you' questions call for a 'yes' or 'no' response to them. The 'what' question asks for information without saying yes or no."

"As you observe the 'what' question, what other information do you notice that it asks for?" I politely ask.

Silence again.

"Well," says a quiet voice from the front of the room. All eyes are on Maria. "It asks for recollection."

"What word tells you that it asks for recollection?" I continue.

"Recall," she says.

"What do you mean by recollection?" I say as I turn away from her and face other teachers in the class in order to take some pressure off Maria and indicate that others could respond to the question.

"You know," Jerry says, "from memory."

"So how is the 'what' question different from the other questions?" I ask the whole group again, positioning myself in the back of the room. They all turn around in their seats to follow me. They look uncomfortable with their bodies twisted.

"Well," says Sarah, "the first three questions ask students to determine if they know the answer; the fourth question asks them to remember the answer—because it was memorized before."

"Oh," I say, moving quickly to the front of the room again, "so there are words in the question that provide clues for the students in answering questions."

Our inquiry into the nature and function of questions has begun. The teachers' faces are covered with interest.

Reflection on Teacher Learning

The study of questioning becomes a comic drama as teachers (our students) struggle to unlearn nonproductive questioning practices and replace them with questioning practices that engage students in the production of language, exemplifying their thinking. The first aspect of nonproductive questioning teachers must unlearn is the closed question.

Many of our students think that picking on the first words of a question is unimportant and frivolous. You may also think that the opening words of a question are nonsense to belabor. However, we assure you that it has been our experience that closed questions interfere with student confidence in answering questions and hinder teachers' insights into how students arrive at their answers. Let us give you an example of how asking closed questions deters students in responding.

We've observed adults, even us, after years of practicing productive questions, ask children, "Can you tell me your age?" In asking the question, we know that the child knows his or her age. However, we insist on asking the child to tell us his or her age by asking them *to decide* if they know it or not. Why? Often, the child is silent. We assume shy. But, it could well be that we have signaled to the child that we are not sure if they can tell us the answer. Another popular phrasing of a question for children begins with "Do you know *(fill in the blank)*?" We ask the question knowing that the child knows, but our phrasing insinuates doubt.

We maintain that closed questions are interpreted by children as meaning that we are not confident that they know what they know. The child may very well interpret such phrasing of a question as reason not to respond, because the answer is obvious. There is no way to ask a closed question that communicates anything but doubt. Try asking the following questions, emphasizing through intonation the italicized words: "Can *you* share your story with us?"; "*Can* you share your story with us?"; "Can you *share* your story with us?"; "Can you share *your story with us?*" Any way you ask it, you impart to the child that you are uncertain that he or she can answer the question.

We also want to sensitize teachers to the issue that asking closed questions infringes on opportunities to discover how students think about things. When we ask, "*Can you tell me about* your house?" or any other way in which you fill in the content of the question, if the child responds with "no," there's nowhere to go to discover how the child thinks about his or her house. If the child responds, "yes," we still have to ask, "What is your house like?" or some other question that provides the child with a clue to use more words to describe the subject of our question. Why ask two questions when one well-phrased question will do?

The only way teachers can enlighten themselves about the effects of closed and open questions on student responses is to play around with question phrasing and concentrate on the responses that they receive from people to various kinds of words used in the opening stems of questions. We've found that when teachers focus on the first words of their questions, they quickly resolve that closed questions limit responses and do not generate the use of language in answering the question.

SELF-STUDY DISCUSSION

Questions that begin with "Do you know," "Can you tell me," "Don't you think," or "Have you ever had the experience" must be dropped from the teachers' repertoire of questions, especially if our intent for instruction is to qualify students' understanding of subject material and refine their thinking. Closed question stems result in students' deciding yes or no—determining whether or not they are going to answer the question before they ever think about the answer.

The most notorious, rhetorical closed question used for punctuating our important points or closing our lessons is *"Do you understand?"* What do we learn about students' understandings by the phrasing of this question? What do we think they are going to say? What do we want them to say? Most often, when we ask this question, students sit silently, often avoiding eye contact. Why do we accept their silence? Why do we encourage it with how we ask the question? At best, the question *"Do you understand?"* signals to students that the last thing the teacher said was important; at worst, it communicates to students that the lesson is over. Period.

Closed question stems can be replaced by asking questions with open stems that require students to converse and by using language in answering the question without deciding yes or no before responding. Questions beginning with *"what," "how," "why,"* or *"in what way"* open up the windows of students' minds for using language in responding to questions. These question stems do not permit students the option of deciding not to answer. They elicit ideas and affirm students' understanding and cognitive operation.

In asking "What is your age?" "What kind of house do you live in?" or "In what way is your story interesting?" students must formulate a response or be silent. Additionally, by asking the open question, the teacher is assuring the students that he or she believes that the students know the answer. Students read intonation. The intonation of an open question is one of affirmation. For example in the question, "What do you remember about the discovery of America?" no matter what word the teacher emphasizes in the question, the implication is that the answer is known by the students and they must respond.

Sometimes, however, because students are used to being asked closed question stems, they don't know how to respond to a teacher who is using open question stems. The question is intimidating to them because they don't have the choice not to respond. In this case, the teacher needs to make the students aware of the change in question phrasing and to assure students that the questions are not intended to threaten them. Teachers must let students know that the questions are intended to create opportunities for students to share their knowledge, thinking, and understandings with each other. Once students understand and respond to questions with open stems, they are eager to participate in instructional conversations.

The phrasing and intonation of an open question confirms for students that the teacher knows they know and all that is left for them to do is answer the question. By replacing the initial word of our questions—"can," "do," and "will"—with the words *"what," "why," "how,"* and *"in what way"* unlocks the boxed answers of "yes" and "no," opening opportunities for students to engage in meaningful instructional conversations. This is most important when we want to find out if students thoughtfully have engaged in reflecting on important points of the lesson or to discover what students know as a result of our instruction.

The subtle rephrasing of the question from "Do you understand?" to "What do you understand from our lesson today?" changes the entire posture of the intent of this question. The open-stem question invites a response from students. It affirms their knowledge through our expectation that they will share their understandings with us. This slight, yet significant, change in asking questions can be the difference between empowering students as learners or diminishing students' confidence in learning.

Closed Question Stems	**Open Question Stems**
Do you . . .	What are . . .
Can you . . .	In what way . . .
Will you . . .	How . . .
Do you know . . .	Why . . .
Do you have . . .	What is there about . . .
Are you . . .	How do you know . . .
Have you . . .	

INQUIRY SUGGESTIONS AND QUESTIONS

To continue developing your awareness of productive questioning practices, do some of the following inquiry before reading the following chapters:

- Observe for ten minutes a teacher in your school conducting a discussion or recitation. Count the questions the teacher asks that require a "yes" or "no" for an answer. The question stems begin with "Can you," "Do you," "Have you," "Will you," "Should you," or some other closed grammatical structure.
- Without planning a lesson, conduct ten minutes of dialogue between you and your students and tape-record the lesson. Listen to the tape. Count the number of closed questions you used in the dialogue.
- Plan a lesson, writing out open questions. Conduct the lesson and tape it. Listen to the tape. Count the number of open and closed questions you asked.
- Review the tape to find out how students responded to your closed and open questions. Review your tape to discover what you did after asking a closed question.
- Write a reflection about your and other teachers' use of open and closed questions. Focus on these questions:
    - What have you learned about the number of open and closed questions teachers ask?
    - In what situations do teachers tend to ask open questions?
    - In what situations do teachers tend to ask closed questions?
    - When you didn't plan your questions, what kind of questions did you ask?
    - When you planned your questions, what happened in conducting the lesson?

- What insights do you now have about open and closed question stems?
- How did students react to the questions with open stems?
- What effects did open question stems have on student responses?
- What will you do to help yourself become more conscious of the openness or closeness of your questions?

▶ 12

"Who Asks a More Beautiful Question"

e. e. cummings, 1968

FACILITATIVE SET

There is beauty in questions. Poets and educators use questions in a similar manner. Questions illuminate our ideas. Questions that are richly structured, more profound in nature, and more clearly articulated receive complimentary responses. Everyone has experienced the "burning question": the question that begs asking, resulting in an answer that uncovers or discovers a new way of looking at something or solves a problem. In the quest for the answer, we gingerly pose the question and mystically a new idea bursts forth, rendering us both comforted and energized by our new knowledge.

Our instructional questions have the power to unlock trapped knowledge. Yet, most of the time, when teachers ask questions, they include only content cues. The hiatus in teachers' instructional questions is the action word that informs students as to how to think about the content. When we omit the verbal cues that specify the thinking operations needed to answer the question, we negate the process in learning. To neglect the role cognitive processing plays in instructional questioning transforms students' potentially rich conceptual understandings into rote learning.

Signaling Thinking

In order for our questions to produce productive instructional conversations, teachers must attend not only to content issues, but also to the kinds of thinking learners must do to acquire and process the content. By methodically wording our questions, framing them with thought cues, we provide students a myriad of opportunities to explore curricular content and to make connections among concepts they understand and concepts that are puzzling or confusing to them.

Effective instructional conversations commence with productive questions that broadly encompass the content and specify the thinking operation(s) needed to achieve the goals and objectives of the lesson. Productive questions that signal the cognitive operation of the lesson are *core questions*. Core questions are the hub of our instructional conversations. Placing an action word in our questions to signal the kind of thinking we want students to do equips our instructional conversations with guideposts. These guideposts constitute the framework for our interactions with students. Core questions can be used to initiate a particular kind of thinking operation, to refocus student thinking when it drifts off-center, and to scaffold various kinds of thinking operations needed for constructing and better understanding concepts.

To familiarize you with the nature and function of core questions during instructional conversations, we present the following activities for our readers:

1. A vignette focusing on the study of core questions;
2. Our reflections about teachers in the process of studying core questions;
3. A self-study discussion that analyzes the concept attributes of core questions;
4. Inquiry suggestions and questions to assist our readers in investigating the use of core questions during instructional conversations.

Vignette: Cueing Thinking

The classroom smells like popcorn. The teachers, our students, are busily popping the kernels of corn into their mouths and talking loudly at the same time. They are obviously excited. As I enter, I notice that they have rearranged the desks from the normal straight rows to a horseshoe. They are standing in small groups within the horseshoe.

Jerry turns to me and blurts out, "Well, you were right! I observed three teachers in my school and they all asked closed questions. I never heard them until we started discussing them. And you know, some students did say no to their questions." She laughs and the others join in laughter. They continue sharing their stories with each other, ignoring me.

When there is a slight lull in the noise, I sneak into their conversation. "You appear to be uplifted by your observations and reflections on teachers' closed questions. Tonight, we are going to talk about another aspect of productive questioning—putting the cognitive operation in our initial question. Our lesson could be summed up in this way: If you don't know where you are going, you might end up somewhere else."

I have their attention. I noticed that the lights are not on in the room. I turn on the lights. Each teacher selects a desk, takes out pen and paper, and looks at me. I look around. Everyone has a front-row seat. *Such control*, I think to myself, amused about their eagerness to start.

I begin. "Suppose you want students to recall information from a news article that they read last night. Your objective of the lesson is for students to recall specific details about the article related to the journalistic questions of who, what, when, where, how, and why. Your goal is for the students to tell you why the information in the article is newsworthy."

I pass out the article, handing one to each student. "I want you to read the article and write down some questions that you think will elicit conversation about the article." I give them about five minutes to work.

"OK, what questions have you decided are important to ask in order to initiate students' recollection of the information in the news article?" I ask.

They all begin to shout out their questions, and I back up against the board telling them to wait until I can find a piece of chalk to record their questions. I list their questions on the board:

> What is the article about?
>
> How does the writer inform us about where the story takes place?
>
> What information does the article talk about?
>
> Who is the article about?
>
> When does the story happen?
>
> Why is the news important?

"OK, I see that you are asking open rather than closed questions. What we need to concentrate on now is what the question is asking of students. In all of your questions, you have words that specify the content. What word or words suggest the content?"

Almost in unison, the teachers respond: "Article, story, news, important news, story takes place." I nod and smile, then ask: "What words or phrases in your questions signal the kind of thinking you want students to do about the content?" There is silence for about fifteen seconds. The teachers are becoming comfortable with silence.

Jack states that the thinking for the questions is implied. "We all know that it is recall," he offers.

"So why don't you use it in the question?" I ask.

"You don't need to," Jack retorts. "Students know what you want when you ask those questions."

"OK, let's take the first question, 'What's the article about?' What kinds of things could students say to answer the question?" I wait and then answer my own question, my voice picking up speed as I imagine what students could say to answer the question.

I tell the teachers that students could recall information. They could give the main idea of the story. They could tell you the article was too long. They could tell you that they didn't like the article. They could tell you that it is like another article they read. They could tell you they didn't read the article. They could tell you anything they wanted about the article using any kind of thinking they wanted because the question doesn't specify the kind of processing you want students to use in answering the question.

I take a breath and ask the following series of questions. "Which of the responses would you accept as an appropriate response for your question? Which of the responses received were intended by your question? Which responses addressed the purpose of your lesson? You intended for the students to recall the specifics of the article. How will they know to do that? What words in your question suggested to students that you wanted them to *recall* information?" I elongate the pronunciation of the word "recall."

"It's obvious," Trisha remarks. "Students know what we mean."

"No, it's not obvious. We assume that it is obvious and that most students infer that we mean recall, but some students may infer a different cognitive process. If our questions don't explicitly inform students as to the kind of thinking they are to use in answering the initial question, then they must play a guessing game, a hit-or-miss game that may or may not engage them in our intended thought focus." I pause.

"Are you going to accept responses that *compare* the article to other articles as answering your question, even though the student does not mention any specific information from the article? Will you accept another student saying that she or he didn't like the article as an appropriate or correct response to the question? In this response, the student *evaluated* or *assessed* the article using an intrapersonal barometer. Both elicited answers, after all, *are* what the article was about for the responding student.

"However, we know that in these two instances, the students did not engage in *recall* to answer the question. How do we respond to their answers? By not signaling to students the kind of thinking required by the purpose of the lesson, it may become very confusing for students to provide the kind of information *really intended* by your question."

I take a breath and redirect my thinking. "Who gave us this question? 'What is the article about?'" Jane bobs her head up and down. "What did you intend by it, anyway?" I query.

"I would want students to recall specific information from the article," she offers. I continue. "In what way does the question spell that out for the students?" I continue before anyone can answer. My question is intended to be rhetorical. "If you want students to recall information, why not tell them to recall?" Another rhetorical question. A rephrased question that would offer students a thought focus for responding is: "What specific information do you remember from the article you just read?" I write the question large and boldly on the board. Turning to the teachers, I ask, "How is that question different from all of the questions you posed?"

Jane responds, "It tells the students to 'recall.' The word 'recall' sets the stage for the thinking students are to do. Our questions don't explicitly tell the students how they are to think. We're, I guess, more interested in the content. I guess I've never thought about how students arrive at their answers; I've never really considered that in asking questions."

There is a stir of conversation in the classroom. The room is hot. I walk to the door and open it for air. "Before we move on, I would like to find out how well you understand the use of a cognitive signal in asking a core question. On the overhead is a list of questions. I would like you to decide which questions have a thought focus and which do not have a word that cues a thinking operation. Star (⋆) the ones that do. Also, I would like for you to check (X) the closed questions."

Questions	***Thinking Cued***	***Closed***
What do you *notice* about this room?	(⋆)	
What did you read in the story last night?		
How is cream *different* from milk?	(⋆)	
What makes Halloween *like* Mardi Gras?	(⋆)	
Can you tell me the verb in this sentence?		(X)
Have you *determined the causes* for the Civil War?	(⋆)	(X)

Once the teachers have completed the activity, we talk about the words in the questions that give rise to thinking. They agree that it is the verbs or predicates of the questions that hold the kernels for thinking. We also share that questions can have a cognitive focus and be open or closed. Again, the teachers agree that open, thought-focused questions are more productive in attaining student responses than closed questions and questions without a thinking focus.

Following our conversation, I ask the teachers to write an example of an open, clear, thinking-focused question. Before I have a chance to ask them to share their written questions, core questions are popping from all directions in the room. In the vigorous conversation that follows, the teachers seem convinced that the critical characteristics of productive questioning consist of initial questions that are clear and open, and possess a cognitive signal to guide student responses.

Reflection on Teacher Learning

Teachers argue with us all the time about the need to signal the thinking operation of "recalling." They don't think it is necessary. Teachers continually tell us that "students know that we want them to recall—that it is implied in the asking of the question." When the cognitive operation in questions is changed to comparing, classifying, or distinguishing information, teachers believe that the cognitive operation must be a part of the question for students to answer the question appropriately. We see no difference.

We maintain that words that signal cognitive operations, even recalling, must be explicitly stated in the question to initiate and direct the thinking students are to use when answering the question. To erroneously assume that students will infer that recalling, or any cognitive operation for that matter, is intended without an instructional question cueing the thinking results in futile conversations that are confusing and drift aimlessly. If students don't know the thought direction of our lesson, they may well give us what we don't intend. Accomplishing the cognitive purpose of the lesson, without cognitive cues, would be most difficult. If we have no cognitive guideposts within our questions, we can hardly be strategic in guiding student inquiry nor can we assist students in using and monitoring their thinking.

To help us explain our position, we offer the following example. Let's say that you are conducting a lesson in which the objective of the lesson is stated as: *Students will observe the critical characteristics of improper fractions.* As educators we have to ask ourselves the following questions about the objective:

- What is the content addressed in the objective?
- What is/are the cognitive operation(s) students must use to think through the content?

- What are the resources needed in order for students to gather, process, or apply the information?

In analyzing the objective, our answers to these questions are:

- The content under study is the critical characteristics of improper fractions;
- The cognitive operation(s) called for by the objective is observing;
- The resources that we need to engage the students in the instructional conversations are examples of improper fractions—for example, $^5/_3$, $^{10}/_1$, $^{12}/_9$.

Given our answers, we have to make some decisions about the questions we want to ask students in order to facilitate a productive instructional conversation.

If we begin our instruction by asking *"What is an improper fraction?"* we have implied, by our question, that students know the answer and that the "correct" definition is all that we are seeking. The question cues are focused on content only. If students tell us the correct definition, our question for you is: *Has the objective of this lesson been achieved by asking this question?* Obviously, it has not. The objective does not call for the students to state the definition, nor recall the concept definition. It directs us to engage students in observing examples of the concept to arrive at the critical characteristics of the concept, improper fractions.

If we change our initial question to *What can you tell me about the improper factions $^5/_3$, $^{10}/_1$, and $^{12}/_9$?* we more closely approximate the intent of the objective; however, the question still has not identified the thinking operation specified in the objective. We would like to brainstorm some responses students could give us in answering this question. If we have missed a response, please add it on to our list.

Question: What can you tell me about the improper fractions $^5/_3$, $^{10}/_1$, and $^{12}/_9$?

Possible Student Responses to the Question:

- It is not a proper fraction.
- It has two parts like a proper fraction.
- It has a numerator and a denominator.
- It is more than one.
- You have to divide it to find the answer.
- The top number is larger than the bottom number.
- The / divides the top number from the bottom number.

(Your responses:)

- ____
- ____

After reviewing the possible student responses, our question to you is as follows:

- Which of the responses are attained through observing, and which of the responses are results of some other kind of thinking?

Our analysis of student responses for this question is expressed in the following chart.

Marylou's and Paul's Analysis of Student Responses

- *It is not a proper fraction.*—Students may have observed something that made them say this, but we don't know what. They have *classified* these examples as nonexamples of an improper fraction.
- *It has two parts like a proper fraction.*—Students *compared* the examples of improper fractions to imaginary proper fractions. They may have begun with observing but jumped to *comparing* in their thinking.
- *It has a numerator and a denominator.*—They have observed something and have used labels to *classify* their observations; they have not told us which number is which label. They *labeled* and *classified* the fractions.
- *It is more than one.*—Students have told us information about the improper fraction, but they have not told us what they have observed that made them arrive at the response. We think the student *recalled* the information or *solved* the problem.
- *You have to divide it to find the answer.*—Here, the students told what they needed to do to solve the problem. They *recalled* the process.
- *The top number is larger than the bottom number.—Finally,* an answer resulting from *observing.*
- *The / divides the top number from the bottom number.*—Again, an answer that stems from students *observing* the examples of improper fractions.

From our point of view, the question What can you tell me about the improper factions $^{5}/_{3}$, $^{10}/_{1}$, and $^{12}/_{9}$? *did not result in students only observing. They also did other kinds of thinking in responding to the question.* Although we recognize that the kinds of thinking students did in answering the question brought out important information, we most ardently argue that the majority of the student responses given were not attained through the process of observing. *Our initial question did not provide students with an action word to focus and signal their answer formation.* Therefore, we received responses based on whatever thinking students wanted to do with the content.

The point is that if an objective calls for a particular line of thinking, then to fulfill the intent of the objective, students must do the identified thinking to acquire appropriate information. Otherwise, we cannot say that we have achieved the objective with our instruction. *Our questions must provide the* cognitive signals *if we expect students to view learning as a process and not just a game of getting the right answer.*

An instructional question phrased as *What do you observe or notice about the examples of the improper fractions,* $^{5}/_{3}$, $^{10}/_{1}$, *and* $^{12}/_{9}$? contains action words that denote a core or pivotal thinking operation from which students can generate responses specified by this objective. Students can still do other kinds of thinking in responding to the question; however, by including the word "observe" or "notice" in our instructional question, we frame the kind of information acceptable or appropriate for the instructional conversation and signal the thinking operation required to acquire or process the information. Such wording becomes a guidepost for directing instructional conversations. More often than not, you will hear students using the words that cued their thinking in the wording of their responses.

The use of cues or signals to frame the thinking and content of student responses assists us in monitoring their responses during our instructional conversation. It gives us an assessment tool for determining when students are engaged in the appropriate thinking and provides a pathfinder for redirecting student thinking when they are not providing responses using the identified thinking operation. Asking instructional questions that signal both content and cognitive operations constitutes the boundaries for ensuring that our instructional conversations are headed in the direction of achieving the lesson's objective.

SELF-STUDY DISCUSSION

Productive instructional conversations rely on precision in question asking. Well-phrased questions elicit quality responses from students, especially if we and our students understand the kind of information the question seeks and the thinking necessary to fulfill the purpose of our lesson. Questions that specify the content we want students to know help them focus on the material so that they do not become distracted. Questions that provide clues for the kind(s) of thinking we want students to use to ascertain the content furnish them with a means for understanding how to think about their responses. When students are able to *understand how to think* about ideas, we touch a deeper level of understanding that makes it possible for students to use these signals when monitoring their learning.

Cognitively cued questions are referred to as *core questions* in Qu:Est. Effective core questions cue and command the thought experiences for classroom discourse. They focus, direct, and guide particular kinds of thinking operations and the content specified by the goals or objectives of the lesson. Also, they are used to scaffold thinking or to create questioning sequences for moving from one type of thinking operation to another when engaging students in conceptualizing. The phrasing of core questions consists of three distinct, critical attributes.

Attributes of Core Questions

Core questions must be clearly stated using words that students understand. Core questions focus students on the content and thinking operations required by the lesson objective(s) and should be structured broadly to elicit a multitude of responses rather than one correct answer. The syntactical structure of core questions provides clues for students in answering the core question.

The nouns of the core question(s) focus the content under study. The predicate or verb phrase indicates the kind of thinking students are to do in answering the question. Finally, core questions are open, possessing a question stem that begins with words that generate dialogue rather than yes/no responses from students. Well-phrased, succinct core questions engender more productive instructional conversation than vague or convoluted phrasing. The most productive question stems begin with "what," "in what way," "how," or "why." Examples of core questions for the various thinking operations involved in conceptualizing are:

Core Questions for Individual Thinking Operations in Conceptualizing

Observing: What do you notice about __________?

Recalling: What do you remember about __________?

Comparing: What similarities are there between __________ and __________?

Contrasting: What differences are there between __________ and __________?

Grouping: In what way do these *items* go together?

Labeling: What can we call __________?

Classifying: How can we classify __________?

These core questions can be analyzed using the critical attributes of core questions. The nouns of the questions identify the content. In these situations, the *blanks* represent the content. The verbs or predicates of the questions provide an action word that indicates the thinking operation. Finally, core questions are simply stated, constructed with question stems avoiding a yes/no response from students.

The beauty emulating from well-phrased core questions is that they create the parameters through which we enter into instructional conversations with students and establish the reference point for returning to thinking about the content if students wander off course. For students, core questions signal the thinking operation involved in acquiring, constructing, or assimilating relevant content, closing the gap between their current, personal understandings of the content and new learning.

The next chart provides a quick reference to the critical characteristics of core questions.

Attributes of Core Questions

Purpose: To focus, guide, and direct the thinking and content of classroom interactions.

Critical Characteristics

Clear: Uses language that students understand and is not convoluted with questions or information.

Focused: Uses words that specify the content and stipulate the cognitive operation(s) called for by the purpose of the lesson.

Open: Uses words that provide opportunities for multiple and diverse responses from as many students as possible.

Key Words in Core Questions

Nouns cue the content of the dialogue specified in the lesson objective.

Predicates focus the thinking operation using action words to signal the required thinking about the content.

Question Stems begin with "what," "in what way," or "how."

INQUIRY SUGGESTIONS AND QUESTIONS

To further guide your study of productive questioning using Qu:Est Instructional Strategies, we offer the following suggestions for developing your awareness of core questions.

- Listen to questions asked by teachers in your school.
  - How many of their questions include an action word that guides student thinking about the subject under study?
- Analyze the questions in your textbooks for the attributes of a well-phrased core question.
  - What kinds of questions in the textbooks have thinking operations identified to assist students in acquiring and processing information?
  - How many of the questions ask for a yes/no response?
  - What do your findings suggest to you concerning the textbook's emphasis on learning?
- Select or write three objectives that specify three different kinds of thinking operations. Write a well-phrased core question for each objective. Analyze your questions using the Attributes of Core Questions.
  - What words in your questions identify the thinking needed in order for students to achieve the objective?
- Conduct a lesson using your core questions as the initial question of the lesson. First, ask the question without the action, thinking-operation word.
  - What kinds of responses do you receive from students?
  - What kinds of thinking operations do their answers reflect?
- After you have analyzed their responses, repeat the lesson and ask your initial question, making sure that the thinking operation is identified by the action word in your core question.
  - What kinds of responses do students give you?
  - How are the responses different from or the same as when you excluded the action, thinking-operation word?
- Keep a journal of your core questions and the kinds of responses students give to your core questions.
  - What do you notice about student responses as you become more aware of your appropriately phrased core questions?
  - In what ways are students becoming more conscious of learning as a process rather than learning as simply memorization?

- What can you do to ensure that each initial, instructional question you ask during a lesson focuses the cognitive operation students need to use to appropriately answer the question?

REFERENCES

Cummings, e. e. *Complete Poems 1913–1962.* New York: Harcourt Brace Jovanovich, 1968. p. 462.

▶ 13

"Always the Beautiful Answer . . ."

e. e. cummings, 1968

FACILITATIVE SET

How do we listen more carefully to what students are saying? How do we understand their understandings? How do we take their understandings and help them form rich, meaningful concepts, understandings that contribute to their quest for relevant knowledge? With all the pressures we feel to teach the mandated curriculum, in our preoccupation with covering the content, we sometimes assume that if students answer our questions correctly that their responses are meaningful to them. Many times, however, students are simply telling us what they think we expect them to say or what they have memorized. In essence, they understand neither their responses nor the content. Often, what we have succeeded at is separating teaching from learning. To connect teaching and learning, we must engender relationships with our students that are based in authentic communications.

Teachers have the capacity to help students learn or to hinder them from learning. To be effective as teachers, we must create instructional conditions in our classrooms that connect the content and us with our students' life experiences. In order for students to author their own rich, conceptual understandings from curricular concepts, we must engage them in instructional conversations that uncover the ways that they are thinking about the subject. We must also join them in dialogue that keeps learning alive. This means listening carefully to what they are saying and using their responses to frame questions that require them to think consciously and deeply about their answers. To listen adeptly to students requires us to examine how we think about our students: *Are they* objects *of our instruction or are they* knowers *who inform us about our instruction?*

Misty Johnson, a teacher from the Midwest, reflecting on her first year as a teacher, provides us with a lens for understanding our students as knowers.

> *Wow! Everytime I consider this I'm amazed I was allowed to keep teaching. It's been a long evolution. My first school was a very hopeless place to teach. Chemical addictions, teen pregnancy, and a 50 percent dropout rate were my school's claim to fame. When I arrived, I asked for the curriculum, and the principal showed me the textbooks. He told me to cover the text and that was that. The first week taught me that the kids wouldn't stand for such nonsense. They didn't trust the books or me—I was white and they were not. Over time I abandoned most of what I'd learned about student teaching at a local teacher education program and focused on what my kids needed. They taught me how to teach. They taught me to question, evaluate, and reflect on what's happening. It's the most important thing I learned—books can't tell me what my students need. I have to listen to the kids first. Since then it's been trial and error, keeping what works and getting rid of what doesn't. Somehow I built community with them. I still hear from some of those kids. I guess I owe my career to them, I've thanked them but they don't get it. The just tell me all they did was to make me part Chippewa.*

Our willingness and ability to listen to students is powerful, and the beauty in students' answers is revealed in their conversations with us. They tell us how to teach them. Their answers provide the clues for how to connect with them. As we engage students in genuine, relevant instructional conversations, we establish the bond between teaching and learning; however, instructional conversations are only as effective as the questions we ask. We must ask questions that directly relate to student responses, questions that ask them to extend, refine, and personalize their understandings of the content. The coherence between what students have to say and our subsequent questioning of their responses is paramount in assisting students in constructing meaning from unfamiliar curricular content.

To better understand the concept of instructional conversation, we provide the following set of activities:

1. Two vignettes, one focusing on a classroom interaction that is *not characteristic* of an instructional conversation, and a second interaction that *illustrates* the qualities of an instructional conversation;
2. Our reflections about teachers studying instructional conversations;

3. A self-study discussion that analyzes instructional conversations; and
4. Inquiry suggestions and questions to assist you in investigating instructional conversations.

Vignette: Back and Forth We Go

The following is a small piece of the transcript of a classroom discourse that is *not characteristic of an instructional conversation.* Fifth-grade students are learning about the Revolutionary War. Last night they were assigned to read pages 274–284, Troubles with Great Britain and The War Begins, in their social studies book, *United States and Its Neighbors,* 1966, New York: Macmillan/McGraw-Hill School Publishing Company. The following day, they were asked questions to find out what they retained from the reading. The lesson is to concentrate on the events leading up to the American Revolution. The students are seated in straight rows with their books open to page 274.

Teacher: I want to know what you think were the events that led to the Revolutionary War. Let's concentrate on the rebellions and taxes. Jane, what were the important things that happened?

Jane: The Boston Tea Party.

Teacher: OK, who else can tell me something?

Traceana: The first shot was at Lexington. The British fired it.

Teacher: Yes, you're right, Traceana, but what happened before that?

Jane: Oh—the people didn't like taxes.

Teacher: Taxes?

Jane: Yeah, you know, England was taxing everything, and the Americans had to pay it whether they liked it or not.

Teacher: All right, let me list the taxes. *The following list was written on the board.*

Stamp Act
Townshend Acts
Intolerable Acts

Teacher: What were the reasons for these taxes, and why did the colonists not want to pay them?

Brad: They were laws that made the people pay for everything, like food, newspapers, and tea.

Jane: Oh, yes, the Boston Tea Party happened because they didn't want to pay taxes on tea.

Teacher: Who was responsible for the Townshend Acts?

Students (in unison): Townshend.

Reflection on Teacher Learning

The preceding vignette, while typical of recitation, is not an instructional conversation. The interactions between the teacher and the students do not elicit how students are thinking about the events. The teacher's purpose was to provide students the opportunity to *recall* information about the events leading to the Revolutionary War. She asks questions to determine what students remember from their reading. In asking her first question, "Jane, what were the important things that happened?" she opens the door for a variety of responses. However, by calling on Jane before she asks the question, she limits the amount of interactions that could occur in the classroom. Calling on Jane places the responsibility for answering on Jane. Other students are off the hook for answering. As you note in the transcript, there are only two other students who respond.

Most of the interactions that occur are a direct result of the teacher asking a specific question and a student, mostly Jane, giving very specific answers to the questions. No interactions occur among students. Nor does any question prompt students to explain a response. The emphasis is on the book content. It is obvious from the dialogue that the teacher is interested in fact recall only, not what students understand about the facts.

At one point, the teacher provides a list of taxes rather than soliciting the information from the students. She asks, "What were the reasons for these taxes, and why did the colonists not want to pay them?" In this question, the teacher asks two questions, allowing the students to choose which they will answer. When Brad responds with a statement that told *what* the Acts were and *what* was taxed, the teacher, rather than pursuing her initiated focus of "reasons for the taxes," changes the subject to the person responsible for the Townshend Act.

There is no obvious logic to this instructional interaction, except perhaps to get out specific facts. Logic was initiated when the teacher asked for events leading to the Revolutionary War, but none of the student responses are stated in a way that reveals that they understand their answers to be events leading to the war.

The teacher does not ask any redirection or refocus questions when students are not providing their answers in a manner that suggests they understand that their answers are the events leading to the Revolutionary War. Because student thinking is not explicit in their responses, we cannot assume that the students have made the connection that the facts they cited are the events leading to the war. At this point, the teacher's intent for the recitation is called into question. Does she truly want students to understand the events that led to the War, or is she concerned with the students' recollection of specific information?

This vignette is problematic and characteristic of many interactions we have observed in instructional conversations ranging from kindergarten through college teaching. As long as the students are providing correct answers to questions, teachers fail to query student thinking to find out if the content holds meaning for the students. Teachers often are listening for the answers and not listening to the student who is doing the answering.

Unless we listen to what our students are saying and how they are processing what they are saying, we haven't a clue about what students understand about the content. *When we engage in authentic instructional conversations, we must listen carefully to students and converse with them meaningfully, using their responses as prompts for our next questions.* When we use their responses to prompt our next questions, we assist students in thinking more deeply and precisely about their ideas.

Instructional conversation is classroom dialogue that should help us discover how students think about concepts as well as how they make connections between what is known and their new learning. Our students should understand and be able to monitor how they arrived at their understandings. We are not simply determined to cover the content. Likewise, we have to be clear about our intent for the classroom discourse. We must recognize answers that fulfill the intent of our instructional conversations and answers that don't. This means knowing what is expected from student responses before the interactions begin.

Decisions must be made about how to deal with student responses to achieve the intended purpose of the lesson. Often, this requires that teachers ask additional questions of student responses to assist students in processing information and formulating quality responses, questions such as "*What do you mean by* (didn't like being taxed)?" "*How do you know that* (the Boston Tea Party occurred as a reaction to taxation)?" or "*You're telling me that* (the Acts were laws designed to tax the colonists)—*in what way did these* (Acts) *lead to the* (Revolutionary War)?" To ask such questions permits us to engage in instructional conversations with our students that refresh the material, stimulate the ways students think about it, and underscore learning as a process.

Vignette: Making Conversation

The following is a small piece of transcript from the classroom discourse that illustrates the dialogue that can occur during an instructional conversation. Fifth-grade students are learning about the Revolutionary War. Last night they were assigned to read pages 274–284, Troubles with Great Britain and The War Begins, in their social studies book, *United States and Its Neighbors*, 1966, New York: Macmillan/McGraw-Hill School Publishing Company. The following day, they were asked questions to find out what they retained from the reading. The lesson is to concentrate on the events leading up to the American Revolution. The teacher has arranged the students in small groups, three to four students in each group. Students have been directed to open their books to the pages they read last night.

Teacher: Last night you read pages 274–284 in your social studies text. It dealt with the events leading up to the American Revolution. Today, I want to find out what you remember about these events and how they led to the American Revolution. We will be doing two things. First, in your groups, make a list of the events that led to the war. After you have completed your lists, we will talk about why these events led to the American Revolution. Begin making your list as you answer this question: What do you remember were the events that led to the American Revolution?

The students begin to peruse the chapter and write down the events. The class is noisy, but focused. The teacher walks around the room, talking softly with members of various groups. After about three minutes, the teacher begins a large-group discourse.

Teacher: OK, I see that you have made a list of the events. Let's put the information on the board. What do you remember about the events that led to the American Revolution?

Traceana: Pontiac's Rebellion, The Stamp Act, The Townshend Acts, The Sons of Liberty, The Boston Tea Party, The First Continental Congress, The Lexington event, Patrick Henry's speech.

When Traceana stops talking, other students in the room begin whispering. Brad, in another group, says:

Brad: There were two things that happened in Boston, the Massacre and the Boston Tea Party.

Traceana: Oh, yeah, there was the Boston Massacre also.

Teacher: Let's see, Traceana has given us a good list of the events, and Brad has added one. Let's arrange the events in the order in which they happened. Take 5 minutes to do this. I will take your answers on the order of the events once all groups have made an order of the events.

Teacher: Which group would like to share their order of the events? *Many hands go up.* OK, I saw Jane's hand first. Jane, give us your group's list. *The teacher lists the order of events on the board as Jane says them.*

Pontiac's Rebellion
The Stamp Act
The Sons of Liberty
The Townshend Acts
The Boston Massacre
The Boston Tea Party
The First Continental Congress
The Lexington event
Patrick Henry's speech

Teacher: The teacher sits with the students. How many of you agree that this was the order of the events? *Most of the students raise their hands.* All right, let's assume this is the order of events. Make a report sheet. Divide your paper into three sections. On the right put "The Events" and list them in order. In the middle column, write a few words about that event. Place the heading "What Happened" there. In the left-hand column, write a statement telling why your group believes that this event led to the American Revolution. Name that column "Why It Meant War."

Students spend approximately ten minutes generating the report sheet. There is much conversation in the groups.

Teacher: I see that we are ready to begin talking about what we found out concerning the events that led to the American Revolution. Let's begin with Pontiac's Rebellion: What do you remember happened and how did it lead to the American Revolution?

Brad: Well, the Indians didn't want to be pushed off their land, so they burned the British forts and the Americans' houses.

Jane: Yes, that made England make a law that gave land to the Indians, and the settlers didn't like that.

Teacher: What were the reasons for the settlers not liking that?

Chris: Because England taxed them.

Teacher: Taxed them?

Chris: Yes, the settlers had to pay for the army England sent to protect them.

Trevor: It was one more tax, and the colonists were sick of taxes.

Teacher: How do you know the colonists were sick of paying taxes to England?

Carla: Because there was the Stamp Act and The Intolerable Acts.

Jane: Well, the colonists had to pay taxes on everything, and they didn't get any of the money. It went to the King.

Jamie: Yes, the laws were made by the British government to get money from the settlers.

Teacher: What do you remember from your reading that makes you say these laws made the colonist pays money to England? *The children flip through the chapter.*

Shannon: Well, on page 280 it says that the colonists dressed like Indians and threw the tea the British sent them into the water because they didn't want to pay taxes.

Chris: And on page 276 it says that Americans refused to buy British stuff and that the Sons of Liberty pressured merchants not to sell stuff from England.

Teacher: Read that passage to us. *Chris reads.*

Teacher: In what way did being taxed lead to the American Revolution?

Joseph: The Stamp Act made the Americans pay money for their paper to England, and they thought that England had no right to tax them on stamps because the Americans did not vote to elect people in Parliament.

Teacher: We have a lot of ideas here. What do we mean by taxes?

Jane: Money that is paid to a government to run the government.

Trevor: Yeah, you know, like sales tax.

Teacher: How does our sales tax help pay to run the government?

Chris: It pays for schools and roads.

Teacher: How do you know that?

Chris: Well, I went to vote with my parents last month on the law that makes us pay more on what we buy. Now, things cost more.

Teacher: How does that tax help pay for roads and schools?

Carla: That's what the people who made the law said it would do.

Teacher: OK, tell me about the people who made that law.

Bobby: They are people in government.

Hunter: We voted for them.

Katie: They represent us.

Teacher: What does represent mean?

Hunter: Like someone going to talk for you because you can't be there. I remember that my brother went to ask my parents if we could go to Laser Zone. I wanted to go and so did my friends, but only my brother asked my parents.

Jane: It's like what we are doing now. We all said our ideas to each other, but only one person in our group is talking, but we all said it.

Teacher: So your brother represented you, Hunter; and Jane you said that the person doing the talking in your group represents the rest of the members of the group. In what way do people we vote for talk for us?

Katie: Well, we vote for them, and then they take our ideas and make laws to help us.

Brad: They don't represent me. I didn't vote for them. My parents did.

Teacher: Brad makes a good point. *She redirects her next question to the class.* How is what Brad said like the settlers' situation? There is silence, then Traceana speaks.

Traceana: They were giving money, taxes, to the King and the settlers thought that he didn't represent them.

Teacher: In what way did the King not represent them? They were British subjects.

Brad: Yes, but they lived in America, not England. England voted on people for England and America. The Americans could not vote because they lived in a different country.

Teacher: So how is not being able to vote for someone to represent you like your situation with your parents voting and you not being able to vote?

Brad: Well, they choose the people to make the laws, not me. If I can't vote, then my ideas don't count.

Teacher: Oh, now, how is Brad's idea of not being counted like what was happening to the colonists?

Paul: England was making laws that were good for England, and since the colonists didn't vote for the people, they felt like they weren't getting what they needed.

Teacher: So let's go back to the question that started this conversation: In what way would being taxed and not being able to vote for the people who make the tax laws lead to war?

Marcy: If you don't feel like you are getting what you want and other people are forcing you to pay for something, then it makes you mad.

Jane: Yes, the colonists were mad because they were taxed on everything—tea, stamps, everything they bought—and all the money was going back to England. They couldn't see how the taxes were helping them. They thought the British were selfish and so they rebelled by fighting the British.

Teacher: Let's talk about something that you voted on that you are now paying for.

Traceana and others shout out: We voted on wearing uniforms last year.

Teacher: OK, you said uniforms are an example of being taxed. I'm a little confused about how our situation with uniforms relates to the colonists' taxation situation. So, in what way are uniforms related to the colonists being taxed?

Marcy: We wanted them because we thought they would be good for our school, and because we wanted them we don't mind paying for them.

Jane: Well, it's a little different. We voted for the uniforms, and the colonists didn't vote for their taxes but had to pay them anyway. Most of us voted for uniforms, and now we have to pay for our shirts. It's like a tax.

Teacher: But you said that you voted for uniforms and the colonists didn't vote for their taxes. So, again, how is your voting like the colonists not voting?

Brad: Some of us wanted them. I didn't.

Traceana: Yes, but we voted and most of us wanted them, so we got them.

Chris: Yeah, even though we all didn't want them, when the votes were counted, more kids wanted to wear uniforms. So we all wear uniforms. The people who have the most votes get what they want, and the rest have to go along because we all had a chance to say what we wanted. That's not what happened to the colonists. They didn't have a chance to say what they wanted.

Teacher: OK, I'm going to ask a question to help you see the difference between being represented and paying for something and not being represented and paying for something. Listen carefully. How is paying for something you voted on, even if your side didn't win, better than paying for something someone else wants you to have and you had no say in the matter?

Tommy: Well, if you had a chance to tell what you wanted, then even if you didn't get what you wanted, you are willing to pay for it because the rule was made by us—not kids who didn't have to wear the uniforms. If someone else says you have to do something and you don't get a chance to say your side, then you don't want to pay for it.

Jane: Like the colonists. They wanted to make their own laws for themselves, but England wouldn't let them. They thought they should make the laws, and then they would be willing to pay taxes.

Teacher: Jane, where did you get that idea?

Jane: Let's see, I know I saw that somewhere. *She looks through the chapter.*

Chris: Oh, the answer is on page 257. What it says is that the Americans are tired of being taxed and not having a say in how the tax money is being used. They are ready to revolt.

Teacher: Thank you, Chris. Let's think to ourselves for a few minutes about this question: Based on what we have talked about so far, what are the two important issues that would lead to war?

There is a period of silence.

Chris: I think taxes, because people didn't see how the money was helping them.

Jane: And also voting. People in England were making the tax laws for the colonists, not the colonists.

Teacher: OK, so you say that taxes and not being able to vote for people whom you feel represent you are two of the events that led to the American Revolution. Let's look at the other events we listed and see if we can find any other proof for our thinking.

Reflection on Teacher Learning

Here we have an authentic, instructional conversation! The dialogue between teacher and students and students and students flows. Why? The answer to this question is multidimensional. It relies on teachers' knowing that conceptual understanding involves students in a process of learning. In this vignette, it is obvious, in the teacher's questions, that she assumes that students possess the knowledge and ability to use the thinking operations needed to learn the material. Her questions reveal that she views acquiring concepts as a process. She does not assume, however, that all students understand the ideas in the same way. She uses the student-generated examples as a means for inquiring more deeply into how students understand the material. How does she do this?

First, the teacher establishes the parameters of the instruction by organizing students for the conversation. She gives them time to research the information prior to conducting the lesson and structures a chart for them to collect the information—a list of events, what happened during the events, and why the events led to war. Additionally, the teacher places the students in groups to gather the information so that they can share their thoughts. This simulates the concept of representation, which students note in their conversation.

Second, the teacher joins the group, sitting as a participant of the class. She asks questions that directly relate to the student-generated ideas. Her questions ask students to (1) clarify words they use in their answers, (2) verify the facts they state, (3) find examples that personalize the meaning of what they are saying, and (4) support their responses by hooking up what they say to the original focus of the lesson—events that led to the American Revolution. She waits patiently for the students to respond and does not provide them with information, but waits for them to find it or reason through something. The responsibility for gathering and processing knowledge rests with the students.

Third, the teacher accepts all student comments, even thoughts that seemingly stray from the content of the material. As she accepts all student responses, she makes it their responsibility to connect the gaps between their responses and the colonists' experiences. She uses her core question, "What do you recall are the events that led to the American Revolution?" as a guidepost to initiate the conversation, to keep track of student ideas, and to attach students' personal examples to the concepts in the lesson. The core question is the hub by which all conversation flows to and from. By using it often, in different ways, she helps students keep in touch with the purpose of the conversation. Using it as a redirecting question, she encourages a wide variety of responses from many students. Students often add to each other's ideas without her prompting.

Fourth, the teacher encourages students to reason through their responses. The emphasis of the instructional conversation is on both acquiring content and using students' own thinking as they connect the content from the book to their personal experiences. She patiently queries students on the embedded concepts of voting and representation, making sure that students can give responses that personalize the information before she connects the concepts together to establish the relationship—"No taxation without representation."

Frequently, she asks for clarification and evidence of the information they provide. When she asks, "What do you mean by (taxation or representation)?" the students are able to revisit the idea and come up with their own way of expressing the idea. When she asks for evidence, "How do you know that?" she creates the opportunity for students to view the text material and their personal experience as resources for their understandings. Clarifying and verifying questions demand that students think again about the concepts through self-generated definitions and examples that are meaningful in the students' world. By asking, "What is there about the British taxing the settlers that would lead to war?" following a brief conversation using examples from the students' life about voting and representation, she encircles for the students the main idea of the lesson.

Through subsequent, relevant questioning of student-generated responses and using their responses in our questions, we more aptly stimulate students to make connections between the content of our lessons and their life experiences. The conversation flows because the ideas are real to the student. The ideas come from the students' way of understanding—not the textbook. The material comes alive, and students experience it firsthand. The more real the experiences, the more concrete and personal the examples, the more connections students make. As they make more connections, they deepen and broaden their understandings. Thus, the potential for future recalling or remembering is strengthened in the process.

SELF-STUDY DISCUSSION

Taking student responses into consideration when posing additional questions to assist students in refining their understandings means assessing the quality of student responses. We must know what we are listening for in their responses; and likewise, we must not assume that students' vocalization of something means that they understand what they are saying. Nor should we assume that all students understand the material in the same way. And finally, we must be able to characterize the quality of the response and track students' reasoning. Our subsequent questioning of students' initial responses is a tool for discovering how students think while concomitantly assisting them with their thinking and production of quality responses.

Attributes of Quality Student Responses

What do we do with student responses? How do we know that students understand what they are talking about? How did they arrive at their ideas? These are the three important questions that must be answered if we are to engage students in instructional conversations that deepen their understandings. *The critical issues of quality student responses* are reprinted here for your convenience and are discussed in more detail in Chapter 4, *A Story of Light through Yonder Window Breaks.*

Clarity: The learner answers in understandable English without mumbling, failing to finish, or confusing his/her thoughts.

Accuracy: The learner's answer contains no factual errors and is based on accurate information.

Appropriateness: The learner answers the question that was asked.

Specificity: The learner clearly identifies who and what s/he is talking about.

Support: The learner gives reasons, facts, or examples to support his/her statement, or she or he explains the criteria or assumptions on which she or he bases his/her opinion.

Complexity: The learner's answer shows that s/he is aware that there are many ways of looking at the problem being discussed, and that s/he must consider the options before a valid judgment can be reached.

Originality: The learner draws upon current knowledge and past experiences to create or discover ideas that are new (Gall, 1973, pp. 3–4).

If we keep these attributes as a guide for listening to what our students have to say and assessing their understandings, we can make better decisions about what to do with the answers they give us. Likewise, if we value students' understanding, they must process information for themselves. The attributes for quality student responses can be used as a guide for designing and sequencing subsequent questions to enhance student conceptual thinking.

Processing Questions

Subsequent questioning of student responses permits students opportunities to rethink, revisit, or refresh their original responses. Often, students are not explicit in their responses. More information may be needed in order for all students to understand the material. Understanding how students arrived at their responses is a complex undertaking. It requires teachers to present opportunities for students to rethink their ideas, to engage in sharpening their ideas, and to trace their thought experiences.

Not only do we want students to understand what they think, but we also want them to understand how they think, why they think something, and when it is appropriate to engage in particular ways of thinking to arrive at an answer. Processing questions engage teachers and students in understanding the subtle intricacies of student responses. In answering processing questions, students possess the responsibility for constructing their understandings. The teacher's careful, strategic questioning of student responses can create the path for their process of self-discovery.

Processing questions follow the asking and answering of core questions. They correspond to the qualities of student responses, and direct students to inquire more deeply into their thinking. In asking processing questions, teachers must pay careful attention to the phrasing of the student response and use student expressions in asking subsequent questions. Teachers must be careful not to change student wordings. Most importantly, *processing questions, used during instructional conversations, should heighten student awareness about their responses* and should attend to what students are expressing—not what teachers want them to say. For teachers, processing questions are a way of attaining more information about student ideas and how they are thinking about their ideas so that instruction can be designed to promote students' inquiry, that the dialogue among students results in productive understandings of the content, and so that students understand the cognitive operations they are performing.

The teacher must make decisions prior to instruction, as well as during instruction, concerning the type of processing questions that can be asked to assist students in understanding more completely the concepts originating in the study of content. Therefore, in planning lessons, the teacher should think through the kinds of student responses she or he could get to any core question posed and determine the kinds of processing questions needed to assist students in forming more quality responses. In thinking through potential student responses, both on-focus and off-focus responses must be considered. The question the teacher is asking of himself or herself is: "What do I do with the student responses I receive to my core question?" A chart toward the end of this chapter will provide you with ways of responding to student answers.

There are six types of processing questions that elicit some aspect of quality in student responses. The processing questions are: refocusing questions, clarifying questions, verifying questions, narrow focusing questions, supporting questions, and redirecting questions. A chart toward the end of this chapter will summarize the information about processing questions in the following section.

Refocusing Questions

In using processing questions as a means for uncovering student thinking and understanding, the teacher's first concern is the issue of appropriateness. Has the student(s) answered the question asked? If students have answered the question asked, then the teacher moves on to other considerations of clarity, accuracy, specificity, originality, and complexity. If not, then the teacher must pay careful attention to how she or he assists students in refocusing their responses.

Responses can be off-focused in terms of content or process. What signifies an off-focus response? It may be that students are not talking about the initiated content, or that students are not using the appropriate, initiated thinking operation, or that they are not answering the processing question proposed. If teachers permit off-focused responses as the responses to core questions, or any other question, the instructional conversation will meander and the purpose of the lesson will not be accomplished.

To deal with off-focused student responses, the issue of support also will come into play. In order for students to understand how their responses are not appropriate for the question asked, they must understand three issues: the response they gave, what in their response was not appropriate, and the specific focus of the teacher's core or processing question. This is a complex activity requiring students to make decisions about the relationship between their original response and the factors that make it unfitting for the question the teacher asked them. To refocus, students must understand, explicitly or implicitly, what is unsuitable about a response.

Most of the time, a refocusing question will be asked to adjust a student's answer to the core question or narrow focusing question. Its purpose is to assist students who are not dealing with the content or who are using some other thinking operation not designated by the core question. Sometimes students don't answer a clarifying question with a definition, but provide an example instead. You will want to refocus the example to receive a definition of terms. Carefully crafted refocusing questions can assist students in these complex tasks. The teacher's refocusing questions must restate the student response, tell the student what was not appropriate about the response, and restate the original question. It is called a mirror technique. Examples of refocusing questions are:

- You said (_________). I asked you to (_________). So, (ask your original question again).
- In your answer, you stated (_________). I'm not sure how that relates to (_________), so let's rethink your answer in relation to this question, (ask the original question again).
- In your answer, you said (_________). I'm a little confused about how your answer relates to the question, (ask the original question again).

Clarifying Questions

The characteristic of clarity centers on language usage, definition, and the appropriateness of words to describe an idea. It provides students with opportunities to use *their* expressions to explain *their* understandings of something. Often, the teacher may want several students to define words.

This practice offers a means for examining language as a precision tool for eliciting precision in communication. It sensitizes students as to how words can be used to illuminate understandings or to obfuscate meanings.

Using clarifying questions following a student response is an efficient way of building vocabulary, especially vocabulary specific to the class or subject. These questions relate directly to the clarity, specificity, and complexity of quality student responses. The teacher must make sure that, in answering a clarifying question, students are defining their words rather than giving examples of what they mean. Examples of clarifying questions are:

- What do you mean by (_________)?
- How can you state that in different words?
- How do you define (_________)?
- What would be another word we could use to describe (_________)?

Verifying Questions

Verifying questions promote accuracy and originality in student thinking. When asking a verifying question, teachers are listening for students to provide examples, give personal experiences, cite authorities or references, or associate their responses to generalizations most appropriate for further exemplifying or providing evidence for the content under study.

Verifying questions engage students in validating the accuracy of their information or ideas. In doing so, students relate what they are studying to what they already know and can use to better comprehend the concepts of the subject matter. The quality response categories of accuracy and originality are highlighted by asking verifying questions. Examples of verifying questions are:

- How do you know (_________)?
- What examples can you give for (_________)?
- Where did you find that information?
- When or where have you experienced this before?
- Point to (_________).
- Who do you know that supports (_________)?
- In what way is (_________) like (_________)?

Narrow Focusing Questions

Narrow focus relates to the specificity of the student responses. It asks students to refine their responses for greater depth. If students have shared information that is very broad about the subject or if they don't attend to specific content that is a part of the critical characteristics of the concepts, then the teacher must initiate students' thinking about specific conceptual attributes. The narrow focusing question is designed to investigate particular issues of content using the appropriate, cued thinking operation of the core question.

For example, if students are studying sentence structure and they have talked about everything except the punctuation of the sentences, then the teacher specifies or narrows the focus to punctuation. The structure of the narrow focusing question is as follows:

- What do you (thinking operation) about (specific content or critical characteristics not yet addressed by student responses)?

Supporting Questions

Support deals with tying together relationships among information and suspending judgment until all ideas have been considered before rendering a decision. They ask the students to hook-up evidence to their ideas. Supporting questions also ask students to state reasons for their thinking. They are used when forming concepts and when the examples or ideas expressed by students are not linked to the labels given or the definitions provided.

For example, in an instructional conversation about sentence structure, students may have identified each word in a sentence that is a noun but not stated how they know the word is a noun. To hook-up the identified nouns with the critical attributes of a noun, the teacher must ask the supporting question, "What is there about our identified words that make them nouns in our sentences?" The answer to this type of question informs the teacher about how students have attained, determined, or reasoned that a word in a sentence is a noun. Such questioning also ensures that students understand how they arrived at their responses. The stating of reasons for something is a sure measure that students understand the relevant issues of curricular concepts.

The structure of the supporting question should embody the framework for the response. Simply asking the question "Why" does not set the boundaries for constructing a response. The flippant answer to a "Why" question is "Why not?" or "Because." Examples of properly phrased supporting questions are as follows:

- What is there about (________) that makes you say (________)?
- How did you determine that (________) is a(n) (________)?
- On what basis did you decide that (________)?
- In what way does (________) suggest (________)?

Redirecting Questions

Redirecting questions are questions that call for more student-to-student interaction. It is also a way of generating and eliciting more variety in ideas. Redirecting questions support all the critical issues of quality student responses, especially complexity. They can be asked of any type of question in order to elicit more dialogue. They should be asked often during the lesson to solicit a variety of responses from as many students as possible. Some examples of redirecting questions follow:

- Who else (ask your question again)?
- What other (ask your question again)?
- What are some other ways we can think about (ask your question again)?
- What other information do you have about (ask your question again)?

The more processing questions that are asked during the lesson, the greater the opportunities students have to elaborate on their ideas, rethink and qualify their responses, and trace their thinking. Processing questions provide us the answer for "What do we do with student responses?" The following questions may help in planning for student responses.

Planning for Student Responses

Questions teachers need to ask themselves when planning instructional conversations

- What thinking do I want students to do about the content that is specified in the purpose of the lesson?
- How do I want to express the content in my core question?
- How do I want to express the thinking operation in my core question?
- What are some possible student responses to my core question?
- How will I deal with the possible student responses?

Processing questions bring out the beauty in student thinking. They refine and reshape student responses. They assure students' confidence in their abilities to know that they know. Through our use of processing questions, we will develop a better understanding of what students think, how they arrived at their responses, and why their responses are important.

Processing questions connect concepts to students' personalized understandings, making the study of school subjects relevant and justified. By using processing questions, teachers aid students in their understanding of how specific questions can become *their* learning tools. In a sense, the answers to processing questions create opportunities for students to become the masters of their own learning. And that is what the beauty in student responses is all about.

INQUIRY SUGGESTIONS AND QUESTIONS

To further guide our readers in their study of processing questions, we offer the following inquiry suggestions and questions.

- Review each vignette in this chapter for the processing questions. Determine if they are appropriate.
- Observe teachers in your school. Listen for processing questions.
  - What kind of processing questions do they use most often?
  - Under what conditions?
  - How many?
  - Which processing questions don't they use?
  - If you could give feedback to the teacher you observed, what would you say about his or her use of processing questions?
- Plan and conduct a lesson focusing on your processing questions. Tape it.
  - When do you tend to use processing questions?
  - What kinds and under what conditions?
  - How can you better engage your students in instructional conversations?
  - What guidelines would you set up for yourself and your students' interactions?
  - What do you notice about student responses when you use processing questions?

REFERENCES

cummings, e. e. *Collected Poems 1913–1962*. New York: Harcourt Brace Jovanovich, 1968. p. 462.

Gall, February 1973. "What Effects Do Teachers' Questions Have on Students?" Paper presented at the annual meeting of American Educational Research Association, New Orleans.

▶ 14

Dealing with Correct and Incorrect Responses

FACILITATIVE SET

Correct answers to questions are highly prized as an outcome for instruction. We judge our instructional success in teaching on students' knowledge of the content. Historically, American curriculum and classroom instruction have focused on learning content while vocalizing support for the importance of teaching thinking. However, teaching for content and teaching for thinking, at times, appear to be at opposite ends of the instructional continuum. If we use the time-consuming methods of teaching for thinking, we feel we lose valuable time toward teaching content that is important for passing standardized tests. On the other hand, if we consciously don't teach for thinking and spend our time on content objectives, we compromise our basic democratic value of developing citizens who can make well-informed decisions and who can solve problems facing our nation and the world.

In practice, we are preoccupied with making sure that students have the "right" facts. When teachers first begin to use the productive questioning practices, the dichotomy between content teaching and the teaching for thinking explodes. A constant concern gnawing at teachers is the dilemma of what to do with student responses that are clearly "wrong" answers. As educators, we value correctness. If students give wrong answers to our questions, we feel the need to make sure that in some way, when they leave our classrooms, they will know the right answers.

However, what we do with student responses tells them much about what we value. Basically, students learn by our questioning practices that right answers are expected and that wrong answers are questioned or criticized. What this says to students is that if you don't know the "right" answer, it is better to be quiet. This often limits the number of student interactions and their willingness to risk answering future questions.

Time on task is at play here. The time spent on student responses is when students learn. If we spend our time correcting "wrong" or "incorrect" answers rather than elaborating on "right" or "correct" answers, we do a disservice to our students. We limit conceptualization of the content material and may even be reinforcing the wrong information, especially if we teach students who have attending problems or who cannot discern important information. Often, what we lose in our preoccupation with correcting incorrect responses is helping students understand why their incorrect responses are not appropriate.

Likewise, the time spent on correcting wrong answers gets in the way of processing correct responses in ways that assist students in developing meaningful knowledge, building conceptually on the content, and understanding how they arrived at their answers. Students learn very quickly that the goal in instruction is not to think through ideas, but to provide answers that they perceive their teachers want to hear. *When we focus our instruction on making sure students have the "right" answers rather than how they arrive at reasoned responses, we reinforce the erroneous misconception that learning means getting the answer correct rather than help students understand learning as a process.*

In the vignettes below, the following student response issues will be addressed:

- Dealing with right and wrong student answers
- Clarifying students' understanding of critical content words
- Verifying answers for accuracy
- Supporting examples of concepts to the critical characteristics of the concept
- Determining student misconceptions
- Helping students reason through student misconceptions

Vignette: Student Misunderstandings: Students Have Some Wild Ideas

Taught by Kathy, observed by us

Kathy has a group of third-grade students, and she is covering material on the human body. She wants them to know the various systems of the body and their functions. The students read about the body's systems, they drew lines on worksheets connecting the parts of each system, and they demonstrated how the muscles work. There are models of the different systems on posters displayed throughout the classroom.

The students had been studying the body for two weeks when Kathy decided she would have the students answer questions orally. She planned her core question as, "What do we know about the human body's systems?" Throughout the dialogue with students, Kathy continually corrected all answers that students gave her that were incorrect. She spent a great deal of time *explaining* the "right" answers to her questions. For example, during one interaction, Joshua said that babies have fewer bones than adults do. Kathy remarked that the bones in all people are the same. Everyone has 208 bones. Babies' bones are just smaller than adult bones.

Keisha reported that the stomach is where juices that are acids digest the food. Kathy nodded in approval and quickly changed the direction of the recitation by asking, "What other things do we know about the human body's systems?"

John said that when babies fall their bones break easier than adult bones.

Trying to use questioning to correct John's misconception, Kathy grimaced and asked, "Why do you think that?"

"Because," said John, "they are not built as well because they haven't had time to grow."

Kathy was perplexed. She knew that they had just covered the bones yesterday. The day before she *told them* that babies bones are soft and are not as brittle as adult bones.

"John," Kathy said, in an attempt to review the previous lesson, "don't you think that soft things, if they fall, are less likely to break than hard things?"

"Yes," John responded.

"Well, then, babies' bones are softer and more flexible than adult bones, so they would be *less* likely to break if they fell," Kathy reasoned.

"But babies' bones are not well made—that would make them break more," John protested.

Teacher Reflection

I was amazed at what the students said. I couldn't believe the misconceptions the students had. I knew that I should have clarified and verified their responses, but I was really concerned with their misunderstandings. I realize now, as I look over the transcript of the lesson, that John may not have known what the word *brittle* meant and that he was associating "soft" with "not well developed." I should have asked him to clarify those words. I also told the answers when I should have had the students give me the answers.

SELF-STUDY DISCUSSION

In looking at this situation, there are many issues that must be dealt with: misconceptions, core questions, clarification of words, verification of ideas, narrowing the focus of specific content, and so forth. In her reflection, Kathy is obviously concerned with content. She knows that process is important; however, Kathy has spent instructional time trying to correct "wrong" answers at the expense of attending to correct responses. She fails to use the student responses to further probe their understandings. By her own admission, she *tells* students what the answer should be instead of probing their thinking.

At one point in the recitation, Keisha gives her a correct response that provides opportunities for building on a concept: *The stomach is where juices that are acids digest the food.* However, because Kathy's concern is "correct content," she simply nods approvingly at Keisha's "right" answer and redirects to receive another response in order to cover the material. By not spending time enriching Keisha's response, Kathy misses an important opportunity to reinforce and to add depth to the concept of digestion.

Had she worked with Keisha's correct response and spent time clarifying *acid* as a means for breaking down food and focused on the digestive process, she could have used students' knowledge to deepen their understanding to include how the body is nourished in that process. Second, by Kathy not attending to correct responses, students may not attend to these responses. Students may forget Keisha's correct response as they listen to Kathy trying to help John understand the waywardness of his response.

Joshua's and John's responses, because they are wrong, get all of Kathy's attention. Yet, the attention she gives the responses is centered on content and efficiency. She does not probe to understand how the students arrived at their misconceptions. She simply infers what the students' misconceptions are and tells them the correct answers.

The point is that if students aren't doing the talking and aren't doing the reasoning, they aren't doing the learning. By spending instructional time only on "wrong" answers and giving students the "right" answers to save time, we miss opportunities to assist students in learning *self-monitoring* techniques that they can use as learning tools. Had Kathy asked students to verify their information through their texts or notes, Kathy could have reinforced the value of the textbook information as a resource for validation, and students could have discovered, on their own, the inappropriateness of their responses.

Teachers' preoccupation with right and wrong answers, during recitations and discussions, subtly reinforces that content is more important than developing and using one's cognitive abilities. When we spend all our instructional time correcting wrong answers, often at the expense of elaborating on "right" answers that could provide a vehicle for conceptualizing the content, we lose opportunities for enriching students' relationships with concepts. Our preoccupation with right and wrong answers and using our instructional time in correcting the wrong answers dismiss learning as a process.

If Kathy would have encouraged students to think about their responses, rather than just provide content information, she could have made more productive use of instructional time. In processing both types of responses, she could have discovered what students were thinking that made them respond in the ways they did.

INQUIRY SUGGESTIONS AND QUESTIONS

- What will students remember from this slice of instruction?
- Because Kathy told students the correct answers, what will the students retain from the interactions?
- How does Kathy know that the students heard her explanations and will make meaning of them in the manner she intended?
- How could she have used Keisha's response to develop students' understanding of the digestive process?

VIGNETTE: TRACY DISCOVERS HOW CHRISTY THINKS

Taught by Tracy

I teach second grade. After giving my students a test on declarative and interrogative sentences, I realized that there were some students who didn't understand the difference between the two sentences. I was curious as to why they were confused. I asked the students to tell me topics that were of interest to them. I told them that tomorrow we would punctuate the sentences. I thought that if I had sentences that interested them they would do better. From the topics they gave me, some of the sentences I made up were:

1. John has a pet snake
2. Do the Power Rangers come on at 4:00
3. Is the school lunch bad
4. We have Fall break on October 10

I selected five students who had done the poorest on last week's test and conducted a Classifying lesson. I asked the students to separate the sentences by the ones they would put a period at the end and the ones they would put a question mark at the end. Here's what Christy did.

Period sentences	***Question mark sentences***
1. John has a pet snake.	2. Do the Power Rangers come on at 4:00?
3. Is the school lunch bad?	4. We have Fall break on October 10?

Taking one sentence at a time, I asked her to support her punctuation. This is what happened:

Teacher: What makes you say sentence number 1 should end in a period?

Christy: Well, John does have a pet snake so it is a statement.

Teacher: What makes it a statement?

Christy: It tells what John has.

Teacher: What other information in the sentence do you have that makes it end in a period?

Christy: It has a noun, *John,* and a verb, *has.*

Teacher: OK, what makes you say sentence number 2 is a question?

Christy: The Power Rangers come on at 6:00, not 4:00.

Teacher: So what makes that sentence a question?

Christy: They don't come on at 4:00. I was baffled, but I continued.

Teacher: Let's leave sentence number 2 and talk about sentence number 3. What makes sentence number 3 a question?

Christy: I don't think the school lunch is bad. Some kids do.

Teacher: So why does it end with a question mark?

Christy: Because we can't agree.

Teacher: If you don't agree with something, it's a question?

Christy: Yes.

Teacher: Hmm, what about sentence number 4, what makes you say that it needs a question mark?

Christy: Fall break is on October 3rd, not on October 10th.

Teacher Reflection

I don't believe it. I have been teaching declarative and interrogative sentences for five years. I never really probed my students' thinking to find out why they punctuated correctly or incorrectly. I now realize how valuable this is. When I asked the other students about Christy's punctuation of the sentences, some agreed with her reasoning. I now realize that the students who don't punctuate correctly may be using some other criteria for making decisions about punctuation.

In Christy's case, she was determining if something was true or not. If it was true, then it had to end in a period. If it wasn't true or she was unsure about the answer, then it ended in a question mark. I neglected to help her understand how her reasons for punctuation were causing her to punctuate incorrectly. Christy obviously did not understand the concepts of declarative and interrogative sentences. I wonder how many other students I've taught were thinking the same way? I now know that I have to stress the important things to look at in sentences, rather than just teach that declarative sentences end in periods and interrogative sentences end in question marks. What is so obvious to me is not so obvious to my students. Also, I now realize that how students think about something might interfere with coming up with the right answers.

SELF-STUDY DISCUSSION

Understanding how students think is the first step in helping them use their own resources to discover their misunderstandings related to content study. Through the teacher's use of supporting questions, students have the opportunity to share with the class and with us the thinking they used to arrive at their answers. Questions like *What makes you say that?* or *How did you decide that sentence number 1 is a statement and should end in a period?* require that students review the critical characteristics of the concept and how they applied it. To do so puts the power of learning in the students' hands. Additionally, by probing students' thinking, teachers discover the subtle misconceptions students may use when deciding on their answers.

In this situation, while Tracy has not addressed Christy's misconceptions about declarative and interrogative sentences, she certainly understands the importance of discovering how kids think. Her use of the supporting question "What makes you say this sentence should end in a period?" has helped her make sense of Christy's mistakes. Tracy's reflection indicates that she is now aware that students are using criteria other than the rules of grammar to punctuate sentences. In knowing this, Tracy can deal more effectively with Christy's punctuation errors by focusing on Christy's mistaken assumptions about punctuation.

The power of using the supporting question after students have classified something provides opportunities to share their reasoning with each other. When teachers know how students have reasoned through something, we have greater opportunities to pinpoint their misconceptions and to help them unlearn erroneous ideas. However, knowing what the misconceptions are is not enough. We must go further to assist students in understanding the critical characteristics of concepts, to use their information to correct their mistakes, and to help them understand their thinking. More often than not, students need to think more critically about concepts. Our questions can facilitate their learning about learning.

INQUIRY SUGGESTIONS AND QUESTIONS

- How could Tracy have simplified the lesson so that she could have dealt with Christy's misconceptions as they occurred?
- What other follow-up questions could Tracy have asked of each response so that Christy could use information to correct her understanding of sentence punctuation and her thinking?

VIGNETTE: CLEARING UP STUDENT MISCONCEPTIONS IS NOT SO SIMPLE

Taught by Sandra

Grammar is tough for students, especially the finer points. I decided I would give productive questioning a try in teaching a lesson on simple sentences. My eighth-grade students understand that simple sentences are complete thoughts possessing one subject and one verb. As long as the sentences were written with one subject and one verb without any other grammatical devices, they understood the simple sentence.

When gerunds, infinitives, or introductory phrases were added to the simple sentences, my students said they were complex sentences. I started out with a Recalling lesson, asking them what they remembered about simple sentences. They gave me the textbook response, "Simple sentences have one subject, one verb, and express a complete thought." Great! I thought. They know what one is. Wrong!

I wrote the first sentence on the board: *Jimmy fell out of the tree.* All the students correctly identified it as a simple sentence. I asked, "What about the sentence makes it simple?"

Todd replied, "It has one subject and one verb."

I asked for verification. "What is the subject and what is the verb?"

Todd answered again, "*Jimmy* is the subject and *fell* is the verb."

I put the next sentence on the board. *After leaving the party, Jane had an accident.* Well, several students said that it was not a simple sentence. They said that it was a complex sentence because it had a dependent clause. I then asked them to recall what a complex sentence was. Again, they gave me a textbook answer: Marshall offered, "A complex sentence has one independent clause and one dependent clause."

I said, "What do we mean by dependent clause?"

Richard said, "A dependent clause can't stand alone in the sentence."

"OK," I said, "What do you remember an independent clause is?"

"You know," Ellen said, "it's like a sentence. It is a complete thought."

Verifying, I asked, "And what is the independent clause in our sentence on the board?"

Immediately, Ellen answered, "Jane had an accident."

"Is that all?" I asked.

"Yes," several students said.

Richard added, "*After leaving the party* is the dependent clause.

"What makes it a dependent clause?" I was trying to get them to see that it tells more about Jane's accident.

In unison, they responded, "It can't stand alone."

It was at this point in the lesson that I realized that the students did not have a complete understanding about modifiers. They were confusing modifiers with dependent clauses. I put the following sentence on the board—*After I left the party, I had an accident*—and asked the students to tell me what the dependent and independent clauses were. They correctly identified them. I then separated the independent clause from the dependent clause and asked them to notice the words in the sentence.

Dependent Clause	*Independent Clause*
After I left the party	I had an accident.

They discussed that the independent clause could stand alone. After telling me, again, that the dependent clause couldn't stand alone, that it was hooked onto *I had an accident* by the use of a comma, I called their attention to the grammatical parts of the dependent clause. "What do you notice about the words in the dependent clause?" They noticed that the dependent clause, even though it could not stand alone, had a subject, *I*, verb, *left*, and a word, *after*, that answered the question of when.

I went back to the sentence, *After leaving the party, Jane had an accident*. I asked them to tell me what they knew about the words in this sentence.

Terrance said, "It has a subject, *Jane*, and a verb, *had*, and *after leaving the party* tells when the accident happened.

"Let's look more carefully at these two sentences." I put one sentence underneath the other.

After I left the party, I had an accident.
After leaving the party, Jane had an accident.

I asked, "How are these two sentences different in the way they are constructed?"

Chris said, "Both have a comma, and the part before the comma tells when the accident happened."

"Chris, you are telling me how they are similar. I'm looking for how they are different, so what is different about the way the words are put together in the sentences?'

He looked confused. There was silence for about twenty seconds. I waited it out, but I really wanted to tell the class the answer. Finally, Todd said, "The first sentence part before the comma has a subject and verb, but the second sentence has only a verb.

"What is the verb in the second sentence?" I probed.

"Leaving," he responded.

Good grief, I thought. This is tedious. I'm just going to tell them that *leaving* is a gerund, a verb used as a noun in this sentence. Just as I was about to say that, Sarah, a student who rarely talks in my class said, "Oh, *leaving* is used as a noun, tells what was going on."

A miracle! I thought, "Sarah, tell me about the word *after*."

She thought for a few seconds and said, "*After* tells when the accident happened.

"Wait a minute," Todd said. "If leaving is a noun, then there is no verb. The second sentence doesn't have a verb, but the first sentence has a subject and verb after the word *after*.

"Oh," said Richard, "if you take away the word *after* in both sentences, the first sentence would have two complete thoughts, but the second sentence wouldn't."

"Let's see," I said. I erased the word *after* from each sentence. What remained was:

I left the party, I had an accident.
Leaving the party, Jane had an accident.

Where do I go now? I wondered. How do I get back to simple sentences? Then it occurred to me. I asked, "What words in the second sentence tell when the accident occurred?"

Again, a response in unison, *"Leaving the party."* I was almost afraid to ask the next question, "So what do you remember about words that tell when?"

Jill responded, "They are adverbs. 'Leaving the party' tells when the accident occurred. You could write the sentence, *Jane had an accident (after) leaving the party.*"

"And what kind of sentence is that?" I asked in fear of the response.

Todd shouted, "A simple sentence!" In almost the same breath he said, "It has one subject and one verb."

"Oh, I get it," said Chris, "if you don't have a subject and verb in the dependent clause, then it's still a simple sentence."

"Yeah, the dependent clause has to have a subject and verb and can stand alone once the other words are gone. What you get are two complete thoughts."

"Let's try it on a new example," I offered. I decided we needed some humor. It had been a hard time getting to here. I wrote on the board:

While loosening her belt, Mary's skirt fell down.

After the kids laughed about the sentence, they said that it was a simple sentence.

"What makes this a simple sentence?"

Marshall responded, "It doesn't have a complete thought before the comma, so it must tell about why or when her skirt fell off." Laughter, again.

"I think you have it. So tell me how can you tell whether a sentence is a simple sentence when it has a phrase before the complete thought, or a complex sentence?" Boy, I thought, their answer to this ought to be interesting. I closed my eyes.

Sarah stated, "If the words before the comma in a sentence don't have a subject and verb in it, it is a simple sentence."

"OK," I breathed easier. What had seemed an eternity had taken only twenty minutes of class. Although my lesson was just going to be on simple sentences, my questioning of the students' thinking got them to also understand how to tell the difference between a particular kind of complex sentence and simple sentences. I was delighted.

"Keep these ideas in mind. Tomorrow we're going to practice this some more." The next day I gave the students ten practice sentences; some were simple sentences and some were complex sentences. They got them *all correct* and they knew why the simple sentences were simple. I am amazed.

Teacher Reflection

This was a difficult lesson to teach. I was really thinking throughout the discussion that I should just give them the answers, but a voice in the back of my head kept saying to let them discover it for themselves. I thought they never would! I hadn't realized before this how literally students take everything. When I taught this before, I always told students that the dependent clause could not stand alone and that a comma separates the dependent clause from the independent clause.

I can see from this lesson that they knew this, but what I didn't know was that they would generalize that rule to all phrases that had a comma before the main clause of the sentence. By sticking to this questioning practice and by using the narrow focusing question once I realized what they were not attending to, I was able to clarify for the students the kind of grammatical constructions that were really dependent clauses and the phrases that really modified a simple sentence. I not only taught simple sentences in this lesson, but I also dealt with complex sentences. When I think about it, the questions I asked helped me teach two or three lessons in one.

When I began this lesson, I was thinking only about simple sentences. By the time it was done, we had covered simple sentences and dependent and independent clauses, as well as confusing issues related to simple sentences. I can't tell you how excited I was when they all got the practice sentences right. I know that this sounds like I am still focused only on the content, but I also know that by being patient and working with their responses, I "uncovered" their thinking and was able, this time, to help them discover some other attributes of concepts that helped them better understand sentences.

SELF-STUDY DISCUSSION

Listening to student responses can be tedious, and working with their responses can be messy. To expertly guide student thinking about content issues, the teacher must have a solid understanding of the content, as well as know which questions to ask to help students work through their misconceptions. Most of the time it means analyzing how students are thinking and using subsequent processing questions to direct students to problem areas. In this situation, Sandra used three processing questions for instruction: clarifying, verifying, and narrow focusing questions.

The importance of using concrete, specific examples of the concept facilitates students' abilities to discern critical characteristics of concepts. In this case, placing the two sentences together and having the students focus on the differences in the grammatical signals assisted Sandra in helping students to discover that dependent clauses have both subjects and verbs, whereas phrases that do not have both subject and verb modify the simple sentence. Because students discovered this, through their own verification of examples, it supplied them with information that made the instruction more meaningful to them. They also learned that they could solve grammatical problems by attending better to the structure of sentences. Theoretically, these students have a better grip on the critical characteristics of the concept and how to use their knowledge and cognitive operations to solve similar grammatical problems.

The processing questions used in this lesson each contributed to students' collection of information about the concept, which aided their analysis of sentence structures. Asking clarifying questions—for example, *What do you mean by _______?* or *How do you define _______?*—encourages students to put unclear content into their own words. It is important that students be able to state in their own words what is meant by specific words, and not just repeat textbook definitions. When students simply repeat textbook definitions without thinking about what the words mean to them, they tend to accept ideas rather than critically explore the ideas so that the ideas or words become relevant to them.

Another avenue to pursue in helping students to better comprehend meanings is the use of the verifying question. Asking *How do you know _______?, Where is _______ found?*, or *Give an example of what you are referring to* enables students to generate new ways of looking at something and to validate their ideas. It offers students a means for validating responses and checking their responses against the critical characteristics of a concept. In asking students to use the information they gathered from clarifying words and providing their own examples, we provide a valuable lesson in how to use these questions in exploring their own thinking.

The supporting question *What makes you think that ________ is an example of ________?* or *On what basis did you decide _________?* engages students in hooking up their responses to the critical characteristics of concepts. When Sandra asked at the end of the vignette *"What makes this a simple sentence?"* and Marshall responded *"It doesn't have a complete thought before the comma, so it must tell about why or when her skirt fell off,"* he had connected the critical attributes of determining how a phrase modifies a subject and verb. In doing so, he extended his understanding of the various constructions of a simple sentence. Marshall's answer was further reinforced by Sarah's response, *"If the words before the comma in a sentence don't have a subject and verb in it, it is a simple sentence."*

Sandra's skillful use of the supporting question to "hook-up" the critical characteristics of when words modify something engaged students in carefully observing and studying the construction of simple and complex sentences. They extended their understanding of the concepts. Through her expert questioning, she exhibited for them valuable learning tools that they can use in their own learning.

INQUIRY SUGGESTIONS AND QUESTIONS

- What questions helped Sandra understand how students were thinking about the concept?
- What questions assisted the students in collecting information about the examples that helped them find new ways of understanding the concept?
- What was the value in asking how simple sentences were different from complex sentences?

Part V

Journeys into the Study of Productive Questioning

Research has shown us that the extent to which teachers engage in learning impacts student learning and achievement (Rosenholtz, 1991). Learning is a two-way street: The more teachers learn, the more students learn. The more students learn, the more learning teachers need. "Students *do* what they see their mentors do. We must make conscious, deliberate efforts, as teachers, always to demonstrate or exhibit the kinds of thinking behaviors and dispositions, or habits of mind, that we want our students to develop" (Beyer, 1997, p. 78). If we want students to view learning as a process, then we must understand that teaching is a continual learning process. In these closing chapters, we discuss teaching as learning. In Chapter 15, we present one of our student's journey into learning about questioning. In Chapter 16, we describe a talent development model we use in working with teachers in order to assist our readers in their journey into learning to question and questioning to learn.

To keep up with the calls for reform, educators find themselves in the position of sharpening and expanding their repertoire of teaching behaviors. One way to do this is through the academic pursuit of advanced degrees. The more knowledgeable we become, the more we are able to incorporate one's academic learning into one's teaching repertoires. Another way to continue our growth and development as teachers is to study instructional practices within the instructional work environment through self-study (Knowles & Cole, 1996; McNiff, 1993; McNiff, Lomax, & Whitehead, 1996; Russell & Korthagen, 1995; Whitehead, 1994, 1995). Self-study is inquiry through reflective practice (Schön, 1983, 1987). Reflective practice is a means for studying our instructional practices to inform both our theories of learning and our practices in the classroom.

Jack Whitehead, at the University of Bath in the United Kingdom, is well known within the self-study of teacher education practices community. He refers to self-study as "living educational theory" (Whitehead, 1994). He and others who have been doing work in self-study of teacher education believe that self-study is a means through which teachers and teacher educators illuminate their understanding of educational theories and values through practice and reflection. In doing so, teachers become accountable to themselves and their students.

The purpose of self-study is to investigate one's personal and professional development or to deepen and broaden one's understanding of classroom pedagogy. In Chapter 15, Steve examines his use of questioning. He invites us to view his journey and discoveries. Steve's journey into questioning is a lonesome journey. However, self-study can be performed also by teachers involved in collegial coaching (Dantonio, 1995). Through the process of collegial coaching, educators establish trustful relationships and establish the support they need to investigate teaching and learning. By combining self-study and collegial coaching, teachers can build a support network in their schools to encourage and refine the development of each other's instructional talents while attending to the demands of instructing students.

In Chapter 16, we explore a professional development model that is site-based and teacher sponsored and driven. Teachers form learning communities for studying the Qu:Est Instructional Strategies. A community of learners possesses common goals, shares common visions and practices, and creates and sustains a synergetic spirit. It is what Bryson and Scardamalia (1991) call a "knowledge-building culture." In a professional learning community, each teacher is a teacher, coach, and learner. Together, they assist each other in their practice and thinking about teaching and learning.

The professional learning approach described in the last part of this book is referred to as the Talent Development Model (TDM) (Dantonio, 1990). It provides a framework to assist teachers in forming collegial teams for the self-study of productive questioning practices. TDM is a learning process and a series of developmental rehearsal contexts. It requires rigorous attention to the critical issues of productive questioning, an open attitude toward changing or enhancing one's instructional behaviors, and creating time and opportunities to meet and practice the Qu:Est Instructional Strategies with other teachers.

The TDM is based on our work with teachers over the past twenty-five years. We have found that teachers who use this process to practice the Qu:Est Instructional Strategies have greater success with the strategies when working with students. We offer the Talent Development Model to our readers as a way to commence their journeys into the study of productive questioning practices. We invite your participation and welcome your insights and suggestions.

REFERENCES

Beyer, B. K. (1997). *Improving student thinking* (pp. 86–87). Boston: Allyn & Bacon.

Bryson, M., & Scardamalia, M. (1991). Teaching writing to students at risk for academic failure. In B. Means, C. Chelemer, and M. S. Knapp (Eds.), *Teaching Advanced Skills to At-Risk Students* (p. 162). San Francisco: Jossey-Bass.

Dantonio, M. (1990). *How can we create thinkers? Questioning strategies that work for teachers.* Bloomington, IN: National Education Services.

Dantonio, M. (1995). *Collegial coaching: Inquiries into the teaching self.* Bloomington, IN: Phi Delta Kappa.

Knowles, J. G., & Cole, A. L. (Eds.). (1996). Beginning professors and teacher education reform (theme issue). *Teacher Education Quarterly, 23(3).*

McNiff, J. (1993). *Teaching as learning.* New York: Routledge Press.

McNiff, J., Lomax, P., & Whitehead, J. (1996). *You and your action research project.* New York: Routledge Press.

Rosenholtz, S. J. (1991). *Teachers' workplace: The social organization of schools.* New York: Longman.

Russell, T., & Korthagen, F. (Eds.). (1995). *Teachers who teach teachers: Reflections on teacher education.* London: Falmer Press.

Schön, D. A. (1983). *The reflective practitioner: How professionals think in action.* New York: Basic Books.

Schön, D. A. (1987). *Educating the reflective practitioner.* San Francisco, Jossey-Bass.

Whitehead, J. (1994, April). *Creating a living educational theory from an analysis of my own educational practices: How do you create and test the validity of your living educational theory?* Paper presented at the Annual Meeting of the American Educational Research Association, New Orleans, Louisiana.

Whitehead, J. (1995). Educative relationships with the writings of others. In T. Russell & F. Korthagen (Eds.), *Teachers who teach teachers: Reflections on teacher education,* pp. 113–129. London: Falmer Press.

15

Steve's Journey into Learning to Question and Questioning to Learn

This book has emphasized that learning to question and questioning to learn is a journey of discovery about who we are as teachers and how we can evolve our instruction to include effective practices for helping students think and learn conceptually. Most important are the experiences and reflections of teachers. Through teachers' stories, we come to know the process we must all engage in if we are to evolve into talented educators. As a way of highlighting the evolution of developing teaching talent, this chapter will provide our readers with a snapshot of one of our students' journey into using the Qu:Est Instructional Strategies to discern his students' understandings and his efforts to develop and refine their conceptual thinking.

STATUS OF QUESTIONING AS A LEARNING PROCESS

By STEVE SAUCIER
Director and Teacher, Waldo Burton Memorial School, New Orleans, LA

Many years ago when I was in informal education—museum education—I was introduced to scaffolding, originally developed by Vygotsky. I recently pulled some old resources regarding his work because I am struck by the parallels between what I recall of his work and the questioning techniques I have been introduced to through Qu:Est. In Berk and Winsler's book, *Scaffolding Children's Learning* (1995), they write, "The social environment is the necessary scaffold, or support system, that allows the child to move forward and continue to build new competencies" (p. 26). Earlier they wrote, in Vygotsky's words, "the social dimension of consciousness is primary in time and fact. The individual dimension is derivative and secondary" (p. 20). But the "Tool of the Mind" of preeminent importance in Vygotsky's theory is language, "the most frequent and widely used human representational system" (p. 21). How poignant and relevant this is to me now that I have been introduced to productive questioning practices and the concept of instructional conversation. I tend to boil things down—in this case, to find a central meaning to the art of teaching. The meaning or "big picture" that I continue to return to is the idea of how organic these instructional conversations really are. They are, for me, a return to natural processes.

I use the term "return" because much of what I have learned about teaching, either through example as a student or through formal training at the college level, has caused me to be in conflict. The conflict was more of a feeling or intuition. I was learning one way to teach while my intuitive sense wanted to go in another direction. I, due to my new formal learning, have been forced to face these feelings of conflict because I now understand the source of the conflict. My study of productive questioning practices and the personal development I am experiencing are acting to realign my intuition toward teaching and the natural or organic way in which children and all people learn.

Over time, I feel that I am going to be able to be extremely proficient at these questioning practices. One reason is due to the return to the natural order of things as discussed above, but also because I have been using questions and providing scaffolding already in my instruction, if only in a segmented way. It feels right, for some reason. I feel that I am supposed to teach this way or I have an undeveloped template, a natural gift, regarding proper questioning. I understand that my learning of questioning through Qu:Est has only acted to introduce the concept. I know it will take years to bring my skills to the level of what I am really capable of performing. I am but a child with a new BIG toy who fails to fully understand its power and impact, although I realize that I am growing and so is my ability to make use of this new information.

One reason I remain confident that my questioning abilities will continue to develop is that I am blessed with the vision of being *effective* in my teaching. All teachers teach, but not all of them fall at the same location on the spectrum of effectiveness. Teaching is not an act of the teacher but a process of collaboration between teacher and student. Questioning, when done correctly, generates that collaboration and advances the learning process. The fact that I am aware of this concept, and am now equipped with effective practices that I can further develop, puts me on the path to greater effectiveness and improved teaching.

How then am I going to make use of questioning? First, an explanation of my current state of affairs is in order. I began the 1998–1999 school year as administrator, principal, custodian, superintendent, disciplinarian, and . . . oh yes . . . TEACHER of an alternative school within a boys' home. Every day has been new. I developed a curriculum making use of Jefferson Parish's Curriculum Guides and state benchmarks, and making every attempt to meet the needs of my students and to prepare them for the required standardized testing. Most things worked, but there was certainly room for improvement. Now that I am beginning to look toward the second year of the program, I see that my effectiveness can be raised by fundamentally changing my approach to interacting with each student. It is productive questioning and using instructional conversations that will somehow, through concentrated planning, become infused into much, if not all, of my program.

Each of the students I deal with is unique; however, there is a commonalty among students. They have had behavior problems in previous school settings, and this, I believe, is due to the fact that their learning needs have not been met. Boredom has set in, and the snowballing effect of becoming more disconnected with their schooling experiences has been set in motion. Receiving little attention because of their lack of performance, my students engage in behavior that will elicit attention, even if it is negative. That brings them to the home, my school.

How then do I reengage them in the learning process? My answer, in simple terms, is through reawakening and stimulating their desire to learn. In a short period of time, I have seen how productive questioning leads to instructional conversation, which socially engages these students in ways they have never experienced before. It awakens their thinking processes to bring about real, meaningful conceptual understanding and allows me to access the learning needs of my students.

To help you understand my journey into teaching for understanding and helping my student think conceptually, I have submitted some lesson plans my students and I have experienced. Following the lesson plans, I have included brief transcripts from the instructional conversations, and an analysis of the instruction by coding the interactions and reflecting upon my experience learning to question.

LESSONS, TRANSCRIPTS, CODING, AND REFLECTIONS

Recalling Lesson: "Cloud Formation"

Purpose: To provide learners with opportunities to recall specific details about the physical properties and processes of cloud formation.

Reason: Prerequisite information to developing the concept of thunderstorms and tornadoes.

Content Characteristics:

- The atmosphere
- The water cycle: Energy from the sun > Evaporation > Condensation > Precipitation
- Cloud nuclei: Dust, smoke, airborne particles
- Condensation on cold objects
- Three phases of water: Liquid water, solid ice, water vapor (steam)
- Humidity/relative humidity

Resources: Classroom science demonstration, student science experiments, board diagrams, films

Core Question:

- What do you notice about clouds and how they form?

Possible Learner Responses:

- Water vapor rises in the air. (VR)
- Clouds occur during storms. (VR)
- Clouds sometimes look like objects or people. (RF)
- When the air gets cold, it condenses. (CL)
- Water evaporates, rises, and collects into clouds. (CL/VR)
- Clouds occur when it gets warm. (VR/NF)
- There are many clouds today. (VR/RD)

Processing Question Stems:

- RF 1. What are you recalling about cloud formation that makes you say clouds sometimes look like objects or people?
- CL 2. What do you mean by condenses?
- VR 3. How do you know that water evaporates in the air?
- NF 4. Tell me more about clouds occurring when it gets warm.
- RD 5. Who else noticed that there are many clouds today?

Transcript

Teacher: What do you recall about clouds and how they are formed?

Anthony: Clouds are formed when rain gathers in a lake or any source of water, then evaporates into the sky, which gathers together and . . . umm . . . and acts on itself to cause . . . umm . . . clouds.

Chad: Clouds are formed when low air and high air . . . no . . . when a cold front hits or collides and moisture collects.

Teacher: What do you mean by evaporates?

Anthony: The heat . . . umm . . . the heat around you makes the water warm up and turn into like steam sort of.

Ernie: Can I restate his umm . . . .answer?

Teacher: (nod)

Ernie: All right . . . . It's not that it's formed by rain gathering . . . It's . . . ahh . . . it's water that's been evaporated and gathers up that causes the clouds.

Teacher: Come and draw that for us.

Ernie: Cool . . . If I can get my desk. OK. The sun, water, heat . . . so the heat makes the water evaporate and become a . . . ah . . . gas which kind of like mystifies its way up and it accumulates.

Anthony: Like a sponge.

Ernie: The color of the cloud depends on how much water there is.

Coding of Transcript

T:	RL		CL				VR		
S:	+	+	CL	–	CL	–	VR	CL	RF

Reflection on the Lesson

I feel this went surprisingly well, now that I have analyzed it. As a class, we have done several activities regarding this subject, including a condensation demonstration, followed by students' experiments conducted in groups of two. I conducted the recall lesson two days after these activities for two reasons: to test the students' recollection as well as to require them to respond using their own words.

I know that I am still in the early stages of acquiring this new skill. This is evident by my confusion during the lesson and my lucid analysis as I review the tape. I am clearly aware of when I have coded questions appropriately and inappropriately during the analysis. However, during the lesson, there is so much to think about and anticipate that I quickly become confused and end up disturbing the pace of the lesson. I'm really not sure my coding is correct.

Observing Lesson: "Classical Music: Capriccio Italien" (Tchaikovsky)

Purpose: To provide learners with opportunities to gather the elements of a classical piece of music through auditory observation.

Reason: Prerequisite to experiencing this same piece of music performed live.

Content Characteristics: Pitch, timber, tempo, instrumentation, orchestration, dynamics, style, lack of vocal music

Resources: The class has listened to this piece of music from CD, board, overhead projector

Core Question: Observing

- What do you notice about this piece of music?

Possible Learner Responses:

- I don't like that type of music. (O)
- It kept changing. (RF)
- I heard violins. (VR)
- There were no singers. (CL)
- It reminded me of a movie. (RF)

Processing Question Stems

- RF 1. What are you noticing about the music that makes you say it kept changing?
- CL 2. What do you mean by "type" of music?
- VR 3. Where in the music did you hear violins?
- NF 4. Tell me more about why you noticed that there aren't any singers.
- RD 5. Who else noticed that there were violins?

Transcript

Teacher: What do you notice about this piece of music?

Ernie: The music was constantly changing. The concentration of it was different every time. The violins would go from less to more. They would slack off and rise up.

Teacher: What do you mean by slack off?

Ernie: Less people playing. The louder they go, the more people are playing. The lower they go, fewer people are playing.

Gary: I don't see the point to that type of music.

Teacher: I asked you what do you notice about that piece of music and you made a value judgment about the music.

Gary: It has no real point to it. It didn't go anywhere.

Teacher: What do you mean anywhere?

Gary: It doesn't come back to a point of conclusion.

Ernie: OBJECTION! That's an opinion.

Teacher: What else did you notice about that piece of music?

Chad: It's like music that like goes along with action or drama.

Ernie: YEAH!

Teacher: How do you know that it is supposed to go along with action or drama?

Chad: It's like the action is the fast part and the drama is the slow part.

Gary: It slows down and speeds up.

Ernie: Remember, it doesn't have any point, GARY!

Gary: EXACTLY!!

Chad: The drama has more violins, and the action has more other instruments.

Coding of Transcript

T:	OB	CL	OB/RD	TT
S:	OB	CL	O	OB
CL		OB/RD		VR
CL	O	RD	O	CL
		VR		
CL	O	O	½VR	

Reflection on the Lesson

This was a very successful lesson even though the coding may not indicate it. I conducted this lesson as a precursor to going to the symphony. We did the lesson in the morning and went to the concert later that day. I strongly feel that the lesson heightened the musical experience. My students were making comments and recalling the piece being played in the classroom. They continued the lesson on their own after the concert while we were walking back to the van. There was an "instructional conversation" going on as we walked beside the theatre, and I was but a witness to this thing that seemed to have a life of its own. These students were having open debates, they were recalling specific musical passages and orchestration, and they were making well-stated positions. I WAS PLEASED! The experience will never be forgotten.

Similarities and Differences Lesson: "Water Cycle/Weather"

Purpose: Provide learners with opportunities to compare and contrast the attributes of the water cycle and weather

Reason: Extends students' understanding of the attributes of and relationship between the water cycle and the weather

Content Characteristics: Similarities of Water Cycle and Weather

- *Water*
  Both have water as a component.
- *Energy*
  Both are powered by the sun and earth forces and movements.
  Both involve the loss and gain of energy.
- *Temperature*
  Both concepts include thermal differentials.
- *Phases of Matter*
  Both involve the three states of water (liquid, solid, gas).

Differences between Water Cycle and Weather

Water Cycle

- *Water*—Movement of water through the atmosphere and earth
- *Energy*—Sun powers the movement of water. The loss and gain of energy by water
- *Temperature*—Thermal differentials of water throughout the cycle
- *Phases of Matter*—Water, ice, water vapor (clouds, fog, and so on)

Weather

- *Water*—Water is one of four major components (water, air, the sun, and the movement of the earth) that comprise weather
- *Energy*—This is the engine that powers all weather activity and the movement of all the components of weather. Air and other materials lose and gain energy. The level of energy determines the air's ability to hold moisture.
- *Temperature*—Thermal differentials in air, the surface of the earth, and water
- *Phases of Matter*—Water, ice, water vapor

Resources: Library materials, the Internet, lecture notes on weather and the water cycle, board

Core Question: (Contrasting)

- From your readings, what differences are there between the water cycle and weather?

Possible Learner Responses:

- The water cycle and weather are the same thing. (O)
- The water cycle is the movement of water, whereas weather is all that goes on in the atmosphere. (CL)
- The water cycle is part of weather, whereas weather is not part of the water cycle. (CL/VR)

Processing Question Stems:

- RF 1. You have told me that the water cycle and weather are not the same thing. Is there some weather that does not include water?
- CL 2. What do you mean by movement?
- VR 3. How do you know that the water cycle is part of weather and not the other way around?
- NF 4. Tell me more about the differences in temperature in the water cycle and differences in temperature in other materials in weather.
- RD 5. What other information have you found regarding the differences between the water cycle and weather?

Transcript

Teacher: From your readings, what differences are there between the water cycle and weather?

Anthony: Well . . . wait . . . They're the same thing . . . wait. There is some weather that is not . . . does not have water.

Teacher: Phrase that using contrasting terms.

Anthony: The water cycle is always part of weather, but weather is not always part of the water cycle.

Ernie: YEAH! Like when it includes water runoff or groundwater. That's not weather, I don't think.

Teacher: Is that action occurring in the atmosphere?

Ernie: No . . . so, no, it isn't weather. I was right.

Teacher: What other differences are there between the water cycle and weather?

Justin: The water cycle isn't about air . . . but . . . umm . . . wait, the water is in the air.

Teacher: Try to phrase it correctly.

Justin: The weather includes mainly air and water, whereas the water cycle includes mainly water.

Coding of Transcript

T:	CT		TT		CL	CT	TT
S:	O	CT	CT	VR	CL	O	CT

Reflection on the Lesson

Transcribing this lesson was frustrating. From what I remember, it went pretty well; however, I couldn't hear the responses very well due to background noises. What I transcribed was all that I could verify. After that I am unsure of the responses. For this reason, the transcription and coding are a little short.

This was a difficult lesson for my students to grasp. It is difficult to distinguish between the water cycle and weather. However, the questioning lesson helped to bring to light misconceptions about these two concepts. One student refused to distinguish between the water cycle and weather, insisting that they are one and the same. "You can't have weather without water, so how can there be any differences?" he said. Even after providing him with examples, he continued to make his argument. I can see that the questioning lessons require students to process information in ways lectures cannot, even if there is no complete resolution.

Grouping Lesson: "Erosion"

Purpose: To provide learners with opportunities to group causes of the erosion process regarding water and watersheds

Reason: To develop understanding of the various ways in which things are eventually classified, as well as to build an understanding that the same things can be grouped for different reasons.

Content Characteristics:

- Causes of erosion
- Dynamics of water
- The water cycle
- Watersheds: rivers, streams, lakes, oceans
- Landforms
- Gravity
- Human impact on the land

Resources: The class has recently been on a canoeing trip, board, Internet research, stream tray activity, list of unsorted causes.

List of Words:

erosion	trees	canoes	rocks	camping
land	gravity	people	pollution	students
water	wind	houses	air	storms
floods	hills	rivers	bridges	crops

Core Question: Grouping

- From what you know about erosion, which of these words go together for some reason?

Possible Learner Responses:

Group 1	*Group 2*	*Group 3*
gravity	wind	people
hills	air	pollution
land	storms	houses

Group 4	*Group 5*
floods	crops
rivers	people
hills	water
land	

Processing Question Stems:

- RF 1. You are telling me the reason for your group; what are the specific items in your group?
- RE 2. You are telling me a label for the group; state the words that you have put together.
- SP 3. Thinking about the words that you have placed together, what are your reasons for thinking they go together?
- SP 4. On what basis did you put crops, people, and water together?
  - *Group 1:* Severe weather causes erosion.
  - *Group 2:* Causes water to move within a watershed.
  - *Group 3:* Human impact on land.
  - *Group 4:* The changing courses of water.
  - *Group 5:* Agriculture affects erosion.

- CL 5. What do you mean by "watershed"?
- CL 6. What are you referring to when you say "human impact"?
- VR 7. How do you know the words in Group 5 are all effects of agriculture?
- VR 8. Give me an example of agriculture.
- NF 9. Group the words in the list because they are something you have seen.
- RD 10. Who has another group for different reasons?
- RD 11. Who has the same group for different reasons?

Transcript

Teacher: From what you know about erosion, which of these words go together for some reason?

Anthony: OK . . . gravity, land, rocks, hills, floods, storms, rivers, trees because these are things . . . erosion is caused by these things.

Teacher: You gave me a list of the things in your group, and then you gave me a label for the group. All I want at this point are the words . . . the words that go together for some reason, not the reason. Does anyone else have these same words in their group?

Ernie: I would add air and water to the group.

Anthony: No, man!! Make your own group.

Ernie: We're supposed to work as a group. What do you think this is, a competition?

Teacher: Let's add those words to the group. What are your reasons for thinking all of these go together?

Anthony: Like I said, they are causes for erosion.

Ernie: Look at the big list, though. There are more reasons up there for erosion.

Anthony: All right man! Then . . . they are . . . natural . . . you know they cause erosion without our help.

Teacher: What do you mean by our help?

Anthony: You know . . . people. Nature causes erosion and people cause erosion.

Gary: So people aren't natural. What do you think, I was made by some machine or something?

Anthony: I don't know, man, you're kind of weird.

Coding of Transcript

T:	GR	TT/RD		
S:	GR/LB	GR	O	O
SP			CL	
SP	RF	SP	CL	CL
O				

Reflection on the Lesson

As you can probably perceive from the transcript, these boys are ready and willing to communicate with each other and not always in the most pleasant way. Although this kind of "bickering" continued throughout the lesson, all in all, I feel the lesson was successful. We used some of the same terms in a different group for a different reason, and this seemed to amaze them that there could be such flexibility in the reasons for the same terms.

For some reason, I feel that this lesson lent itself to more group discussion than the previous ones. This, perhaps, could be accounted for by the frequency with which I now conduct Qu:Est lessons. They see my not only allowing class discussions (something I have done even prior to this questioning class), but my encouraging it, or insisting on it.

One wonderful, and a bit frustrating, outcome is that I had a hard time ending the lesson. They kept rearranging new groups and providing reasons for the grouping. They did not want to cease the lesson. One reason is that it provides freedom of thought, and also they knew we had other work to do. The strategies students will use to avoid work! But something tells me that "ain't" so bad—wanting to remain in an instructional conversation as a sanctuary away from more menial tasks.

Labeling Lesson: "Erosion"

Purpose: Provide learners with opportunities to generate causes of erosion for various reasons, including natural causes, man-made causes, and indirect occurrences

Reason: Facilitate the communication of a set of characteristics assigned to grouped causes of erosion, as well as extend vocabulary development

Content Characteristics:

- Causes of erosion
- Dynamics of water
- The water cycle
- Watersheds: rivers, streams, lakes, oceans
- Landforms
- Gravity
- Human impact on the land

Resources: Groupings of causes (see Grouping Lesson)

Core Question: Labeling

- Based on the reasons given for grouping the causes of erosion, what would be an appropriate name for the group(s)?

Possible Learner Responses:

- Group 1: Severe weather causes erosion, storms, violent winds
- Group 2: Causes water to move within a watershed; water goes downhill
- Group 3: Human impact on land; people change the land
- Group 4: The changing courses of water, winding rivers, meandering
- Group 5: Agriculture affects erosion, fertilizer, cutting down trees for land

Processing Question Stems:

- RF 1. You are giving me a reason for the group; what would be an appropriate name for the group?
- CL 2. What do you mean by "violent winds"?
- CL 3. What are you referring to when you say "watershed"?
- SP 4. Why do you think "natural causes of erosion" is an appropriate name for Group 1?
- SP 5. What is there about Group 1 that makes you say "agricultural causes of erosion" is an appropriate name for this group?
- VR 6. Give me examples of some severe weather that would cause erosion.
- RD 7. Who has another name for Group 3?

Transcript

Teacher: Based on the reasons given for grouping the causes of erosion, what would be an appropriate name for this group?

Gary: All right . . . these are things that cause erosion naturally, like storms—you know, the wind blows, trees fall, stuff goes into the river, like when we went canoeing.

Teacher: What you are doing is giving me reasons for the group; what would be a good name for the group?

Gary: Effects of a storm.

Anthony: No, man . . . things that erode because of storms.

Teacher: What are you referring to when you say "things that erode"?

Anthony: No . . . wait . . . these are not the things that erode. These are the things that cause things to erode.

Teacher: So what would be a good name for the group?

Ernie: Stormy Erosion

Teacher: Ricky, why do you think "Stormy Erosion" is a good name for this group?

Ricky: Because . . . those things . . . huh . . . 'cause. . . . When there is a storm, it . . . erosion happens because of the storm.

Justin: You know . . . when the wind blows or rain, this would cause that . . . the banks of that river we were on to fall in the river.

Teacher: Give me more examples of what storms do to cause erosion.

Gary: Mr. Steve, I said that trees fall, wind blows, also water would do it, from the river, you know.

Coding of Transcript

T:	LB	RF/LB		CL
S:	O	LB	O/LB	CL
RF/LB	RD/SP		VR	
LB	SP	SP	VR	

Reflection on the Lesson

I don't know if you can perceive it from the transcript, but my students had great difficulty participating in this lesson. There were long pauses in between most responses. Later, a student asked me, after the lesson was over and we had achieved our labels, "What did you want us to say?" He did not realize that I had completed the lesson and what was said was fine. I believe that this state of frustration is the leading edge of learning. If you can get students to periodically exist in a state of frustration and, in addition, get them to "work" their way out of that state of mind, they are making progress, pushing that leading edge.

This is another reason why I am convinced that proper questioning techniques and designed lessons, such as this, are part of a new paradigm of teaching that I must adopt. Teaching is not an act performed by a teacher; rather, it is a process set in motion by the teacher and reverberates through the experiences of that teacher's students. Like the finger that disturbs the pond, when the finger pulls back it allows the ripples to run their course.

Classifying Lesson: "Erosion"

Purpose: Provide learners with opportunities to collect information about examples of a concept and to determine the appropriate category for the example based on the critical attributes of both

Reason: Facilitate learners' comprehension and retention of concepts

Content Characteristics:

- Causes of erosion
- Dynamics of water
- The water cycle
- Watersheds: rivers, streams, lakes, oceans
- Landforms
- Gravity
- Human impact on the land

Resources: Examples of "man-made causes of erosion"

1. Development of housing
2. Clear-cutting forests
3. Termite intrusion
4. Hurricanes
5. Drought
6. El Niño
7. War

Core Question: Classifying

- Which of these causes of erosion is an example of man-made causes?

Possible Learner Responses:

- Numbers 1 and 2 are man-made causes of erosion

Processing Questioning Stems:

- SP 1. What makes you say Number 1 is an example of man-made causes of erosion?
- SP 2. What is there about Number 2 that makes you say it is an example of a man-made cause of erosion?

- VR 3. How do you know that clear-cutting forests is a man-made cause of erosion?
- CL 4. What do you mean by "this exposes the soil to runoff"?
- CL 5. What are you referring to when you say that "the land can only take so much" with regard to erosion?
- RD 6. Who else thinks that clear-cutting forests is a man-made cause of erosion?

Transcript

Teacher: Which of these causes of erosion is an example of man-made causes?

Gary: Clear-cutting forests because when you cut trees . . . all of the trees . . . OK, you have your forest, right?

Teacher: You are giving me a lot of information from a simple question. Listen carefully to the question. Which of these causes of erosion is an example of man-made causes?

Anthony: I know . . .

Gary: Hold up!! Let me finish. Clear-cutting forests, war, development . . . that on. . . . Is that building like people's homes?

Teacher: Yes.

Gary: Development of housing, El Niño.

Ernie: El Niño? What?

Gary: Look out there. See those cars, man. We . . . people cause pollution, like no more ozone because of us. This is causing El Niño. So El Niño is causing erosion. We did that.

Teacher: How do you know that people caused El Niño?

Gary: It was on the news one day. They said that we are changing the planet.

Ernie: Yeah! But El Niño . . . that's natural. We don't know. It might have been happening for a long time before we started screwing things up.

Teacher: Josh, remember we were talking about erosion? If El Niño is caused by man, what is there about El Niño that would make you say it is a man-made cause of erosion?

Josh: I don't know what that is. Doesn't that make it rain a lot?

Teacher: Yes. During El Niño some areas on Earth get more rain then they usually do. What is there about this that would make you say it is a man-made cause of erosion?

Josh: That rain . . . like with the stream tables. The water makes the mud go into the . . . water . . . the river.

Ernie: But it's natural, not by man.

Coding of Transcript

T:	CF	TT/CF		TT
S:	CF/SP	O	O/CF/VR?	CF
		VR		TT/SP
VR?	VR	VR	VR	O
TT/SP				
SP	O			

Reflection on the Lesson

After working through the Grouping and Labeling lessons regarding the same subject, the students seemed much more willing or equipped to participate in this Classifying lesson. One thing that facilitated their ability to understand what we were doing is that by this time they had dealt with the causes of erosion over a protracted period of time, giving them a more developed vocabulary on the subject. They had developed a degree of articulation. This can be seen in quicker responses to my questions and a greater willingness to participate in class discussions.

Later on in the lesson, we became more informally involved, having a loose conversation. Students began to refer back to the initial lesson—the Grouping lesson. Without my leading them, they began to see the connection between the three thinking operations (Grouping, Labeling, and Classifying), and what began was an instructional conversation, which spanned those lessons. What was additionally rewarding is that I was not involved very much in the conversation. At times, the conversation got heated, but they were discussing the content of the lesson and the associated thinking operations. Each student (some better than others) was supporting his arguments with a high degree of articulation, so that I became very satisfied as a teacher. Not only do the questions work, but they can teach! It was rewarding!

Vignette: Reflections on Erosion—Moving the Thinking of Students

It was Monday, and like all Mondays things don't go quite as planned. In fact, things never go quite as planned, but actual events usually come closer to the plan on Tuesday through Friday. All but two of my students go home on weekends to see their parents, guardians, or whomever it is they go home to see. Monday acts to reintegrate them back into the environment of the group home. What takes place in the class is a derivative of that reintegration. This, I guess, is a long explanation, for it was simply MONDAY.

On the Friday before, I had taken all of my students on a canoeing trip to Mississippi—part recreation and part of an ongoing lesson on watersheds and erosion. I began the lesson with the list of terms regarding erosion. Some terms were about naturally caused erosion, and some man-made. Others were, somehow, indirectly related to erosion, but I wanted students to process them and explain how they could be related even if indirectly.

I broke the students up into two groups (three in one group and four in another). I presented the core question: *From what you know about erosion, which of these words go together for some reason?*

The groups began their tasks as asked of them. However, one group quickly had three groups and a clear reason behind the grouping while the other group was still struggling with their first. The three terms the second group had written down were not there "for some reason." In fact, they were there for no reason. "I thought you wanted us to start writing some words down," said one student in the second group. Apparently, they didn't hear the reasoning behind it. I again asked the core question and then witnessed one of the blankest stares ever since teaching here. I believe they thought that the act of writing—remaining busy with pencil and paper—was the point of the lesson.

I quickly took them away from this obviously daunting task and presented an analogous lesson using something quite familiar and, to them, interesting—FOOTBALL. I placed the names of six NFL teams on the board, carefully selecting certain teams. Than I said, "From what you know about football, which of these teams go together for some reason?" They quickly began shouting out, "The Cowboys, 49'ers, and Broncos go together because they all have won a Superbowl." They continued to group and regroup for various reasons. I then returned to the erosion lesson. It was still difficult, and they still needed my help, but they got it.

One thing I observed about that difficulty was that they grouped several terms but could not articulate the reason, although I believe they had some justification. This is, I believe, the leading edge of learning—finding oneself in a state of frustration and working your way out. The path you develop to emerge from that frustrated state is a pathway that becomes imbedded and can be accessed again in the future. String enough of these together, and you begin to have a network of thinking processes.

I continued to conduct the lesson, again including the entire class. What was once hard to begin was now hard to stop. I believe that the Grouping lesson lends itself to class discussions (instructional conversations), and this is why I believe I had a hard time moving on to the next activity. Of course, I want to maintain my daily pace, but my inner teacher can't help but recognize the value of students wanting to remain engaged in a lesson.

While I have had many adventures in conducting these lessons, I remain confident that I am evolving and developing my talents in teaching students to think conceptually and understand their thinking. To give you an idea of how I have used the Qu:Est Instructional Strategies with my students, I offer the preceding lesson plans, brief transcripts, coding of the transcripts, and my reflections on the lessons. I hope that my journey into learning how to question and questioning to learn inspires the readers of this book to commence their own journeys.

CLOSING REMARKS

For many years I have taught Earth Science in one form or another, and my favorite topic to cover, which I usually cover early and for an extended period of time, is Plate Tectonics. I like this topic because it is the new paradigm in geology. This topic has forced a reassessment of all geologic processes and features because of its systemic importance. This questioning process, I believe, forces a reassessment of the learning process in much the same way.

In every activity I am engaged in with my students, I find myself organizing my questions into a process to best facilitate the students' learning. I'M HOOKED!! Even with my four-year-old daughter, I do the same. She has caught on to my scheme, though. She now says, after a few of my strategic questions, something like," . . . DAD!! Stop doing that again. I already told you about __________ . . . " She sees it coming. OOPS. I've been caught.

My students have also caught on. They have caught me using a word to define that same word. They will call me on it, turning the tables. I must admit that I like when I make mistakes—it gives my students some temporary control and proves to them that teachers are not all-knowing bodies of perfection, although we strive for such status.

As much as I love these new practices, I find myself mired in the frustration of newness. I must do far too much thinking while I'm conducting the lesson, which affects the pace and my ability to dedicate myself to listening and creating the perception that I'm listening. This, with practice, will fade. However, my understanding of the usefulness and effectiveness of this process far outstrips my current abilities.

One of the most wonderful effects of using Qu:Est Strategies is watching the students attempt to use it on each other, even if it is not of the academic variety. One of my students, it was later determined, had taken a fancy pen from another student. When the second student (the one who really owned the pen) approached the first, the first attempted to distract him by employing the Observing questioning techniques. "What do you mean by a pen?" he asked. "The one that had the shredded $5 bill in it," said the second student. "What do you mean by shredded?" "The $5 bill was torn into little pieces." "How do you know that pen was yours?" "It was given to me by my grandmother." "Can you draw it on the board?"

My students seem to sense the power of these questions. I realize, now, that everything I do is being absorbed by them. Their interactions may not have had the content of a lesson, but they knew the questions they needed to ask. It was an instructional conversation that had personal meaning to them.

With the current students I teach, I find it tempting to release these lessons from the requirements of meeting the content characteristics after a while and let the students truly engage in instructional conversations. This has been extremely rewarding, watching my students engage in grounded discussions and substantive debates. They are slowly evolving their conversation skills, improving their probing questions, and being more thoughtful about their answers. It seems that productive questioning is working.

▶ 16

The Talent Development Model

FACILITATIVE SET

"Teaching is a performing art. Like other performing art fields, such as acting, music, or gymnastics, the talents of performers must be developed and refined through a nurturing process that integrates practice and reflection on practice" (Dantonio, 1990). This reflective practice process becomes a means for developing technique and style. For practice and reflection to become reflective practice, the nurturing of talents first requires that performers possess a mental picture of what the perfected practice looks like in a well-executed performance. Second, reflective practice requires that performers study the practice(s) by observing carefully aspects of their execution of the technique in practice situations while constantly analyzing and measuring their execution of the technique against their internal vision of a well-executed delivery of the technique within a performance situation. Often, this is done through self-study and with the guidance of a coach.

In this chapter, we present our readers with a collegial, self-study approach for learning productive questioning practices within the Qu:Est Instructional Strategies. To implement the collegial, self-study process, teachers need to form Collegial Analysis Self-Study Support Teams (CASSST). The members of the team work together to develop and refine the productive questioning practices through planning Qu:Est lessons, conducting the planned lessons, and analyzing teacher questions and the effects productive questioning practices have on instructional conversations.

Whereas the scholarly research on effective questioning practices provides a foundation for the theory of questioning, CASSST offers a means for teachers to engage in reflective practice to construct a personal understanding of productive questioning and to inquire into how the Qu:Est Strategies play out in classroom discourse.

REFLECTIVE PRACTICE

Reflective practice demands that performers study their art form in a manner that assists them in perfecting individual techniques in specific contextual situations prior to integrating the techniques in a performance. In the study of individual questioning practices through reflective practice, performers have opportunities to try out various ways of executing questions and to gain control over technical aspects in order to develop a delivery style. Thus, reflective practice allows for the conscious internalization of techniques in safe rehearsal settings prior to integrating them in a performance situation.

Once the techniques are internalized, performers are then able to combine the specific techniques into larger units of performance. For example, pianists may practice the same notes or scales over and over, perfecting their touch of the keys and listening for the quality of sound as they play the notes and scales. Following this, they practice larger sections of the composition. This concentrated practice automates their technique so that, in the total performance of a composition, the notes and scales flow naturally, without conscious effort. *By internalizing a technique, we mean that it becomes first nature, like breathing.* We do it, but we don't think about doing it. It is a natural process.

The same is true for developing and refining individual techniques related to delivering quality instruction. Concentrated development of individual techniques must be nurtured in order for teachers to integrate the techniques into a repertoire of instructional behaviors. This requires a talent development process that provides opportunities for teachers to attain command over the individual techniques in safe learning environments before integrating them into well-orchestrated performance contexts.

For example, in order to question productively and effectively, teachers must first build a knowledge base about what effective questioning entails and then be committed to practicing aspects of productive questioning in various rehearsal contexts that permit experimentation and conscious reflection on the development of the productive questioning practices. Gaining control over one's questioning practices is prerequisite to using productive questioning effectively during instructional conversations with students.

To question effectively and productively during instruction, teachers must keep their attention focused on the objectives of the lesson and pay careful attention to what students are saying. The art of asking productive questions requires that teachers understand the science of questioning and be able to expertly execute the questioning practices so well that responding appropriately to student talk is first nature. Appropriate teacher responses to student talk are questions or prompts that engage students in shaping more quality responses that add depth and understanding during instructional conversations. The specific aspects of effective, productive questioning have been introduced in Chapter 4 and embellished in Part IV of this book.

THE TALENT DEVELOPMENT MODEL

The Talent Development Model (Dantonio, 1990) described in this book engages teachers in a series of rehearsal situations that become a continuous cycle for acquiring specific productive questioning practices and learning how to conduct the individual Qu:Est Strategies. The components of the Talent Development Model include:

- Understanding the nature and function of productive questioning;
- Determining the individual practices involved and combining them to form an instructional strategy;
- Rehearsing the questioning practices in safe learning environments through the use of reflective practice;
- Inquiring into productive questioning by establishing a Collegial Analysis Self-Study Support Team (CASSST) to develop informed insights as team members plan lessons, perform lessons, and reflect on the performance of each team member.

Purpose of the CASSST

The CASSST consists of a small group of teachers, usually five to eight people. The goal of the CASSST is to form a community of learners who safeguard opportunities for rehearsing. During rehearsals, CASSST members gather and analyze information about the Qu:Est Strategies in order to engage in constructive conversations for integrating productive questioning practices into their instructional repertoires. As a team, they create ongoing opportunities for shared understandings and enhancement of individual, productive questioning practices during the rehearsal contexts. Members of the team do not evaluate each other during the rehearsals or performance; rather, they coach each other in developing expertise in conducting the Qu:Est Strategies, paying attention to the syntactical structure of questions, the sequence of questions, and the effect productive questioning has on eliciting quality student responses.

Learning to question in this manner is a reflective, skill-acquisition process and not simply memorization of information. Teachers cannot learn to conduct the Qu:Est Strategies by just reading about them: They must *practice and reflect on their practice* in a variety of rehearsal situations to attain competence in planning and conducting lessons prior to implementing these techniques with learners during instructional conversations.

To appropriately implement this Talent Development Model, two issues must be understood by the CASSST. First, CASSST members must be familiar with the content of effective questioning as it relates both to the literature on questioning and the implementation of the Qu:Est Instructional Strategies. Second, the CASSST members must be cognizant of the types of rehearsals involved in the Talent Development Model and be willing to participate in the learning process.

TYPES OF REHEARSALS

There are several different types of rehearsal contexts in the Talent Development Model. The first rehearsal focuses on planning lessons and practicing the productive questioning practices and individual Qu:Est Strategies. Practice should take place in a safe setting where teachers can make and correct mistakes without worrying about the effects on students. These rehearsals continue until the team becomes fluent in asking various types of productive questions and in each Qu:Est Strategy.

The second rehearsal context focuses on the relationships between productive teacher questions and quality learner responses. Again, this is a learning process for teachers. They should feel safe to make mistakes and to talk about the conditions necessary for effecting quality instruction for learners using the Qu:Est Strategies. During the second rehearsal, teachers attend to the management issues related to conducting effective instructional conversations by attending to the responses their questions elicit. The second rehearsal should continue until teachers are comfortable enough with an individual Qu:Est Strategy to competently conduct it with learners before moving on to another instructional strategy.

In the third rehearsal context, a Qu:Est lesson is conducted with learners in an instructional setting. It should be audiotaped or videotaped so that teachers can use the lesson as a learning experience. In a sense, it is a dress rehearsal for reflecting on how productive questioning affects instructional conversation. In no way should the content taught in the third rehearsal be required for student learning. The third rehearsal is still a learning context for teachers. It is in this context that teachers gather critical information they will need to fine-tune their developing questioning talent and study the impact that teaching Qu:Est Strategies has on eliciting quality student responses.

Each rehearsal context will be explained in more detail below. We describe the learning environment for each type of rehearsal, specifying the productive questioning practices that should be addressed during each rehearsal session, and provide suggestions and questions to guide the CASSST in their collegial self-study.

FIRST REHEARSAL: LINE TRYOUTS

Each Qu:Est Strategy will possess critical attributes of the instructional strategy that must be attended to in the performance of instructional conversations. The first rehearsal, called *Line Tryouts,* provides opportunities for teachers to plan lessons and to practice asking specific questions that cue and process learner responses. Guidelines for planning Qu:Est Strategies are described in the Framework for Lesson Design following the Guidelines for Line Tryouts.

In Line Tryouts, CASSST members focus on question syntax and fluency in asking the processing questions. Through reflective practice, the teacher will begin to internalize the formats for productive questioning. This process is similar to learning lines in a play or isolating and practicing a routine or skill in sports until it becomes automatic. As teachers become more comfortable with the techniques by internalizing them through their reflective practice, they will become more expert in hearing inappropriately asked questions, or questions that do not meet the syntactical structure of questions that cue a particular thinking operation. This analysis is necessary in order to familiarize teachers with both what to listen for in conducting instructional conversations and how to assess their abilities for sustaining a particular thinking focus.

Making Errors

During Line Tryouts, teachers may make many errors in conducting the questioning practices and Qu:Est Strategies because they are concentrating on precision of delivery. For this reason, teachers must trust each other and feel comfortable in conducting the questioning practices among themselves. They must establish a supportive climate so that they can make mistakes freely and reflect upon the mistakes in order to attain informed insights about how the productive questioning practices work together to produce instructional conversations.

In the Line Tryout, the members of the CASSST must call attention to an inappropriately performed question by a teacher. Because we have developed habits through our experience, some of them must be broken if we are to question productively. Do not permit teachers to ask questions in an inappropriate manner. It is much more difficult to unlearn inappropriate questioning behaviors than to learn them appropriately the first time.

This constant interruption of the teacher performing the lesson may create frustration, but it enables the team to attend to issues of appropriateness and accuracy when asking questions. Moreover, the first few teachers to demonstrate the questioning practices will make many errors, but as teachers listen to their ongoing analyses, subsequent demonstrations will contain fewer errors because teachers have opportunities to incorporate the experiences of other teachers from prior demonstrations. In turn, teachers who were the first to demonstrate the lesson will begin to hear the errors and will begin to contribute to the analysis for teachers who follow.

Guidelines for Line Tryouts

Listed below are the guidelines for engaging in Line Tryout rehearsals.

- During Line Tryouts, lessons are planned as a team, using as a guide the sample lesson found in each individual Qu:Est Strategy.
- Once planned, the lessons are conducted with each other. CASSST members alternate roles as teacher and students.
- Each teacher in the CASSST conducts a two- to three-minute sample of the team-planned lesson.
- The focus of analysis in the Line Tryouts should center on the thinking operation identified in the lesson design, the syntactical structure of the core question, and the relevance of the processing questions in eliciting quality responses.
- In the analysis, CASSST members should concentrate only on the questions—not on the responses they receive to their questions.
- Repeat the Line Tryout for each Qu:Est Instructional Strategy.

FRAMEWORK FOR LESSON DESIGN

Planning is essential for guiding, developing, and refining learners' thinking. Qu:Est lesson designs are highly structured instructional maps that stipulate the core and processing questions needed to guide and to qualify learners' responses and interactions. Core questions are derived from an analysis of the objective and content attributes of the lesson. The processing questions are determined and planned by predicting possible student responses to the core question. Also of importance are the specifications of management issues related to productive student participation, the identification and allocation of needed lesson resources, and the allotment of time for the lesson activities. Lastly, the lesson design must specify the results of the lesson in terms of the accomplishments of students.

Analyzing Objectives for Content and Thinking Operation

To plan and execute lessons through which learners identify and process information for themselves, teachers must think through four important planning issues when analyzing objectives. The issues, stated in a question format, are:

- What knowledge, attitudes, and/or skills does the objective call for?
- What are the critical characteristics of the content, or what are the concept labels, concept attributes, and concept examples that must be addressed?
  - *Concept Label:* *Triangle*
  - *Concept Attributes:* (Three lines intersecting to form 3 angles that add up to 180° degrees)
  - *Concept Examples:* ▲ ▶ ▼
- What thinking operation(s) must learners use to collect, build, or anchor the concept(s)?
- In what order must the thinking operations occur in order for students to form an initial concept, differentiate between similar concepts, or extend an initial concept to include related subconcepts?

Planning Core and Processing Questions

The adage "If you don't know where you're going, you'll probably end up somewhere else" is a definite reality in conducting lessons aimed at the development of student thinking through instructional conversations. Productive questioning practices should enable students to examine and put into practice their metacognitive processing, or how they have arrived at and/or monitored their thinking. Planning and conducting effective lessons using productive questions that address particular kinds of thinking require that teachers understand the attributes of the thinking operation. Likewise, teachers must be cognizant of the nature and function of questions that cue thinking and facilitate complete quality learner responses. The nature and function of productive questioning and how questions are combined to form a Qu:Est Instructional Strategy are important in teaching learners about thinking operations and how to process information using various thinking operations.

Planning Guidelines

Planning lessons for the development and/or refinement of learner thinking operations consists of a number of considerations.

- First, teachers must determine the objective(s) of the lesson, analyzing it for content attributes and thinking operations to be used by students to acquire, construct, or anchor the content.
- Second, the content-critical characteristics and resources needed to teach the lesson must be well thought out. The analysis of content results in a conceptual map, or a picture of the critical attributes of the concepts or subconcepts to be learned (Dantonio, 1988). This includes the concept labels, concept attributes, and concept examples to be used when conducting the lesson.
- The design of the core question(s) is the third consideration. The core question(s) must initiate or cue the type of thinking operation(s) students must use to "learn" the content.
- Along with the formation of the core question, teachers should predict possible student responses. Predicting possible student responses during the planning of a Qu:Est lesson not only helps teachers envision what students may say to the core question but also ensures that appropriate processing questions will be incorporated into the design of the lesson.
- Finally, processing questions must be planned and identified for quick reference when conducting the lesson.

SECOND REHEARSAL: BLOCKING

Blocking rehearsals provide an opportunity for teachers to hear and to code their questions and student responses. Again, CASSST members are in a practice context that provides opportunities to reflect on and to develop expertise in productive questioning. During the Blocking rehearsal, CASSST members *focus on both teacher questions and learner responses.* It is an opportunity to gain control over the questioning sequences needed to conduct productive instructional conversations. Analysis and discussions center on the relationships between teacher questions and the learner responses, as well as emerging patterns of interactions. Additionally, this is the time to discuss thinking operations and the sequence of Qu:Est lessons needed to address conceptual development.

Within the Blocking rehearsal, teachers, again, plan and conduct a two- to five-minute teaching episode using as a guide for planning the sample lessons found in each Qu:Est Instructional Strategy. The lessons conducted during the second rehearsal should be developed individually by each teacher in the CASSST, focusing on content that can be used with learners in their respective classrooms. There is a distinct difference between the Line Tryout rehearsals and the Blocking rehearsals. During Line Tryouts, the emphasis of the analysis was on question syntax and fluency. The emphasis of analysis in the Blocking rehearsal centers on question/response patterns. To assist the CASSST in this endeavor, a coding system is used to identify and trace questions and responses.

CASSST members must become familiar with the Qu:Est coding system. The coding system is described in this chapter under Framework for Coding. Through coding questions and responses, teachers further extend their abilities to hear appropriate and inappropriate interactions. By coding, CASSST members will shift their attention away from the questions they ask to listening to the responses elicited by their questions. Coding facilitates CASSST members' awareness of effective and ineffective question/answer patterns. At first, teachers will feel discomfort concerning which processing questions to ask; however, as they continue with their collegial self-study, they will become quite knowledgeable and skillful in asking core questions and sensing when to ask various kinds of processing questions.

During the Blocking rehearsal, the CASSST members rotate the roles of teacher, learners, and coders. Following the conducting of a lesson, the coders share their coding chart. The entire CASSST analyzes the conducted lesson using the coding chart and reflects on the experience of a lesson. At first, teachers will not be able to code quickly; but as they practice the coding, time after time, and if the lessons are audiotaped, teachers will become quite masterful at the coding process as well as at discussing the specific issues of productive questioning.

By emphasizing the relationship between the teacher's questions and the student responses, teachers will become more cognizant of the importance of using processing questions to elicit quality student answers. Likewise, teachers will continue to mature in their understanding of how appropriate, productive questioning leads to depth of student understanding.

Guidelines for Blocking Rehearsals

- Listed below are the guidelines for engaging in Blocking rehearsals.
- A teacher is selected, and coders and peer learners are appointed. The teacher teaches, the learners respond, and the coders code the interactions.
- Each teacher conducts a brief lesson, usually lasting no longer than five minutes, concentrating on asking processing questions that follow up on learner responses.
- As the teacher is conducting the lesson with the peer learners, the coders classify the interactions using the Guidelines for Coding following this section.
- Following the conducted lesson, the CASSST discusses the coding of the lesson, paying particular attention to the types of questions asked by the teacher and the relationships they find between the teacher's questions and type of student response(s) to the questions.

FRAMEWORK FOR CODING

The coding process assists teachers in analyzing both teacher questions and student responses to discern patterns of appropriate and inappropriate interactions. Teachers, by coding, become more sensitive to listening to student responses and become more adept at asking appropriate processing questions to elicit quality responses. Likewise, teachers become more cognizant of when to move to a different thinking operation to assist students in constructing concepts. The Qu:Est Instructional Strategy coding system is based on the "Discussion Analysis Form" developed by Ehrenberg and Ehrenberg for the Institute for Staff Development (1978) for the Hilda Taba Teaching Strategies Program.

Guidelines for Coding

The general guidelines for coding the questioning practices are:

- Determine the coding symbols needed for each Qu:Est Strategy. (Coding symbols for teacher questions and learner responses are found in each Qu:Est Instructional Strategy in Part III, Learning to Question, of this book.)
- Develop a grid that looks as follows:

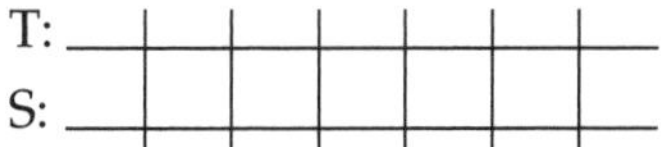

- Every question that the performing teacher asks is recorded in sequence by placing the appropriate symbol in the "T" line.
- Every answer or question that learners provide is recorded by placing the appropriate symbol in the "S" line as it relates to the teacher question.
- If a learner response directly follows a teacher question, then the symbol for the response falls directly beneath the symbol for the teacher question. (The example below uses the Observing Questioning Strategy.)

  T: OB CL VR OB

  S: OB CL VR OB

- If more than one learner response is given to any question, then the "S" line reflects the interactions. (The example below uses the Observing Questioning Strategy.)

  T: OB CL

  S: OB OB OB OB CL CL VR

- Use the appropriate coding symbol for what you hear teachers and students asking or saying, even if there is a mismatch between the teacher's question and the learner's response. (The example below uses the Observing Questioning Strategy.)
- T: OB CL CL CL RD VR
- S: OB OB CL VR RL OB OB CL
- Make brief notes about the interactions. Note especially the discrepancies between teacher questions and noncorresponding learner answers. Also note the manner in which teachers handle the noncorresponding answer.
- Analyze both the grid symbols and your notes. Provide analysis using the following questions as a guide for analysis and discussion.

Discussion Guide

- Are the learner responses an answer to the core question?
- Does the elicited response attend to the thinking and content focus of the core question?
- Does the teacher ask additional questions to assist learners in qualifying their responses?
- Are the processing questions asked of responses appropriate for the responses?
- Does the teacher refocus the response if the response is off-focus?
- Does the teacher clarify words used by the learner to elicit additional language?
- Does the teacher verify responses in order to attain accuracy?
- Is support of the response needed? If so, does the teacher ask for the "hook-up" response from learners?
- Does the teacher redirect questions in order to provide opportunities for many students to engage in the cognitive operation?
- Does there appear to be an appropriate pattern of questions that pace the lesson and extend learner understanding of the thinking operation?
- Is there an inappropriate pattern of questioning (closed questions, no refocus, no redirection, little clarifying, verifying only inappropriate responses)?
- What is the impact of the observed patterns on the learners?
- What patterns need to be maintained in order to facilitate learner development and refinement of the thinking operation?

- What patterns need to be changed in order to facilitate learner development and refinement of the thinking operation?
- In what ways can teachers maintain and/or change existing patterns?
- What questions appeared to give learners trouble?
- What did the teacher do to assist the learner in understanding troublesome questions?

THIRD REHEARSAL: DRESS REHEARSAL

The Dress rehearsal is performed in a classroom setting with learners and is the third practice context. Although the context is a classroom with learners, this is still a learning experience for the teacher. This is the first opportunity for teachers to perform a Qu:Est lesson with students to discover the challenges that they may face in conducting the lessons with real learners. Issues of classroom management and control over the questioning practices begin to become a reality. The difference between planning lessons and conducting them to achieve specific purposes with learners creates opportunities to discover instructional issues that could not be anticipated during the prior rehearsals. The outcome of the third rehearsal determines the need for further study of the Qu:Est Instructional Strategies. Any critical issues should be brought back to the entire CASSST for discussion using the Blocking rehearsal Discussion Guide found in the Blocking rehearsal section.

Because teachers are practicing Qu:Est lessons within the context of their respective classrooms, it becomes necessary to work in pairs, rather than a team. During the Dress rehearsal, it is important for teachers to participate in the roles of teacher and coach. There are several reasons for this. First, if teachers work in isolation to implement the Qu:Est Instructional Strategies, they may run into difficulties that they feel have no solutions. Feeling isolated, they may decide to quit developing their productive questioning practices.

Second, the coaching partners can empower each other to overcome their individual struggles to implement the Qu:Est Strategies. Through their dialogue about teaching and learning, as well as their exchanges concerning the challenges and successes in using productive questions to promote instructional conversations, they evolve an esprit de corps that spreads to other teachers, helping other teachers to become aware of the advantages of collegial self-study.

Third, it is hard to observe and analyze one's own performance. The coaching partner is an objective observer. Through coding and analyzing another teacher's attempt at using productive questioning in instructional conversations, the coach can provide a lens for the performing teacher to view the lesson. Likewise, the coach is in a position to learn about productive questioning from the performing teacher's successes and challenges. By studying together, teachers will develop their confidence and refine their abilities to conduct the Qu:Est Strategies. By working together to solve instructional challenges and share in successes, CASSST members will fashion strong professional friendships among teachers.

Guidelines for the Dress Rehearsal

The following information details the experience of the Dress rehearsal.

- Each member of the CASSST selects someone whom they trust to observe and record the lesson's interactions. The paired teachers become each other's mirror or lenses for the purpose of gathering information about the planning, conducting, and analysis phases of the instructional conversation. Using Collegial Coaching (Dantonio, 1995), described in the next section, the paired teachers engage in the study of their classroom performances of the Qu:Est Strategies.
- The paired teachers meet in a Planning Conference to design the lesson and to discuss any issues related to conducting the lesson. *The Planning Phase* is described in the Collegial Coaching section of this chapter, and the *Planning Guidelines* can be found in the Tryout section of this chapter.
- Following the planning of each other's lesson, the paired teachers alternate roles between teacher and observer as they conduct their respective lessons. To facilitate data collection, again, an audiotape or videotape is useful.
- After conducting and taping each teacher's lesson, the paired teachers exchange tapes, code the instructional conversation using the *Guidelines for Coding* found in the Blocking rehearsal section, and analyze the performance.
- *Reflection Time* provides the teachers with an opportunity to collect their thoughts. When each teacher has had time to analyze their teaching performances, they meet to discuss each other's lesson in a *Debriefing Phase* (described in the Collegial Coaching section of this chapter).
- Once all of the members of the CASSST have conducted and reviewed each other's classroom experience, the entire team meets to discuss the next steps. Next steps may be to focus on specific instructional issues arising from the Dress rehearsal, to view and analyze each other's lessons, to begin a Line Tryout rehearsal on a different Qu:Est Strategy, or to develop curriculum using the Qu:Est Instructional Strategies.

COLLEGIAL COACHING

Collegial Coaching (Dantonio, 1995) is a collaborative, teacher-driven process for investigating and experimenting with instruction. Collegial Coaching offers teachers opportunities to discuss instructional goals and practices in order to develop shared visions about effective instruction. Four phases are involved in the Collegial Coaching process. They are:

- Planning Phase
- Observation of Teaching Performance
- Reflection Time, and
- Debriefing Phase

Planning Phase

During the Planning Phase of the Dress rehearsal, the paired teachers prepare a lesson that will be conducted by one of them while the other teacher observes the performance. They discuss the objectives of the lesson, determine the kinds of cognitive operations learners are to use when engaged in instructional conversations, structure the types of processing questions needed to facilitate the learning, anticipate the problems that the teacher may encounter while conducting the lesson, and agree on the intended learning outcomes for students. The goal of the planning phase of Collegial Coaching is for both teachers to form a clear and concise picture of what they expect to happen during the lesson.

Observation of Teaching Performance

During the Observation of Teaching Performance, the coaching teacher observes the teacher conducting the planned Qu:Est Strategy. While observing, the coaching teacher jots down specific notes about the teacher's use of questions, the learner responses, and any management issues that are apparent. Videotaping or audiotaping the lesson will assist both teachers in coding and analyzing the performance during the Reflection Time.

Reflection Time

Following the viewing of the lesson, the coach and the teacher, independent of each other, reflect on the lesson and code the lesson. This Reflection Time is needed to discover important relationships between teaching and learning. In their reflections, the coaching partners should pay close attention to the intended plan for the lesson as it compares to the actual conducted lesson. They will also independently code the interactions and analyze the instructional conversation for patterns. Before the coaching partners meet to discuss the instructional issues, they need to decide if problems or successes encountered during the instructional conversation resulted from the planning or the implementation of the plan.

Debriefing Phase

The Debriefing is a problem-solving arena. The coaching partners come together to share their coding and analyses, as well as to explore the ways in which they can further inform their understanding and abilities to conduct instructional conversations with learners. The coaching partners may want to continue working together on another Qu:Est lesson. After each completed Collegial Coaching cycle, the entire CASSST should meet to investigate and to solve commonly shared problems that arose in conducting the Qu:Est Instructional Strategies. The CASSST may also want to redefine, redirect, and reassess their investigations into the study of productive questioning to determine how to best impact student learning.

CLOSING REMARKS

The Talent Development Model offers teachers a vehicle for their collegial self-study of the Qu:Est Instructional Strategies to gain proficiency in productive questioning to carry out thoughtful instructional conversations. We have found that teachers who integrate Collegial Coaching into their ongoing study are more likely to continue the development of their instructional talents. Through coaching, teachers are supported in their experimentation with instructional methods, and they build ardent professional relationships within the school faculty.

Although talent development places many demands on teaching time, the time spent developing shared instructional goals for the school community and developing strong professional commitments to each other and to our students is time well invested. It only stands to reason that the more we understand our instructional efforts, how students learn, and the ways we have to improve upon instructional delivery influences the quality of education we can provide our students.

Quality in students' educational experiences depends on the instructional talent and leadership of caring, talented teachers. If we want our students to emerge from our schools as wise and courageous citizens, capable and ready to investigate tomorrow's perplexing situations and determined to contribute productively to our society, then we must make it our priority to employ methods of instruction that foster students' abilities to think critically and creatively. Teaching for conceptual understanding cannot be just a call for reform in education, it must be a reality in American classrooms. Through sharing our instructional journeys, we may discover deeper understandings of how questioning confronts us with learning and how learning demands that we question. The inquiry is yours. We invite you to share your learning passionately with others.

REFERENCES

Dantonio, M. (1990). *How can we create thinkers? Questioning strategies that work for teachers.* Bloomington, IN: National Education Service.

Dantonio, M. (1995). *Collegial coaching: Inquiry into the teaching self.* Bloomington, IN: Phi Delta Kappa.

Ehrenberg, S. D., & Ehrenberg, L. M. (1978). *Building and applying strategies for intellectual competencies in students.* Miami, FL.: Institute for Curriculum and Instruction.

Index

A Nation at Risk, 25
accuracy, 167, 170
analysis, 62–64, 225–226
anchoring, 56–57, 105–120
answer(s)
  right, 174–178
  uncertainty of, 20
articulation, 210
assessment, 129
attributes
  concept, 53, 57, 96–97
  content, 220
  critical, 106

behavior
  unlearning of, 134
Biological Sciences Curriculum (BSCS), 11
blocking, 221–222
brain storming, 21
brainteasers, 62–63

characteristics
  concept, 79, 88, 89, 90, 185–186
  content, 73, 79, 98, 107, 114, 196, 198, 200, 202, 206, 208, 213
  critical, 106, 109–111, 117, 146–147, 185–186
  distinguishing, 109
characterization, 6–7
clarification, 77, 84, 94, 103, 112, 126, 165–166, 169–170, 175–176
  elementary, 19
clarity, 42, 167
classification, 54, 57–58, 148, 150
  analyzing lessons for, 118–120
  cognitive operation of, 116–118
  examples/nonexamples for, 106
  labeling and, 106
  lesson design for, 114–116, 208–210
  reasons for, 116
  strategy chart for, 114
  systems of, 37
classroom
  cognitive operation in, 39
  observation in, 49–50
  observations on, 24–26
clause
  dependent, 182
  independent, 182
closed question(s), 134, 136–140, 142–143, 145–146
  stems of, 138–139
clues, 42, 136
coaching, collegial, 227–228
coding, 197, 199, 202, 205, 207, 210
  guidelines for, 222–225
  reflections on, 78, 85, 95, 96, 104, 113–114, 120
  symbols for, 77, 84–85, 94–96, 102–104, 112–113, 119–120
cognitive abilities, 27–28, 32, 35, 37
  concepts and, 34
cognitive operations, 146–147
collecting, 71–85
Collegial Analysis Self-Study Support Teams (CASST), 214–219, 221–222, 225–226, 228
comparison, 41, 54–55, 57–58, 148, 150
  analyzing lessons of, 92–96
  lesson design for, 89–90
  similarities and, 91, 126–127, 129
  strategy chart for, 87–88

comparison (*cont.*)
subconcepts and, 86–87
thinking operations of, 90–92
concept(s). *see also* characteristics
critical characteristics of, 185–186
distinguishing between, 58
forming of, 86
initial, 57
labels of, 116–117
subconcepts and, 58, 86–87, 96–97, 100
conditional statements, 91–92
confidence, 136
connections, 34
constructivism, 34
content, 149–151, 165, 175, 185. *see also* characteristics
critical characteristic of, 220–221
contrasting, 54–55, 57–58, 150, 200–202
analyzing lessons of, 92–96
difficulty for, 91
discrepancies and, 91–92
lesson design for, 88–89
subconcepts and, 86–87
thinking operations of, 90–92
conversation. *see* instructional conversation
core question(s), 39–40, 45, 61, 73, 75, 77–79, 84, 88, 90, 94, 98, 107, 115, 117, 119, 121, 142, 145, 165, 168–169, 196, 198, 200, 203, 206, 208, 211
attributes of, 150–153
planning for, 220–221
Council for Basic Education, 22
cues, 81, 145
cognitive, 146, 149
content, 141
nonverbal, 60, 68–69
verbal, 39, 141

debriefing, 226, 228
definition
concept, 115
Dewey, John, 23, 34
differentiation, 41
Distant Thunder (Wyeth), 4–5
doubt, 136–137

education
definition of, 22
inquiry, 1
empowerment, 5, 9, 33, 52, 225
errors, 218–219
evaluation, 144
peer, 129
examples
concept, 54, 97, 115, 117, 220
nonexamples, classification and, 106, 117

facilitative set, 112, 141, 154–156, 174–175, 214–215
focusing, 73–74, 77, 80, 84, 89–90, 94, 100, 103, 112, 119, 169, 170–171, 185

gestures, 69
group consensus, 221
grouping, 54–55, 57, 130–132, 150, 202–205
analyzing lessons of, 101–104
facilitative set for, 96–97
inductive strategy of, 97
lesson design for, 98–100, 202–205, 210–211
strategy chart for, 97–98
subconcepts and, 96–97
thinking operation of, 96–97
understanding differences in, 101

ideas
student-generated, 165–166
inferences, 75–76, 78
inferred qualities, 6–7
inquiry
approach of, 17–18
education through, 1
John Dewey and, 23–24
science and, 12–13
teacher's experience in, 14–15
instructional conversations, 17, 35–36, 121, 142, 149, 154–164, 168, 171, 194–195, 199, 205, 210, 213–214, 216, 226
procedures for, 164–166

instructional methods, 1, 3
  change in, 14
  dialogical approach with, 36
  experimenting with, 9–10
  missing value in, 12
  three Taba, 24
internalization, 215, 218
interpretation, 62–63
intonation, 138
intuition, 194
issues
  positioning, 69

knowledge
  internalizing of, 45–46
  three forms of, 44

lab
  as playtime, 11
labeling, 130, 148, 150,
  analyzing lesson for, 111–114
  concepts and, 109
  groups and, 105–106
  inductive process of, 108–111
  lesson design for, 107–108, 205–208, 210
  process of, 56–58
  reasons for, 108
  strategy chart for, 107
  thinking operation of, 109–111
labels
  concept, 53, 57, 86, 96, 115, 220
  technical, 110
language, 194
  precise, 38, 73–74, 80, 89, 90, 99–100, 108, 110, 116, 210
learner
  objectives and, 26
learner response, 73, 76–77, 79, 83–84, 88, 93–94, 98, 101–103, 107, 111–112, 114, 118–119, 196, 198, 201, 203, 206, 208, 223
learning
  basis of, 53
  excitement about, 46
  heightened awareness in, 52
  illogical discussions in classrooms and, 24
  mental pictures and, 45
  ownership of, 6
  as a process, 14, 149, 189
  reciprocal value of, 189
  responsibility of, 20–21
    rote memory, 14, 23, 25, 28, 49, 52, 53, 86, 87
  spiral, 35
  teaching connected to, 154
  tool of, 8
  understanding basis of, 33–34
lecturing, 19
lesson(s). *see also* strategies
  classifying, 208–210
  concept development and, 128
  design of, 219
  discovery, 128
  grouping, 202–205, 210, 211
  labeling, 205–208, 210
  objective of, 147
  observing, 197–199, 224
  performance of, 216–217
  planning of, 168, 217, 220–221
  processing planning and, 172–173
  questioning, 126–129
  recalling, 195–197
  similarities/differences, 200–202
  student's response and, 158
line tryouts, 218–219, 226

memorization, 49, 52, 53, 81, 86, 87
metacognition, 43–44, 75, 220
mirror technique, 169
misconceptions, 177, 180–181, 202

observation, 41, 54–55, 57–58, 148, 150, 197–199, 213, 224, 227
  analyzing lessons for, 76–79
  lesson design of, 73–74, 197–199, 224
  process of, 75
  questioning strategy and, 71–72
  recalling questioning for, 79
  thinking operation of, 74–76
on/off-focus responses, 76–77, 78, 83–84, 93–94, 101–103, 111–112, 118–119, 168–169

open question(s), 137–140, 145–146, 150–151
  stems of, 139, 150
originality, 42, 167, 170

patterns
  comparison and, 91
  discovery of, 53, 67
  interative, 69
  questioning of, 40–41
  repeating, 124
  understanding of, 77
pedagogy
  new policy for, 29
  principles of, 8
perception
  sharpening of, 74
Piaget, Jean, 24
principal
  resistance by, 7–8
process skills, 14

Qu:Est strategies, 9, 10, 17, 45, 49, 51, 56, 60, 66, 68, 70, 76, 81–82, 87, 101, 110–111, 117, 121, 134, 150, 190, 194, 212–214, 216–220, 223, 225, 227–228
question function, 68–69
question(s), 152. *see also* closed questions; core questions; open questions
  analysis of, 152
  clarity of, 28
  cognitive, 27–28
  cognitively cued, 150
  conceptualizing with core, 150–151
  effective, 36–37, 38, 215
  experience and, 133
  follow-up, 20
  four basic, 17
  frequency of, 25
  guiding of, 8
  higher-level, 26–27
  inappropriate, 218
  instructional, 32, 40, 49, 66, 141, 149, 153
  learner objectives and, 26
  lower-level, 26–27
  nature of, 66–67
  patterns of, 222
  phrasing of, 39–40, 45, 68, 70, 137–138
  practicing of, 217
  processing, 39, 43, 73, 80, 90, 108, 116, 129, 167–168, 172–173, 186, 196, 198, 201, 203–204, 206, 208–209, 218, 220
  productive, 45, 60–61, 66, 195, 213, 214, 215, 217
  purpose of, 67
  recall-oriented, 23–26
  rhetorical, 137, 145
  sequencing of, 37–38, 40–41, 66–67
  subsequent, 167
  supporting, 101–103, 110–111, 112, 117, 119, 171, 180–181
  systematic way of, 4–5
  thought-focused, 66
  threatening, 138
  understanding of information from, 8
  wait time and, 61, 68, 123

recall, 41, 55, 57, 135, 143–146, 148, 150, 157, 195–197
  analyzing lessons for, 79–85
  collecting and, 81
  lesson design for, 79–80
  strategy chart for, 79
  strengthening of, 166
redirection, 77, 84, 94, 103, 112, 126, 158, 165, 172–173
refinement, 166
reflection
  metacognitive, 44
reflection time, 226–227, 227–228
reflective practice, 190, 214–216, 218
refocusing, 73, 77, 80, 82, 84, 89, 90, 92–93, 94, 99, 101–103, 108, 112, 119, 158, 168–169
rehearsals, 215–216
  blocking and, 221–222
  dress, 225–227
  errors in, 218–219
  line tryouts and, 218–219, 226
  types of, 217–218
report sheet, 160

scaffolding, 40–41, 193–194
science
  inquiry in, 12–13
Science: A Process Approach
seating
  U-shaped, 4
self-actualization, 1
self-expression, 3
self-monitoring, 177
self-study, 190, 214
sentences
  simple, 185
signal
  cognitive, 145, 146, 149
specificity, 167, 170
storytelling, 17
strategies. *see also* lessons
  anchoring, 56–57, 105–120
  bridging, 55–56, 86–104
  classifying, 105–106, 114–120
  collecting, 55, 71–85
  comparing, 86–88, 89–95
  contrasting, 86–96
  grouping, 86, 96–104
  instructional, 5, 51, 54
  labeling, 105–114
  observing, 71–79, 213
  recalling, 71–72, 79–85
student(s)
  answers inspiring to, 6
  empowerment of, 5, 9, 33, 52
  frustration of, 211
  "hook up" characteristics by, 102
  interaction within, 172
  knowledge through questions for, 43
  learning responsibility of, 127
  older, 27
  participation of, 73–74, 80, 89, 90, 100, 108, 116, 148, 155
  quality of responses by, 41–42, 166–167
  questions guided by responses of, 9
  reasoning of, 166, 171
  self-directed, 35, 38
  shaping of, 68
  specificity of, 42
  younger, 27
synthesis, 27–28
Taba Teaching Strategies (Ehrenberg), 4
Talent Development Model (TDM), 190, 216–217, 228
teacher(s)
  acceptance of students by, 165
  changing of instructional behaviors by, 9
  clarifying questions by, 169–170
  clarity of questions of, 28, 112
  Collegial Analysis Self-Study Support Teams (CASST) and, 214–219, 221–222, 225–226, 228
  discovering student's process of thinking by, 62–66
  diversity, learning and, 25
  effectiveness of, 9
  experimentation by, 9
  as facilitator, 36, 38
  first year of teaching by, 11, 14
  focused questions by, 170–171
  learning by, 136–137, 146–149
  lecturing and, 19
  listening to students by, 155
  master-disciple, 22
  as participants with students, 165
  preservice, 12–13, 130
  probing by, 43
  process-centered methods by, 14, 24
  pseudo-Socratic, 21
  reactions of, 61
  redirecting questions by, 172–173
  re-enforcement for learning/change in, 14–15
  refocusing questions by, 168–169
  rethinking of teaching by, 62–65
  social dialogue of, 35–36
  Socratic, 19, 21, 22
  supporting questions by, 171, 186
  teaching of thinking by, 13
  teaching self as, 133
  threatened feeling of, 8
  understanding, learning and, 25, 33–34
  verifying questions by, 170, 186
teaching
  academic learning and, 189
  audio/videotape of, 217, 222

teaching (*cont.*)
  constructivist, 34
  follow-up of student's responses in, 42–43, 67
  internalization of techniques for, 215, 218
  learning and, 154
  as performing art, 214
  as a process, 208
testing, 19–20
think time, 61, 67
thinking
  analyzing of, 220
  characteristics of, 61
  conceptual, 33, 34–35, 40–41, 44, 50, 150, 175
  cueing, 141–142
  difficulty of, 22
  as ends in itself, 36
  focusing of, 38–40, 73–74, 80
  individual, 40
  inferential, 27–28
  innate, 1
  listening *vs.*, 212
  monitoring of, 44
  operations of, 210
  refinement of, 45, 52
  signaling, 141–142
  teaching of, 13, 60–62, 65, 174
  types of, 61
time
  factor of, 175
truth
  test of, 20

understanding
  arrive at, 66
  conceptual, 18, 53–54, 164
  individual, 20
  lack of, 33
  teaching for, 8, 25, 28–29, 32, 33–34, 37–38, 45–46, 49, 51
  thought process and, 44, 167, 180
university
  teacher's continuation in, 14
unlearning, 65

verification, 74–75, 77, 84, 80, 82, 83–84, 89, 90, 94, 100, 103, 108, 112, 116, 119, 170, 175, 176, 186
vignette, 61, 121, 135, 142, 155, 175

wait time, 61, 68, 70, 123, 144